BITTER CHOICES

BITTER CHOICES

Loyalty and Betrayal in the
Russian Conquest of the
North Caucasus

Michael Khodarkovsky

CORNELL UNIVERSITY PRESS

Ithaca and London

First published 2011 by Cornell University Press

Printed in the United States of America

Library of Congress Cataloging-in-Publication Data

Khodarkovsky, Michael, 1955–
  Bitter choices : loyalty and betrayal in the Russian conquest of the North Caucasus / Michael Khodarkovsky.
      p. cm.
  Includes bibliographical references and index.
  ISBN 978-0-8014-4972-7 (cloth : alk. paper)
  1. Atarshchikov, Semën, 1807–1845.   2. Revolutionaries—Russia (Federation)—Caucasus, Northern—Biography.   3. Cossacks—Russia (Federation)—Caucasus, Northern—Biography.   4. Caucasus, Northern (Russia)—History—Autonomy and independence movements.   5. Caucasus, Northern (Russia)—History—19th century. I. Title.
  DK511.C2K494   2011
  947.5'207—dc23   2011020199

Cornell University Press strives to use environmentally responsible suppliers and materials to the fullest extent possible in the publishing of its books. Such materials include vegetable-based, low-VOC inks and acid-free papers that are recycled, totally chlorine-free, or partly composed of nonwood fibers. For further information, visit our website at www.cornellpress.cornell.edu.

Cloth printing   10 9 8 7 6 5 4 3 2 1

To the memory of my parents,
Klara and Efim Khodarkovsky

and to Loïc and Tosya,
children of several cultures

Contents

Maps

Acknowledgments

THE idea to write a book about the North Caucasus occurred to me sometime in early 2000 during the bloody fighting in Chechnya that became known as the Second Chechen War. While news reports and journalistic accounts focused on the Chechens' fierce resistance in the face of an overwhelming Russian force, they had little to say about the history of the region and its peoples. For Russians, the references to Chechnya or Daghestan were likely to conjure up negative stereotypes, and for Westerners these names simply drew a blank. Writing a book that would introduce a basic historical, ethnic, and geographical mosaic of the region enticed me. But it was not clear how to turn this mosaic of disparate ethnic and clan identities into a coherent picture.

It was not until 2001, while on leave thanks to a grant from the American Council of Learned Societies, that I stumbled on a biography of Semën Atarshchikov. It was a short description of the file that M. O. Kosven discovered in the Russian Archive of Military History and provided in his classic book on the ethnography and history of the Caucasus. I realized that Atarshchikov's biography could serve as a metaphor for the history of the North Caucasus's indigenous peoples. This was the beginning of the project. My first and foremost debt, therefore, is to Mark Osipovich Kosven (1885–1967), a great Russian ethnographer and scholar of the Caucasus.

This book benefited greatly from the help, advice, and critical comments of colleagues and friends to whom I owe many thanks: Vladimir Bobrovnikov, Igor and Liza Gomberg, and Igor Kurukin in Moscow; Vladimir Kolesov and Igor Kuznetsov in Krasnodar; and Sufian Zhemukhov in Kabarda. Sufian deserves a special thanks for his prompt responses to my queries and generosity in sharing his knowledge.

My thanks to Robert Dankoff, Valerie Kivelson, Barbara Rosenwein, and Lucette Valensi for reading early versions of the manuscript and offering valuable comments. My thanks to the reviewers at Cornell University Press, and in particular to Bruce Grant, who went far beyond the call of duty in his careful reading and knowledgeable comments. Numerous conversations about the Caucasus's past and present with Georgii Derlugian—over a shot of a local brew he somehow always managed to procure from his native region of Krasnodar—were never dull.

I owe much to Dan O'Connell, a former literary agent who at an early stage of writing offered valuable comments on the style and structure of the manuscript. My thanks also go to the editors of the project, and particularly to Ange Romeo-Hall, for combining so well expediency with congeniality. Finally, I owe even more to John Ackerman, director of Cornell University Press, who took a personal interest in the book. While initially his comments and criticisms made me question whether his close involvement with the manuscript was punishment or bliss, the end result indisputably pointed to the latter. To him I am most grateful.

The final revisions to the manuscript were made in Berlin, where I spent a year as visiting professor at Humboldt University. To Jörg Baberowski who made sure that my stay in Berlin was as comfortable as possible, I am very grateful. I am also thankful to Felix Schnell, Christian Teichmann, and many other colleagues and graduate students who provided good company at our daily gatherings at the mensa, where the conversations, if not the food, were invariably warm. Finally, my thanks to Malte Rolf, without whose collegiality and friendship, my stay in Germany would not have been the same.

Of course, I would be remiss not to mention my two children, Loïc and Tosya, whose daily routines, no doubt, contributed to a protracted gestation of the book; my father, who never ceased to wonder why was it taking so long to write another book; and my wife, Insa, who was patient and tolerant where others might not be. To all of you, thank you for being there.

Chicago and Berlin, 2011

Abbreviations

AKAK   *Akty sobrannye Kavkazskoiu arkheograficheskoiu komissieiu.*
12 vols. Tiflis: Tip. Glavnogo upravleniia namestnika Kavkazskogo,
1866–1904.

GAKK   Gosudarstvennyi Arkhiv Krasnodarskogo Kraia

PSZ   *Polnoe sobranie zakonov Rossiiskoi imperii. Sobranie pervoe,* 45 vols.
St. Petersburg, 1830.

RGVIA   Rossiiskii Gosudarstvennyi Voenno-Istoricheskii Arkhiv

BITTER CHOICES

Introduction

SEMËN Semënovich Atarshchikov was a Russian Cossack officer. A dashing Cossack uniform, a bushy mustache, a tall hat of black wool, a fine saber and dagger—nothing in his appearance distinguished him from his fellow officers, who, like him, were stationed in the frontier regiments of the North Caucasus. Yet his command of four languages—Russian, as well as Arabic and two regional tongues, Chechen and Kumyk—clearly set Semën apart from his compatriots. His intimate knowledge of local languages and cultures made him an indispensable translator and expert on the highlanders of the North Caucasus.

Atarshchikov's professional star rose steadily if not spectacularly. In 1830 his service as a translator was needed in St. Petersburg, where he joined the Caucasus Mountain half squadron, better known as the Circassian Guard. Two years later, as a leading expert on the Chechens, now promoted and decorated, he was dispatched back to the Caucasus, where the third imam named Shamil was about to unite the native peoples in what would become a long and bloody holy war against the Russians. In 1836, Atarshchikov was transferred to the northwest Caucasus and appointed a superintendent of the Karachay people. During all these years, he earned the respect and trust of one of the top Russian military commanders in the Caucasus, the notorious Baron Grigorii Khristoforovich von Zass. An eccentric general known equally for his courage and his cruelty, Zass regularly dispatched Atarshchikov on sensitive missions deep into the mountains, and Atarshchikov always performed admirably. But in 1841, at the age of thirty-four, suddenly and without any apparent reason, Atarshchikov fled to seek refuge among the Adyge highlanders.

Contemporary Caucasus

Such desertions were far more frequent than Russian officials were willing to admit. Typically the deserters were rank-and-file soldiers and Cossacks who fled to escape justice or abuse by their officers. Some simply preferred a few years of freedom to twenty-five years of grueling military service. But a deserting officer, whose previous years of service were an example of diligence and dedication, was not something that Russian officials could easily dismiss or deny.

Atarshchikov's story grew even more intriguing when, four months after his escape, he chose to return to Russia and ask for pardon. When his petition reached the imperial desk in St. Petersburg, the Russian emperor, Nicholas I, convinced by General Zass's assurances, agreed to sign a pardon. But the imperial pardon from the charge of treason did not necessarily imply the imperial trust. Nicholas I, who came to power in the tumultuous atmosphere of the December 1825 uprising, saw sedition and treachery everywhere. The imperial decree ordered Atarshchikov to be transferred to a Cossack regiment—in Finland.

Perhaps the emperor's suspicions were not entirely unfounded, for shortly before his transfer Atarshchikov again fled to the mountains. This time he converted to Islam, married a local noble's daughter, and participated actively in raids across the Russian frontier. In 1845, during one such raid, his companion, the fugitive Cossack Fedor Fenev, shot Atarshchikov while he slept. Fenev had decided to surrender to the Russian authorities, and betraying Atarshchikov, who had become one of the most notorious and dangerous raiders, offered Fenev the best hope for a pardon. Shortly after a party of Cossacks arrived to seize him, Semën Atarshchikov died from his wounds.[1]

Semën Atarshchikov's dramatic life and its tragic end were inseparable from the sense of romance and mystery that early nineteenth-century Russian romantics associated with the Caucasus, which had become at once Russia's "Parnassian sanctuary and a bloody battlefield." An entire generation of Russia's writers and poets was inducted into the military and banished to the "southern Siberia" for their outspoken opposition to monarchy. For many, life ended early and abruptly, as government authorities had intended.[2]

Thus, Aleksander Bestuzhev-Marlinskii, Russia's best-selling author of stories set in the Caucasus, fell in June 1837 during the disastrous Russian landing expedition at Adler on the Black Sea coast. Alexander Odoevsky died from typhus while stationed on the same coast, and Alexander Griboedov was murdered by an angry mob in Teheran. Four years later, in July 1841, Mikhail Lermontov died in his infamous duel with N. S. Martynov at the North Caucasus town of Piatigorsk. Both duelists were enamored of the local culture: Lermontov romanticized the Caucasus in verse and prose, while Martynov emulated the region's martial traditions, preferring a distinctive mountaineer's tunic, a woolen hat, and a large dagger to a Russian officer's uniform. In fact, Lermontov's mocking of Martynov, whom he called "le chevalier des monts sauvages," and his sartorial trappings eventually provoked the fatal duel.[3] In the Caucasus imagination and reality often blended into a typical frontier exoticism.

While many Russian officers transformed their exile into an adventure by romanticizing the region and its inhabitants, the highlanders' experience with the Russians was far from romantic. Concerned with the preservation of their social position, property, and power, the local elite were forced to choose between collaboration and resistance. As was the case with Haji-Murat, immortalized by Leo Tolstoy in the story of the same name, such choices were not always lasting. Haji-Murat was an influential Avar noble who served Russian interests until local political intrigues and the high-handedness of the Russian administration forced him to join Shamil in 1841. A few years later, disappointed by his new ally, Haji-Murat fled back to the Russians, only to be hunted down and killed a few months later as he attempted to return to Shamil. Haji-Murat's story was representative of the experience of many local nobles who searched for political security in the ever-shifting space between the Russian authorities and their own people. Whatever the nature of their relations with Russia, they preserved their indigenous identity and remained strangers to Russian ways.

At the same time, Russia's continuous presence in the region resulted in the growing influence of a different kind of local elite, who were educated in Russia and later returned to serve Russian interests among their own people. Theirs was the third way between collaboration and resistance. Seemingly comfortable in both Russian and their own culture, these men were privileged outsiders in both worlds. Their loyalties remained in doubt, for they often anguished over their complex identity. Even decades of successful service in the Russian military did not preclude their return to their native roots.

One striking example was Musa Kundukh (Kundukhov). Born to a family of Ossetian nobles, he joined the Russian army as an officer and rose through the ranks to become a highly decorated major general. After Shamil had been defeated, however, Kundukh's disgust with Russia's policies toward the local population led him to organize a massive immigration to the Ottoman Empire. In 1865, his ship with hundreds of fellow highlanders docked at an Ottoman port on the Black Sea. Later, Musa Kundukh was given the Ottoman title of pasha-general and served with distinction in the Ottoman wars against the Russians.[4]

The little-known story of Lieutenant Semën Atarshchikov offers valuable insights into the life of individuals indispensable to Russia during its conquest and rule of the indigenous population. For in the end, this model Russian officer turned out to be a native son of the Caucasus. Indeed, his is the story of the Caucasus itself: a region of seductive landscapes, exotic languages, diverse peoples, ancient customs, tangled identities, and divided loyalties. It is a story of the indigenous peoples subjected to Russia's conquest and the empire's struggle to turn the highlanders into loyal subjects. Semën Atarshchikov's life is an illustration of an encounter between the worlds of the colonizers and the colonized, and of those who, like Atarshchikov, were caught in between.

THIS book is an attempt to reconstruct the life of Semën Atarshchikov, a Russian officer of Chechen ancestry. It is a fascinating story of a man who in many ways was a typical product of the Russian imperial frontier. Yet writing a biography was never my primary goal. Instead, Atarshchikov's life serves as a vehicle for a larger story—a history of the North Caucasus during the three centuries of Russian conquest (1560s–1860s).

With remarkable consistency throughout the centuries, both imperial St. Petersburg and Soviet Moscow discouraged projects such as this for fear of revealing less-than-complimentary pages from the history book of Russian rule. Tsarist censors deleted stories of Russia's notoriously brutal conquests, while their Soviet counterparts shaped narratives that emphasized the virtues of the conquerors and the benefits they brought to the natives. The only exceptions were the two decades of imperial interregnum: the mid-1920s to mid-1930s, when the colonial nature of the Russian Empire became an officially sanctioned line, and the 1990s, when the collapse of the Soviet Union produced a number of revisionist studies by local historians in the region. Today Moscow has reverted to the old Soviet canards, and revisionist approaches are once again discouraged, not through the overt censorship of old but through the more subtle pressures of a postmodern authoritarian regime.[5]

Apart from political and ideological issues, the historian of the North Caucasus also faces serious methodological challenges. How should one tell the story of a region that, with the exception of common religious identity, remained fragmented in every other respect—political, geographic, linguistic, ethnic, and economic? How can the history of the indigenous peoples be disentangled from the imperial discourse that has tended to dominate historiography? Moreover, any attempt to step outside the imperial narrative is complicated by the fact that kinship-based indigenous societies leave few written records, certainly not enough to counterbalance the overwhelming weight of written sources produced by the imperial administration.

The life of Semën Atarshchikov allows us to address both concerns. Throughout his career Atarshchikov served in different parts of the North Caucasus, and his path thus traces a narrative that embraces the entire region. At the same time, as a product of both Russian and local cultures, Atarshchikov's life enables us to view the history of the region from both the perspective of the indigenous societies and the more familiar view of the imperial center.

A project of this kind presents the historian with some unusual challenges, and some readers may question the way in which I have chosen to meet them. The facts of Atarshchikov's biography are scant. Most information about him comes from a thin file first discovered by M. O. Kosven at the Archive of Military History in Moscow, where I subsequently found several other documents concerning Semën Atarshchikov. To connect the dots, one is inevitably compelled to make leaps of imagination. For example, we have little information about Atarshchikov's father and the circumstances that brought him to Russia. But it is reasonable to assume that he was sent to Russia as a hostage, a practice that was widespread at the time. Similarly, though Semën Atarshchikov and another Russian officer, Fedor Tornau, took part in some of the same campaigns, and the latter mentioned Atarshchikov's name in his famous memoirs, we do not know whether the two knew each other personally. For the purpose of the book's narrative line, however, I assume that they met.

I do not hesitate to bridge the gaps in Atarshchikov's life by applying information derived from well-known local practices and imperial policies. My main concern is not the veracity of Atarshchikov's biographical data but the larger history of the North Caucasus. I am certainly not the first historian to use this approach in the attempt to create a more consistent narrative and invoke the atmosphere of time and place.[6]

In these pages the North Caucasus emerges as a region with a history of daunting complexity. I focus on a set of themes and issues central to the process by which over three centuries the region was transformed from a quintessential frontier into a part of the Russian Empire. I seek to provide a point of departure for those who choose to explore the history of the region at greater length and depth, in the hope that this narrow mountain trail will one day become a well-traveled highway of knowledge. And even though political, linguistic, geographic, and archival challenges may daunt a future scholar, the promise of fascinating new vistas makes the journey worthwhile.

1

The Frontiers of the North Caucasus

A FTER days of traversing the seemingly endless expanse of Russia's southern steppe, a traveler approaching the Terek River would finally take in the sight of the majestic mountaintops of the North Caucasus. Before crossing the river, an early-nineteenth-century traveler would have felt some trepidation: he was about to leave behind familiar European landscapes and enter the mysterious world of Asia. For contemporary Russians, the Terek formed a mental frontier that separated Europe from Asia, the known from the foreign, civilization from barbarism, rationality from exoticism, prosaic life from heroic deeds.

Cascading down the northern slopes of the mountains and then flowing east until it reached the Caspian Sea, the Terek River was a natural divide between the steppe region and the piedmont of the imposing Caucasus Mountains. It was also a military frontier, separating the Cossack towns and forts along the Terek's north bank from the villages of the highlanders perched on the mountain slopes at a distance.

Of course, the area had not always looked the same. Before Russian colonization of the North Caucasus began in earnest in the middle of the eighteenth century, the steppe north of the Terek was prime pastureland intermittently contested by the Kabardins, Kumyks, and Nogays. A perennial frontier, in the fifteenth century the North Caucasus formed the southern borderlands of the Golden Horde—a Turko-Mongol empire stretching from the Danube River to the Aral Sea. The peoples of the Caucasus had invariably found themselves affected by the political winds coming from the north.

Until Russia's conquest of the North Caucasus, it remained a quintessential frontier zone. Several factors helped to prevent the region's annexation by more powerful states. The traditional primitive economies primarily based on animal husbandry and raiding, inaccessible geography, and little strategic value (with the exception of the Derbend passage) offered little incentive for the neighboring empires to commit large resources for a full-scale invasion, conquest, and annexation of the region.

Throughout the sixteenth and the seventeenth centuries, the Ottoman Porte made a few feeble attempts to establish direct control of the North Caucasus. Distracted by more urgent affairs in the west, the Ottomans were content to rely on the Crimean khans to exercise some control in the northwest Caucasus and provide the Porte with prized Adyge (better known as Circassian) slaves. Likewise, sporadic invasions of the northeast Caucasus by the Safavid Persia were intended only to enforce the collection of taxes and tributes from the local population. Thus it was not until Russia's full-scale colonization and military conquests of the early nineteenth century that the North Caucasus acquired strategic importance as a barrier against Russian designs and became one of the battlefields in the notorious "Great Game."[1]

Moscow's Initial Advance

When in the 1550s Moscow conquered and annexed the khanates of Kazan and Astrakhan—two major political and commercial centers on the Volga River—the significance of these momentous events became immediately apparent to the native elites of the Caucasus. Astrakhan in particular was a major commercial and transportation hub linking the North Caucasus to the trade centers dominated by Moscow in the north and the Central Asian markets in the east. The Nogays, whose pastures were along the Yaik, Volga, and later Terek Rivers, had no illusion about the significance of Moscow's presence in the region. In a 1587 letter to the Ottoman sultan, the Nogay ruler Urus ruefully admitted that "whoever controlled Astrakhan, the Volga, and Yaik, controlled all the Nogays."[2]

Moscow's rapid rise was not lost on Temriuk Aidar (Kemirguko Idar), a Kabardin prince whose people were known to the Russians as the Circassians of the "Five Mountains" (Beshtau in Turkic and Piatigorsk in Russian). In 1557 Temriuk dispatched his envoys to Moscow to seek alliance against the traditional foes besieging the Kabardins. In the west the Crimeans were demanding increasing numbers of celebrated Kabardin slaves, and in the east the Kumyks were laying claims to the villages that had formerly paid tribute to the Kabardins. Seeing his power eroded, Temriuk also needed help against the rival Kabardin princes.

The Kremlin was most enthusiastic about the new ally, who was immediately considered the tsar's new subject. In the short term the two could form a common front against their mutual antagonist, the Crimean khan. This alliance also provided an invaluable opportunity to gain a foothold in the Caucasus and advance Moscow's long-term commercial and religious objectives: access to the fabulous riches of the Persian cities on the Caspian Sea and the eventual return of the Black Sea to the Orthodox Christian fold.

In October 1558, Temriuk's two sons, Bulgeruko and Sultanuko, arrived in Moscow to enter the tsar's service. They were baptized Andrei and Mikhail and in a short time reached high military rank. In time, the descendants of Temriuk, known as the Cherkasskiis, became one of the most prestigious and wealthiest clans among the Russian nobility.[3]

The significance of the North Caucasus for Moscow's geopolitical ambitions became fully apparent in 1561. Upon the death of his first wife, Anastasia Romanov, the Russian tsar, Ivan IV, sought a new wife among the Kabardins. In doing so he was following in the footsteps of his famous contemporary, the Ottoman sultan Süleyman the Magnificent, whose first wife was also an Adyge. Ivan's choice fell on one of Temriuk's daughters, Guashene, whose two brothers and a brother-in-law were already in the tsar's service. Brought to Moscow and baptized Maria Temriukovna, she remained Ivan's wife until her death in 1569.

Ivan's marriage to Temriuk's daughter was, among other things, intended to enhance his claims as a new suzerain over the lands that belonged to the Golden Horde. In the complex world of steppe politics, only the Chinggisids, the princes descending from the Chinggis khan's royal lineage, were entitled to lay such claims. Though he was not a Chinggisid, Ivan IV nonetheless attempted in different ways to present himself as a legitimate heir to the Golden Horde's khans. It was no coincidence that Temriuk's other daughter, Altynchach, had been married to Bekbulat, a Chinggisid and khan of Astrakhan, and that their son, baptized in Moscow as Simeon Bekbulatovich, would be crowned the Sovereign of All Russia in the bizarre incident of Ivan's brief abdication in 1575.

For some time the alliance between Ivan and Temriuk paid off. The detachment of Muscovite musketeers sent to Temriuk helped him to contain the threat from his external foes and Kabardin rivals. In return, Moscow established its first advance outpost in the North Caucasus, Fort Tersk, founded in the early 1560s at the place where the Sunzha River discharged into the Terek. It was from this northeastern corner of the North Caucasus, which today comprises northern Daghestan, that Russia's incremental expansion into the area began in the second half of the sixteenth century.

As always, Moscow's geopolitical ambitions far exceeded its military reach, and the fort had to be razed a few years later upon the demands of the Crimean khan. Another attempt to build a Russian fort was abandoned a decade later when the Ottoman Porte claimed that the Kabardins were its subjects and that the fort was an intrusion into an Islamic realm. Finally, in 1588, Fort Tersk was erected in a different but more secure and permanent location in the estuary of the Terek River closer to Astrakhan.[4]

Tersk remained Russia's principal frontier garrison in the Caucasus until the middle of the eighteenth century, when the expansion of the neighboring town of Kizliar made this once-strategic frontier fort obsolete. Built for no other purpose than to serve as an advance military outpost, Tersk was now left far behind the advancing Cossack settlements and Russian forts and was soon abandoned.

Religion and Conquest

Russia's annexation of the North Caucasus began in earnest in the 1760s with the construction of the Mozdok Fortification Line. By the mid-nineteenth century Russia had succeeded in turning the Caucasus from a contested frontier zone into a borderland of the Russian Empire. Yet even the Russian military conquest had little initial impact on the deeply entrenched traditional identities and economies.

The local economies remained completely peripheral to the markets of the neighboring empires, with the major exception of the lively slave trade. The North Caucasus remained both a source and a transit point of a large number of slaves until Russia finally succeeded in stopping the slave trade by the mid-nineteenth century. Before the Russian annexation of the Crimea in the 1780s, many slaves came from among the Adyge peoples of the northwest Caucasus. Either captured by the Crimeans or delivered to them as tribute payments, they were sold in the Crimean market at Kaffa. In the northeast Caucasus, the largest slave market was located at Enderi in northern Daghestan, where thousands of Slavic, Georgian, and local captives were sold to the slave traders from Persia and Central Asia.

The collapse of the slave economy and the simultaneous expansion of Russian towns and industries led a growing number of natives to migrate in search of new opportunities. In the northeast Caucasus, some chose to leave for the neighboring Azeri cities of northern Persia, but most left for Russian towns and villages, where they settled and converted to Christianity. The northwest Caucasus was essentially emptied of the indigenous population when in the 1860s the Russian authorities conducted their own version of ethnic cleansing by forcing the exodus of several hundred thousand Adyges and other native peoples from the Ottoman Empire.

For centuries a zone of economic and political imperial competition, the North Caucasus had also become a religious battleground during the Russian conquest. Several previous attempts to introduce monotheistic religions into the region—most notably, Christianity by the Byzantines and Islam by the Ottomans—yielded few results. It was not until the nineteenth century that the two religions became deeply entrenched in the North Caucasus. One was the Orthodox Christianity of the recently arrived colonizers, who occasionally made their intentions clear by the names given to their new settlements, such as the short-lived Fort of the Holy Cross near the Caspian Sea and the present-day Stavropol (literally, the town of the cross in Greek). The other religion was Islam, adopted by the indigenous population. It was hardly surprising that the native peoples would perceive Christianity as the religion of the imperial authority, whereas Islam was construed as a religion of resistance.

The hold of Islam over the region remained uneven. The northeastern corner of the Caucasus, Daghestan, came under Islamic influence during the initial Arab conquests of the seventh and eighth centuries and thus became the earliest and most thoroughly Islamized part of the region. Sunni Islam prevailed on the coastal plains of northern Daghestan, while Shi`a Islam took hold in parts of the south.

Apart from coastal Daghestan, however, the influence of Islam among the highlanders of the North Caucasus varied, from its tenuous hold in the central North Caucasus among the Chechens, Kabardins (the eastern Adyges), and some Ossetians, to the northwest Caucasus, where Islam was only nominally accepted by the western Adyges (present-day Karachay-Cherkes Autonomous Republic and the Krasnodar province), and to the Ingush, who largely remained animist until the 1860s.

It was not until the late eighteenth and nineteenth centuries that the North Caucasus experienced what can be termed an Islamic revival. This revival was fueled in part by the arrival of the mystical Sufi orders, in particular the Naqshbandi'ya. By the early nineteenth century, both secular and religious elites in the region found themselves on the defensive against the rapidly growing ranks of the Naqshbandi'ya's followers.[5]

Russia's stubborn expansion and brutal war provided another potent impetus for the revival of Islam among the indigenous population. By the time the Russian government began to realize that its military push in the North Caucasus and General Ermolov's scorched earth policies had driven the native population toward further resistance, it was too late. By

1829 the internal disputes within the Naqshbandis in the Caucasus were resolved, and the influential Naqshbandi sheikh Ghazi Muhammad was declared the first imam and the leader of the *ghazawat*, or holy war, aimed at establishing the Islamic state (the Imamate) in the Caucasus.[6]

For the next thirty years, Ghazi Muhammad and his successor, Imam Shamil, continued to resist the Russian expansion in the North Caucasus. The idea of establishing the Imamate, an Islamic state guided by sharia (Islamic law) and ruled by the Muslim religious authorities, became inseparable from the idea of ghazawat against the Russians. It was not accidental that the Russians used the word *murid,* which meant a disciple of the Sufi sheikh, when they were referring to a rebel.[7]

Shamil's war was as much about instilling true Islam and turning the population of the North Caucasus into genuine Muslims as it was about resistance to the Russian invasion. For Shamil and his followers, Islam and sharia were supposed to separate Muslims from Christians, believers from infidels, victims from oppressors, and indigenous peoples from newcomers.

It took three centuries before Russia was able to claim full suzerainty over the North Caucasus and its peoples. The lack of resources in Moscow, the inhospitable terrain of barren steppes and rugged mountains, and the resistance of the local population inspired by Muslim clergy and aided by neighboring Islamic states—all conspired against a quick and successful conquest.

By 1800 much of the North Caucasus's plain, overwhelmed by settlers, had been secured within Russia's imperial borders, while a continuous chain of fortifications stretching from the Caspian to the Black Sea firmly separated the plains from the foothills and mountains where the native inhabitants continued to reside. By the 1860s the long and bloody conquest of the North Caucasus was over, but it had come at a great price in blood and treasure.

It is impossible to calculate the full financial cost of the conquest. Suffice it to mention that whereas in the 1820s the government's annual military expenditures in the Caucasus were 24,000 silver rubles, in the 1840s the Caucasus consumed one-sixth of the entire imperial budget. But far more shocking were the human losses. It is estimated that the Russians lost a hundred thousand soldiers in battle and nine times that many from disease. If one assumes that an equal number of natives died during the Russian conquest of the region, it would mean that two million people perished so that an estimated population of four million natives could be annexed to Russia.[8]

The Indigenous Societies

The history of Russian expansion into the Caucasus is more than just a story of military conquest and colonization. It is also a story of the encounter between worlds that were structurally incompatible: the world of the highly centralized empire-state and indigenous, kinship-based societies with rudimentary political organizations. In this sense, it is the story of a continuous learning process by both sides. Viewing the outside world through the prism of its own society, each side projected upon the other its own values and expectations. The fact that multiple clan, tribal, linguistic, and later ethnic identities in the region intersected in complex and poorly understood ways did not make communication easier. Thus, Russian government policies must be seen not only as a product of government objectives and ideologies but also in the context of genuine and persistent mutual misperceptions.[9]

Moscow's presence in the region was marked from the very beginning by a single concern: securing the political loyalty of the local peoples. From a Russian point of view this was accomplished through a ritual idiom of pledging an allegiance (*shert*) to the Russian sovereign. But the government's official rhetoric of self-aggrandizement and the ritual of allegiance, which portrayed the natives as the subjects of Moscow, persistently failed to recognize that the reality differed substantially from the official language. The government preferred to deny the uncomfortable fact that Russia's relationship with the local chiefs was more akin to a military-political alliance of unequal but independent rulers.[10]

At various times, Russian officials and military commanders observed that applying the yardstick of the empire's official terminology to the natives was not helpful. Grigorii Kotoshikin noted this in his famous treatise in the 1660s, and so did Prince Alexander Bekovich-Cherkasskii in the 1710s. But if the former could have been dismissed as a traitor and the latter as too sympathetic to his kin, none of this could apply to Russia's legendary commander, the future field-marshal Alexander Suvorov. In 1779, after having received a report about the oath of allegiance taken by the Adyges, Suvorov penned in the margins, "[T]he notion of becoming a subject is not as important in their language as it is in Russian. It is better to avoid such descriptions."[11]

For Suvorov the conceptual differences between Russia and the native peoples implied the need for a better understanding of the other side, but for others they were a call for even harsher measures when dealing with the natives. Such was the case of General Delpozzo, who in 1809 alerted his superior commander, General A. P. Tormasov, that the oath of allegiance was meaningless to the natives and putting it in writing was of no help. Yet, if Russian military commanders allowed such glimpses of reality in their internal correspondence, the same was not permissible in their reports to St. Petersburg. A year later, despite Delpozzo's warning, General Tormasov reported to the emperor that the Ingush people had voluntarily taken an oath and became the eternal subjects of His Imperial Majesty.[12]

At one point, Russian authorities began to use the term "half-loyal highlanders" to capture the ambiguity of the situation. To reconcile Russia's claims to the region and its peoples with the contrasting reality was never an easy matter. The supreme commander in the Caucasus, General I. F. Paskevich, attempted to do so in 1830, following the orders from the capital to compile a map of the Caucasus demarcating the peoples who had submitted to Russian rule. A large part of the map that was eventually sent to St. Petersburg was colored green, indicating the peoples loyal to Russia. Paskevich was compelled to attach a special report explaining that even though "the green line on the map delineated the peoples who swore allegiance to the sovereign and emperor, this did not mean that they had been subdued, because many of them often violated their allegiance which they usually swore as a matter of temporary necessity during the military expeditions against them."[13]

Geopolitical and military concerns notwithstanding, throughout the nineteenth century the Russian government began to show increasing interest in learning more about the region and its peoples. Numerous expeditions ventured deep inside the region to describe the topography and collect information about the local peoples and languages. The Russified native elite were given the task of compiling the codes of the customary laws and composing treatises describing the indigenous peoples and their social organization. By the middle of the nineteenth century, the Russians had a significant body of knowledge at their disposal. Yet how to apply it toward advancing the imperial agenda in the region remained a matter of debate among the military authorities.

Russia's acquaintance with the region began with the peoples of the plains and the foothills of the northeast Caucasus, the Kumyks and Kabardins. It was the Kumyks who provided the Russians with the first glimpses into the native societies of the North Caucasus. The Kumyks were a part of the Turko-Mongol world and spoke a dialect of the Turkic language that was a lingua franca throughout the Eurasian steppe. They possessed the most centralized political structure among the peoples of the region. At the top of the social hierarchy of princes and nobles, known as the *uzden,* was a ruler with the title of the *shamkhal* who exercised substantial political authority.

The Kabardins and their language belonged to a distinct Adyge-Abkhazian branch of the Caucasian language group. The Adyge people, widely known as Circassians, populated most of the northwest and central Caucasus. The Kabardins were the most powerful and numerous people among the various subdivisions of the Adyge, and their territories, largely known as the Greater and Lesser Kabarda, occupied the central part of the North Caucasus. To the east there were clusters of the numerous village societies, later subsumed under the name Chechens; to the southeast were the Ingush, Ossetians, and Balkars.

Kabardin society, like that of the Kumyks, was highly differentiated. The hereditary nobility consisted of the members of the four princely families, the *pshi,* whom the Russian called princes, and the lesser nobility, *uork,* whom the Russians called *uzden.* Applying the term *uzden* to the Kabardins indicated Moscow's tenuous grasp of the social hierarchies of the different indigenous societies. The term, of Turkic origin, was a title of nobility among the Kumyks and other Turkic peoples (the Karachays and Balkars). The Kabardins and other Adyge peoples, however, did not use the term but instead carefully differentiated among the types of uorks.

It was only in the 1820s that the government began to realize the importance of the finer gradation of ranks among the Kabardin nobility. Even then, the subtleties of the indigenous social rules continued to elude the Russian authorities, as they attempted to systematize and divide the lesser Kabardin nobility into the uzden of four different ranks. To the Kabardins the new administrative language made little sense.[14]

Other peoples of the region, most notably the Abadzekhs in the west and the Chechens in the northeast Caucasus, were organized into free societies. Nineteenth-century Russian observers distinguished them from others by referring to them as democratic societies, which essentially were a cluster of villages or clans united by kinship, territory, and a mutual oath; the elders decided common matters in the council, and the most skillful fighters led others in raids and ambushes.

These free societies had little social differentiation and were essentially brotherhoods, alliances of communities bound by mutual oath, which the Russians translated as *soprisiazhnichestvo* (cf. the Eidgenossenschaft of the early Swiss confederations). Among the Chechens, such brotherhoods were known as *tukkhum,* which consisted of a number of clans (*taips*). These alliances functioned as a way of adopting a fugitive individual into the local clan as well as cementing the ties among different clans, which formed complex co-fraternities.[15] The fiercely independent societies of the Chechens and western Adyges offered the most resistance to the Russians and, with no traditional elite to co-opt, proved hardest to subdue.

Yet the fragmentation and lack of unity among the indigenous populations remained their main weakness. One significant attempt to form a larger confederation among the western Adyge was undertaken in the 1790s. With the initial encouragement of the Russian authorities, the commoners of the three Adyge tribes—Shapsug, Abadzekh, and Natukhay—united against the Shapsug nobles and their ally, the Bzhedugs. Later, chastened by the experience of the French Revolution, Catherine the Great decided to switch sides. In 1796, in a major battle on the banks of the Bziuko River near today's Krasnodar, a troop of Black Sea Cossacks armed with cannon and shrapnel played a crucial role in saving the native elite from a complete debacle. If this was an opportunity to form a lasting Adyge confederation, it was cut short by Russian support for the local elite.[16]

One other attempt to create a confederation was undertaken in 1861, when the representatives of the Abadzekhs, Ubykhs, and Shapsugs convened in the valley of the Sochi River to form a collective government that could better resist the Russian invasion. Presented with an ultimatum to resettle in the Kuban plains or face deportations to the Ottoman Empire, the Adyge Grand Council, better known as the Mejlis of the Circassian Freedom, chose resistance and sent envoys to Istanbul, Paris, and London with an appeal for help. When help did not materialize and the resistance proved futile, several hundred thousand Adyges were forced into exile and a mass emigration to the Ottoman Empire during 1863–65.[17]

Russia's attempt to impose its political and legal norms upon the indigenous societies collided with the traditional values and practices forged through the centuries of communal experience. Some indigenous institutions were seen by Russians as particularly invidious in constraining Russia's ability to impose imperial rule and order in the region. For example, native peoples conceptualized their relationship with the Russian authorities through two traditional institutions: the *maslahat,* a truce and an alliance against a common enemy, and the *konak (kunak),* a form of patronage and mutual protection. Neither of these implied the kind of subservient relationship that the Russians expected from their putative subjects.

Many of the same customs that the Russian authorities confronted throughout the entire Eurasian steppe tenaciously stood in the way of Russian colonization of the North Caucasus. The native societies continued to rely on the *barimta,* a widely practiced custom of seizing herds or humans as bargains in adjudicating disputes, which the authorities saw as simple brigandage. The *kanly,* a kin-based vendetta against an enemy and his kin that could involve several generations, often seemed to the Russians to be unstoppable. The boundaries of families and clans were extended further through the institution of *atalyk,* which promoted bonds across different clans and social groups through the adoptive relations between fathers and sons. Another long-established tradition continued to spit out socially ostracized individuals or communities, the *abreks,* who became the most formidable raiders across the frontier. Finally, the institution of the konak had also sealed the bonds of the inviolate hospitality between the individuals and often those seeking refuge as the konaks proved to be outside the reach of Russian authorities.[18]

The peoples of the North Caucasus remained an aggregation of highly fragmented Islamic societies organized on the basis of kinship, language, and common territory. Their social organization varied dramatically, from the free societies of the western Adyges and Chechens to the more complex political entities in the northern Daghestan and among the Kabardins. The local nobles and notables were interested in preserving and augmenting their power through a continued reliance on customary law (*adat*) that privileged the elite. At the same time, the local Islamic judges and scholars, the *ulema,* presented an alternative locus of power, which wanted to extend the rule of the more egalitarian sharia at the expense of the customary law.

By the mid-nineteenth century the Russians were able to provide a sort of Pax Russica that could assure the relative stability and development of the region. But Christian colonial power, which sought to graft itself upon the people of the region through the usual combination of carrots and sticks, was seen as alien and unwelcome by the Muslim population. Not surprisingly, Islam became a rallying force for all those who chose to resist the invaders under the green banners of Sheikh Mansur in the 1780s and three other imams from 1824 to 1859. It was only after the failures to create long-lasting confederations or Islamic states in the region that modern ideas of ethnic and national identities began to reach the North Caucasus as it became increasingly drawn into the Russian imperial orbit.

Methods of Conquest and Colonization

Russia's conquest of the Caucasus was comprehensive. Unlike the Persians, who occasionally sent expeditionary forces into the region to assert their short-lived supremacy, or the Ottomans, whose sporadic military campaigns intended little more than ensuring a flow of taxes and slaves to the Crimea and Istanbul, the Russian government undertook a systematic colonization of the region by stationing troops in the numerous forts; dispatching bureaucrats, merchants, and priests to the newly built towns; and encouraging the newcomers to settle and farm the land.

By the mid-nineteenth century, almost three hundred years after Russia's first attempt to conquer and colonize the region, the North Caucasus appeared substantially altered by the impact of Russian policies. Most of the changes occurred throughout the first half of the nineteenth century. The geography of the region underwent a dramatic transformation as rivers were diverted, primeval forests systematically cut down, and pastureland seized to build forts, settlements, industries, and spas. The traditional economies had become more dependent on Russian products and cash. The large-scale slave trade was formally abandoned, even though it was not uncommon for many native children and women to be sold to Russian officials and end up in bondage across the frontier. Traditional law had increasingly come under the influence of the Russian one, and various peoples began to redefine their identity through modern notions of ethnicity. Finally, Russian policies created a colonial situation that served as a catalyst in intensifying the social antagonisms between the indigenous elite and commoners on the one hand and among different groups of the indigenous elite on the other. The result was the emergence of two sharply polarized factions within native societies: one pro-Russian, the other pro-Islamic and consequently anti-Russian.

Like imperial conquests elsewhere, Russia's expansion into the region had begun with indirect rule: paying off the native elite and manipulating local factions in an effort to secure the political loyalty of the indigenous population. By the late eighteenth century the increasing presence of the Russian military, the arrival of the colonists, and a demand for Russian trade allowed for a shift toward direct rule over annexed lands and subjugated peoples.

In the early 1790s the government decided that the time had come to consolidate Russian rule by introducing a new system of courts and justice. Catherine the Great believed that military force alone was not enough to subdue the highlanders and that "the rule of law was the best way to soften and win over their hearts." In the nineteenth century some government officials continued to envision the cautious and phased transformation of native customs and laws as the only way "to achieve the desired moral and civil development of indigenous tribes."[19]

In an attempt to introduce Russian legal and administrative norms, Russian authorities set up clan (*rodovoi*) and frontier courts. The clan courts, composed of members elected from the local nobles, notables, and some clergy, followed adat. Their decisions could be appealed to the frontier court at Mozdok, which included both native and Russian officials and was chaired by the Mozdok military commander. Ultimately the frontier court was under the jurisdiction of and subordinate to the Astrakhan governor-general. Despite the token native representation in the courts, all major decisions were in the hands of Russian authorities. The new court system functioned as intended by the government: a barely disguised tool of Russian domination.

It is likely that Russian authorities did not quite realize the full extent of damage that the new courts and laws would inflict upon Russia's relations with the native population. This court system effectively excluded the Muslim clergy and sharia courts from decision making. Likewise, a series of measures severely circumscribed the traditional rights of the secular elites by requiring them to seek special permission to travel, to convene public meetings, or to offer refuge and hospitality to outsiders. In other words, the Russian government effectively antagonized both the religious and the secular elites.

With the courts' members turned into salaried officials and much of the secular elite bought off with military ranks and entitlements, the local population increasingly saw the clan and frontier courts as a vehicle of Russian colonization. Election to the clan courts was usually preceded by the deployment of Russian troops among the locals and could not have taken place without the threat of force.[20]

In 1807, a series of insurrections in the midst of the continuous wars with the Persian and Ottoman empires compelled Russian authorities to replace the clan courts with *mahkeme* courts. Composed of native secular elite and Muslim judges (*qadi*), the mahkeme adjudicated cases mostly on the basis of sharia law and did not allow any appeal to Russian authorities. The emergence of the mahkeme signaled a temporary retreat from the government's goals of Russifying the region.

In 1822, continuing his "gradual but persistent conquest," Ermolov announced a new assault on Islamic institutions: the hajj, a pilgrimage to Mecca and Medina, was banned and the mahkeme courts were replaced with the Kabardin Provisional Court. The new court included elements of adat, sharia, and Russian laws. Its members were no longer elected but appointed by Russian authorities. A surrogate legal and administrative body with the task of governing the Kabardins, the new court intruded into the Kabardin local affairs more than any previous Russian attempts at projecting imperial authority. But the court proved to be less provisional than Ermolov had intended. It survived until 1858, when it was replaced by a similarly hybrid court, now renamed the people's court, with better-defined judicial functions.[21]

Throughout this period, Russian authorities relied on an incomplete and fragmented knowledge of both adat and sharia. In 1841, the local military authorities proposed compiling the customary law of the peoples of the North Caucasus and translating it together with sharia into Russian. Four years later, the first of the adats were collected and annotated. In 1847, Captain M. Ia. Ol'shevskii, whose task was to systematize the adats of the North Caucasus, had to admit that his efforts were incomplete and some of his descriptions were likely to be erroneous. In 1849, another captain of the general staff in Tiflis, Baron K. F. Stahl, annotated a large body of the Adyge adats. Yet the progress of collecting adats was slow and continued into the 1860s. The administration's acquaintance with adat and sharia laws remained tenuous, and it continued to rely on the Russified local elite as its guide through the native legal realm.[22]

If various attempts to increase the influence of Russian law often served to alienate the native elite, so too did the policy of encouraging the migration of native commoners to the Russian interior provinces. Throughout the eighteenth century, such migrants were resettled, converted to Christianity, and not allowed to return, despite persistent pleas to authorities from the local nobles. In the 1770s, the government decided to placate the elite and pledged to return fugitives or pay the local nobles compensation for those who stayed behind. Nonetheless, in the early nineteenth century, numerous individuals and groups of commoners continued to seek and were granted refuge across the frontier. They were given tax exemptions and allowed to settle and farm the land.

Driving a wedge between the elite and commoners remained a contentious policy. After all, the commoners were an irregular militia, while the noble cavalry constituted the equivalent of a professional military force, and some Russian commanders believed that turning the local elite into the enemy made little sense. One policy recommendation was simply to deprive the local inhabitants of their herds, make them dependent on Russia, and then resettle them deep inside the Russian provinces.[23]

At the same time, the government's policy continued to divide the native elite by supporting one people or faction against another. Many local chiefs and nobles were successfully co-opted by the numerous advantages that cooperation with Russia had to offer. It is safe to say that at the time, most of the internal conflicts within the indigenous societies were generated directly or indirectly by the Russian policies in the region.

However, winning the allegiance of some chiefs over others was not a one-way street. It also meant that Russian authorities were increasingly drawn into local politics. No longer seen as outside observers or a third party, the authorities were forced to take sides. They now had vested interests and responsibilities to those chiefs and factions that they sponsored while becoming a target of rival factions.

Russia's expansion and its policies of dividing the elite, offering refuge to migrant nobles and commoners alike, and above all, converting some

Muslims to Christianity assured a continuous violent response from the indigenous population. While Shamil's war (1829–59) against Russia attracted most attention, the North Caucasus was in a state of virtually constant rebellion before and long after Shamil. Since the 1760s the repeated outbursts of violence and Russia's repressive measures against the "rebels" had come in cyclical waves. In the 1770s, the government dispatched the military to suppress uprisings among the Kabardins, Chechens, and Nogays. In the 1780s, the government struggled to contain the Sheikh Mansur uprising (1785–91), which threatened to engulf the entire region. In the 1790s, another wave of uprisings and internal wars spread among the Adyges.

Despite Napoleon's threat and the invasion that followed, Russia continued to be actively involved in the Caucasus in the first decade of the nineteenth century. The completion of the Georgian Military Highway in 1799 opened the way for the formal annexation of Georgia two years later and renewed activity in Transcaucasia. The successful conclusion of the wars with the Ottomans (1806–12) and the Persians (1804–13) left most of the Georgian and Azeri territories in Russian hands.

As the Russian grip on the region tightened, the rebellions among the various peoples of the North Caucasus did not abate. Between 1806 and 1813, a series of punitive military expeditions left a trail of blood and destruction in the campaigns against the various peoples of Daghestan, the Chechens, Kabardins, Ossetians, and Adyges. By 1815, with Napoleon's defeat and the renewed sense of confidence and mission in St. Petersburg, the time had come to secure Russia's control of Transcaucasia and to assert imperial rule over the "savage" peoples of the North Caucasus.

2

Atarshchikov's Childhood

SEMËN Semënovich Atarshchikov was born in 1807 in Naurskaia, one of the largest Cossack settlements on the Terek River. Semën was a typical product of the frontier—a first-generation Cossack whose parents had been brought to Russia as teenagers from their native societies. His father was a Chechen from a small hamlet across the Terek River, and his mother was a Nogay whose kinsmen roamed the steppe between the Terek and Kuma Rivers. Our story begins with Semën's father and his odyssey from the family of a lesser chief to the Russian army, where he served as a translator.

The Father

Semën's father, Ismail, was the second son of a prominent Chechen villager from the area of Borokhan, a small sliver of land south of the Terek River and west of the Sunzha's estuary. If the North Caucasus was a contested frontier separating Russia from the Ottoman and Persian Empires, Borokhan—or Braguny, as the Russians referred to it—was a frontier zone claimed by Kumyk rulers in the east and Kabardin princes in the west. The area consisted of a cluster of hamlets (Baragunskie kabaki), mostly populated by Chechens, and a larger Kumyk village of Borokhan. As was typical in the borderlands, the residents of the area were bilingual, intermarriages were frequent, and the local Chechens were thoroughly assimilated into Kumyk traditional culture.

Moscow's expansion was traditionally accompanied by immediate claims of suzerainty over newly encountered peoples, and Braguny was

A decorated Cossack officer with his sword

no exception. Though Moscow mentioned Braguny among "the newly acquired states" as early as 1593, such claims remained a mere rhetorical exercise of political aggrandizement well into the eighteenth century.[1] Even then, the loyalty of the Braguny chiefs could not be taken for granted, and Russian military authorities had to rely on hostages as the best way to assure that Braguny was "a peaceful village."

It was in these circumstances in the late 1780s that Ismail Atarshchikov was delivered as a hostage to the Russian authorities in Kizliar. Russia's immediate demand for hostages was prompted by two events: a rapidly spreading anti-Russian uprising led by a Chechen named Ushurma, better known under his nom de guerre Sheikh Mansur, and the outbreak of yet another war with the Ottoman Empire (1787–91).

The initial success of Sheikh Mansur's call for a jihad—a holy war—against the Russians in the Caucasus and his vigorous support by the Ottoman authorities was a cause of great concern in St. Petersburg. But by 1791 the Russians had proved to be victorious in both crushing Mansur's uprising and making the Ottomans sue for peace. Mansur was captured when Russian troops seized the Ottoman fortress of Anapa on the Black Sea coast. He was promptly dispatched to St. Petersburg and remained imprisoned in the infamous Schlisselburg fortress until his death in 1794. All of this would happen later, but in 1786 the outcome of the war in the North Caucasus was far from certain, and the Russians resorted to a time-honored tradition of demanding hostages from the local chiefs in hope of securing their allegiance or, more realistically, their neutrality.

Taking hostages was a standard practice in Russia's relations with the non-Christian population along the frontier. A typical hostage (*amanat*) was one of the chief's male heirs, who would be sent to a Russian frontier town to reside there in a specially constructed "hostage quarters." The hostages usually lived in squalid conditions and in a state of virtual imprisonment. The measure was intended as leverage against the local chiefs in preventing their hostile acts against Russia.[2]

By the late eighteenth century, the Russian government was slowly turning toward more subtle ways of exerting control over the non-Christian peoples. Hostages were still in demand, but they were now arriving in a new guise—the sons of the local nobles and notables to be schooled and educated in Russia. Prominent hostages were often sent to the imperial court at St. Petersburg to receive an education befitting a noble scion. Ismail, as the son of a lesser chief, was sent to a newly founded boarding school for non-Christian boys in the city of Astrakhan.

This school had just opened its doors through the efforts of the Astrakhan governor, Semën Krechetnikov, who envisioned the Caucasus transformed through the civilizing hand of the Russian administration. A typical product of the Age of Enlightenment, Krechetnikov believed that ignorance, which for him was synonymous with the Islamic religion and the natives' barbarous customs, was a major handicap en route to civilization—the latter equated with Christian and Russian values. The school was supposed to introduce the boys to Russian ways and prepare them to be inducted into the military "so that there would no longer be a need to take hostages, and they would convert to Christianity."[3]

Ismail arrived in Astrakhan at the age of thirteen and was enrolled in the boarding school. The school was an old one-storied building that the governor had selected for this purpose. Its two rooms, the classroom and the bedroom, were not heated. Its fourteen students, between the ages of twelve and seventeen, represented different peoples of the region: the Kalmyks, Nogays, Kabardins, Kumyks, and Chechens. The boys were badly mistreated, poorly fed, and harshly disciplined. The mortality rate in school was usually much higher than its graduation rate.[4]

Ismail was the lucky one. He survived three years of schooling, learning arithmetic, how to read and write in Russian, and of course the fundamentals of the Christian faith. At the age of seventeen he converted to Christianity, was baptized Semën, and was given the last name Atarshchikov. The choice of the converts' surnames varied. They were most often Russified forms of family, ethnic, or birthplace names. In Semën's case, the surname Atarshchikov literally meant "a cattle hand, cowboy" and was derived from his native hamlet of Otar.[5] With the newly forged Russian Orthodox Christian identity, Semën Atarshchikov was drafted into the army and assigned to the Cossack regiment stationed in Mozdok as a translator of the Chechen and Kumyk languages.

The job of a military translator did not allow for much personal life. Yet several times in the following decade, he took leaves to visit his home village, only to be reminded of the stark contrast between his childhood memories and his present life. His parents and elder brother were now deceased and buried at a local cemetery. His sisters were married: one to a minor Kumyk noble in a neighboring village, the other to a Terek Cossack from the Cossack settlement across the Terek. His father had willed the family property to be placed into a charitable trust (*waqf*) endowed to the local mosque. Such an arrangement both satisfied the pious urges of his father (who might have felt guilty for allowing his son to become a Russian) and at the same time allowed the family to draw on a stable income from the trust.

Some time in the early 1800s, during one of the Russian military campaigns, the elder Semën found himself in Karabudakhkent, a distant

Kumyk village on the Caspian shore. This was the place where he had lived and studied for several years before being surrendered to the Russians as a hostage. Tradition demanded that a young boy had to be raised away from home by an adoptive father known as an *atalyk*. Following the complex ties of kinship, Semën had been sent here to live with one of the Karabudakhkent nobles.

The village was still here, nestled in the foothills of the Caucasus among the familiar fields, pasturelands, vineyards, and orchards. But Russia's growing presence was already visible even in this bucolic environment. The rich soil of the village continued to produce peaches, apricots, persimmons, grapes, and honey, all of which were now increasingly sold in Russian towns in the north rather than in the Persian ones in the south. Madder (a type of herb), the source of a bright-red dye, was in particular demand. Russian-manufactured textiles, boots, utensils, and various luxury items were omnipresent. There were even several new houses built in the Russian style by migrant laborers from Russia. They were easily distinguished from the local ones by tin or tiled roofs, glass windows with shutters, and stoves.

Many villagers remembered the elder Semën as a studious young boy who excelled in learning Arabic and memorizing verses from the Quran. But now, in his Cossack uniform he was an outsider, a part of the invading army, a translator for the high-ranking Russian officers. His presence among the villages must have provoked both fascination and dismay. Some despised him for his conversion to Christianity; others were awed by his transformation and success. But all were spellbound by the new world he represented—the little-known but increasingly less distant Christian land called Russia.

After his stay in Karabudakhkent, the elder Semën was determined to settle down and start his own family in his new homeland. The road back to his native society seemed to have been cut off. He was now seen as a Russian, and whether he himself shared that perception mattered no longer. Shortly upon his return, Semën married a Cossack woman, Antonina Urusova. Born in the plain felt tent of a Nogay herdsman, she too was a newcomer to Russian mores and customs. Once the Nogays had formed a mighty nomadic confederation, but now they were dispersed throughout the North Caucasus steppe and utterly destitute.

At the age of six Antonina had been sold by her parents to an Armenian merchant in Kizliar. Even though Russian law forbade the slave trade, such practice was widespread in the region. Purchasing non-Christians was an extremely profitable business, and many local Russian officials received kickbacks and bribes for turning a blind eye to such transactions.

St. Petersburg was conflicted about stopping the trade in human chattel, and it reversed itself on many occasions, permitting local officials, merchants, and Cossacks to buy and enslave the local residents so that they could be civilized and converted to Christianity. There were plenty of impoverished and desperate families willing to part with some of their children in exchange for cash, cattle, or other valuable items.

Taken away from her family at a young age, Antonina never returned to her Nogay past and had a stronger Cossack identity than did her husband, who retained childhood memories, his native language, and a connection to his family and village. It was to this Chechen-born father and Nogay-born mother that the younger Semën was born in 1807 in the Cossack frontier settlement of Naurskaia.

Naurskaia

Naurskaia was no ordinary Cossack village (*stanitsa*). Built between 1642 and 1645 on the north bank of the Terek River, it was one of the oldest Cossack settlements in the steppe. Its early founding date as a small Cossack fort with twenty to thirty defenders would have remained unnoticed had the Cossacks not chosen to rob a prominent Kabardin nobleman on his way to Tersk to join the tsar's military service.

Kambulat Pshimakh Cherkasskii and his retinue of eight uzdens barely escaped alive when a band of Cossacks fell upon their camp near Naurskaia. Their horses and military gear—armor, helmets, bows, and quivers—were seized, and one uzden was killed. When Kambulat appealed to the military governors of Tersk to investigate and return the loot, they professed their inability to deal with the Cossacks for fear of provoking them. The Kabardin nobleman then petitioned the tsar to detain the Cossack ringleaders and subject them to interrogation, which was synonymous with torture. On the reverse side of the submitted petition, the tsar ordered the torture of the ringleaders so that the truth could be found and the stolen items recovered and returned to the chief and his people.[6]

Small bands of Cossacks had been present in the foothills of the Caucasus along the Terek River (the Greben Heights) since the 1580s. By the middle of the eighteenth century, however, Russian military fortifications and Cossack settlements dotted the left bank of the Terek. Naurskaia received a major boost when several hundred Volga Cossacks were transferred there in 1765.[7]

During the late eighteenth century, Naurskaia's military and commercial significance made it an attractive target of several military campaigns. In

1774, when a large Crimean army besieged the town, the hopelessly out-numbered residents were able to hold off against the Crimeans. By some accounts, the Cossacks' wives showed extraordinary courage in this des-perate defense—taking positions on the village walls, pouring boiled water down on the attackers, and cutting with sickles those who managed to climb up the earthen rampart. When the story of Naurskaia's legendary defense reached St. Petersburg, Catherine II bestowed lifetime pensions on the Cossack women of Naurskaia in recognition of their unprecedented valor. From that time onward, the residents celebrated this memorable event on Women's Day, when once a year the women were given full au-thority over men.[8]

But there was more to Naurskaia than the images of military prowess and courage. By the early nineteenth century it had developed into an im-portant regional center set apart from other Cossack towns and forts by its commercial and industrial ties across the frontier. The Naurskaia trade fair was one of the largest among similar fairs and annually drew crowds of visitors from the entire North Caucasus. In 1837, for instance, 6,500 Chechen, Ingush, Kumyk, and other local villagers came to Naurskaia to purchase 39,000 rubles' worth of goods.

Trade had always been an important tool in the overall Russian strat-egy of promoting the natives' dependence on Russia. Trade with high-landers was strictly regulated, and banned items included anything that could be turned into potential weapons: iron, steel, gunpowder, firearms, gold, and silver. As of 1810, such trade was conducted at the specially constructed exchange markets (*menovyi dvor*) on the outskirts of Russian frontier towns and was supervised by Russian officials. The highlanders brought to market the raw materials—hides, wools, horses, local clothing and crafts—that they were permitted to barter but not sell. In return, they were eager to obtain textiles, sugar, grain, soap, paper, mirrors, and all sorts of industrial products from Russia. By far the most valuable com-modity was salt, which was available at an exceedingly high price because of the government monopoly on the salt trade.

By the mid-nineteenth century, Naurskaia's rudimentary industry re-ceived a boost from the increasing demand for petroleum that had been discovered in the natural wells near Fort Groznyi. Together with Mozdok, Naurskaia became the principal center for refining and distilling oil. By 1855, production from these wells reached around 1,400 barrels annually.[9]

Arriving at Naurskaia in the early nineteenth century, a traveler on his way to the Caucasus would not have failed to notice that he had reached Russia's distant borderlands. Naurskaia appeared to be unmistakably different from towns and villages in Russia. The village had been built with no apparent planning. Houses with no yards or fences were smoky huts with adjacent entrance halls decorated with painted and copper-cast icons. Hanging on the walls of these halls were muskets, sabers, saddles, reins, and other essential items of the Cossack lifestyle. Chests and boxes for storage were placed on wide, low-built benches, which also served as beds. They had mattresses and pillows with silk pillowcases in a brightly colored, checkered designs.

The interiors of the houses and the haphazard nature in which the houses were scattered around betrayed the influence of local traditions and styles, formed over the centuries through contact with regional cultures.

The most conspicuous sign of a frontier settlement was the dress of its inhabitants. The Cossack men wore the cloth jackets (*chekmen*) favored by natives, and women wore long dresses (*sarafan*) with short sleeves girded with silk sashes (*kushak*). Gardening, fishing, and raising cattle provided the staple foods. Horses and cattle were kept in pens on the village's outskirts and guarded by Cossack watchmen.[10]

With a population of about two thousand residents, Naurskaia was one of the largest Cossack villages, falling short only of several larger regional centers such as Kizliar, Mozdok, and Stavropol. Similar to that in other frontier settlements, Naurskaia's multicultural environment was a mixture of different peoples, tongues, and customs. Yet the specific ethnic composition of towns varied. For example, Mozdok's non-Slavic population, composed mostly of hundreds of Georgians, Armenians, and Greeks, had been resettled there to develop various industries. Naurskaia's non-Russian residents were mostly converts from among the neighboring peoples: Chechens, Kumyks, and Nogays. There were also plenty of visitors from nearby indigenous villages. Right across the Terek from Naurskaia, there were several villages settled in the 1780s by the Chechens who had migrated from the uplands. Many Cossacks and Chechens chose to become kunaks, forming ties of strong friendship, and exchanged frequent visits.[11]

Like other Cossack settlements in the North Caucasus, Naurskaia was a miniature melting pot that blended the Russo-Ukrainian traditions brought by the Don and Volga Cossacks with those of the native population into a distinct culture of the Cossack Caucasus. Despite their different backgrounds and tolerance for other customs and languages, the Cossacks of Naurskaia had one overarching identity: they were Orthodox Christians.

Despite this fact, the Cossacks were notoriously oblivious to religious matters. Their interest in Christianity was limited to exhibiting icons in their houses and celebrating Christian holidays. The only church in the village was more often empty than not. And yet they regarded themselves as good Orthodox Christians, and any man who wished to become a Cossack and settle in Naurskaia had first to abandon his faith and convert to Christianity. In other words, the melting pot was a distinctly Christian one.[12]

The Cossack Childhood

Semën's childhood in Naurskaia at first seemed remarkably similar to that of other Cossack children. He did what other boys did: learned how to ride a horse and handle a musket and a saber, fished, tended livestock, helped around the house, and waited patiently for his father's return from endless military campaigns. Semën was aware of the respect that his father commanded among the Cossacks, for the elder Semën was one of the few Cossacks who were literate. He could read and write and was conversant in several local languages in addition to Russian. It was his father who taught Semën the alphabet and helped him acquire basic reading skills by the age of seven. Only a few other boys in Naurskaia could boast of being able to read at this early age—the sons of a scribe, a treasurer, and a Cossack commander (*ataman*).

Yet by the time Semën turned eight, his life took an abrupt and critical turn. His father decided that the time had come to send his son across the frontier lest he completely forget the language and culture of his ancestors. The decision was less surprising than it might seem because it was based on the old custom widely practiced by most peoples of the North Caucasus: a notable would entrust his son, and on occasion his daughter, to be raised by one of his own servitors or another notable from a different clan or people. A child could spend anywhere from seven to thirteen years growing up in the family of such a man, who became his atalyk—a combination of adopted father, caretaker, and tutor (in different forms a similar custom has existed in many cultures).

To become an atalyk was an honor, and it was not uncommon that several candidates competed with one another for the privilege of hosting a child. An atalyk could also count on more tangible dividends than honor. He was generously rewarded by the son's father and together with his family was now considered the adopted kin. The institution of atalyk allowed the critical circle of friends and allies to expand, as a child who grew up with an atalyk acquired an adopted father and brothers (*imeldesh,* literally known as milk brothers).[13]

The elder Semën did not follow the atalyk custom to the letter. As it was practiced among the Kumyks—the Chechens did not appear to have

Prince Grigory Gagarin, a Circassian noble with his atalyk

this institution—the child was supposed to be given to an atalyk sometime shortly after his birth or at the age of three or four. Yet the very fact that the elder Semën chose to have his eight-year-old son raised in accordance with the local custom attested to this Cossack convert's continuous links to the indigenous peoples. Likewise, the fact that the Russian authorities did not object to his decision was an eloquent testimony that they understood that frontier identities remained fluid and uncertain.

It is possible that Semën would have arranged for an atalyk earlier had the situation in the Caucasus been safer. But in the first decade of the nineteenth century, the entire region was engulfed in war. In 1804, the eastern part of the Caucasus, and Daghestan in particular, became a principal theater of military conflict in the new war between the Russian and Persian Empires. Two years later the Russians were at war with the Ottomans in the western part of the North Caucasus. The hostilities did not end until 1812, when the anticipated Napoleonic invasion compelled St. Petersburg to seek peace in the region. The first peace treaty was signed with the Ottoman Porte in May 1812 in Bucharest and a year later with Persia at Gülistan. The latter treaty stipulated Russia's control over most of the Caspian Sea coast, including Daghestan and much of Azerbaijan.

It was not until 1815 that the elder Semën felt it was safe to send his son away. It took some time to convince his wife, who was unaccustomed to such practice, that Semën had to spend the next seven years away from home in Karabudakhkent, a large and prosperous Kumyk village where the elder Semën had been raised by his own atalyk some thirty years earlier.

Moreover, his son's atalyk was to be none other than the rluer of Karabudakhkent, Arslan beg. Typically, the atalyk belonged to a lower social rank than the father of his newly adopted son. But the elder Semën's situation was far from typical. He had accompanied the high-ranking Russian officers on important missions and effortlessly navigated between the Russian and Kumyk worlds. During his several visits to the area, Arslan had learned to rely on Semën's indispensable services as a translator and mediator. In appreciation of Semën's role in his successful negotiations with the Russians, Arslan had offered to be an atalyk to his son.

In May 1815, when the preparations for the young Semën's departure were finished, a group of Arslan's uzdens arrived to pick him up. As was customary, the elder Semën put on a feast inviting his Cossack neighbors and friends to celebrate the beginning of an important rite of passage for his son. The boy was expected to return seven years later as a fully grown man skilled in martial arts, steeled by hardships, and schooled in the indigenous languages and way of life.

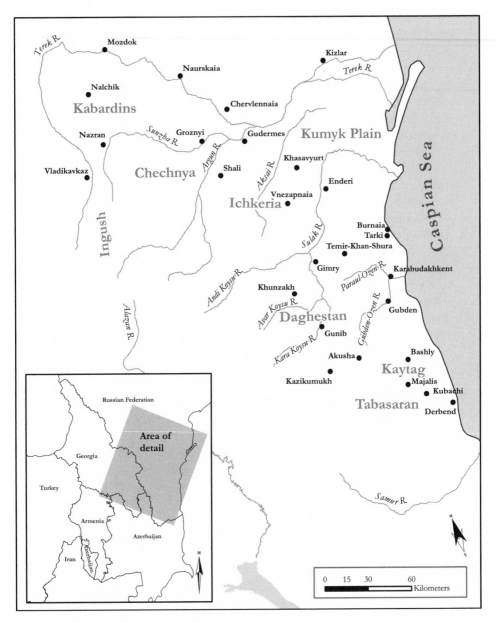

The Northeast Caucasus in the nineteenth century

Departure

In the late spring of 1815, the party with eight-year-old Semën departed for Karabudakhkent. Under normal circumstances the journey would have taken three days. The road from Naurskaia wound along the northern bank of the Terek River, where they could travel under the protection of the Mozdok Fortification Line, which stretched from Mozdok to Kizliar. Thirty miles down the road was the next significant Cossack settlement, Chervlennaia. Founded on the site of the former Nogay winter camp, Chervlennaia had grown up next to a vital ford across the Terek.

The ford was located two miles down the river and guarded by a small Cossack outpost. After checking their travel papers, the Cossacks ferried the party across the rapid and murky waters of the Terek, which at this point spanned about four hundred yards. Across the Terek, the world of Cossack settlements and outposts straddling the river was suddenly replaced by the Chechen *auls* (villages) scattered amid the plains and dense forests in the foothills of the Caucasus. Now Semën and his group had crossed the frontier. The Russian government had long claimed sovereignty over the lands and peoples of the region south of the Terek, finally compelling Persia to recognize it in a diplomatic treaty of 1813. In reality, the Terek River and the Mozdok Line continued to mark the southern boundary of the Russian Empire.

Crossing the Terek offered welcome relief for a traveler, for it meant leaving behind the harsh and barren Nogay steppe that stretched in seemingly endless monotony north of the Terek. It was for a good reason that this steppe was called *solonchaki,* or "the salty lands," referring to its extremely arid and salty soil where deeply dug wells provided the only source of water.[14] The harsh landscape now yielded to the dense forests that graced the right bank of the Terek. In fact, the Cossack towns and villages had traditionally been dependent on the supply of wood from the forests across the river and had had to enter some sharing agreements with the local Chechen auls.[15]

Crossing the Terek also meant leaving behind the relative safety of the Russian frontier. There was, of course, plenty of brigandage in the Russian borderlands, where a good number of Cossacks preferred a harsh life of banditry and freedom to the more predictable and settled life of the Cossack villages. Yet a traveling party faced a much higher chance of ambush and pillage on the other side of the Terek. The Terek's northern bank was part of the Russian Empire—a sovereign and centralized state that attempted to exercise its control and apply imperial law. Brigandage was a crime, and its perpetrators were to be hunted down and punished.

By contrast, the lands immediately south of the Terek were a collection of free Chechen hamlets or Kumyk auls and towns under the loose control of local chiefs. None of these were either willing or able to prevent raiding activity. For many locals, the Chechens in particular, brigandage was not a crime but a manifestation of one's prowess, valor, and skills.

The primeval oak and beech forests stretching virtually uninterrupted between the Sunzha and the Terek Rivers were swarming with Kumyk, Chechen, and Cossack runaways.[16] The region around the Sunzha River had long been disputed between the Kabardin princes and the Kumyk begs. By the eighteenth century, the Kabardins were forced to abandon their claim to lands across the Sunzha, and the river became the principal divide between the Lesser Kabarda to the west and the Kumyks and Chechens in the east.

Two miles west of the Sunzha River estuary, Semën's party reached the first safe haven, a large Kumyk aul of Borokhan, Russified into Braguny. Perched on the slopes of the minor mountain range of the same name, Braguny was in the easternmost corner of the Kumyk settlements immediately bordering the cluster of Chechen hamlets a few miles up the Sunzha River. Semën's ancestral hamlet of Otar was located here. By the early nineteenth century, the residents of the Braguny region found themselves in close proximity to the Russian frontier, making it difficult to engage in any cross-border mischief.

The Great Road (Ullug Yol) passed along the northern slopes of the Braguny range. Next to it, the remains of the once-deep moats were still visible. Legend had it that this was an ancient road used in the time of the famous fifteenth-century conqueror Timur. The same road was also known as the Ottoman road, as it was used in the late sixteenth century by the Ottoman-Crimean armies crossing the Northern Caucasus on their way from the Ottoman fort of Azak (Azov) to the Caspian coast. Their initial success in occupying what were the Persian northern provinces of Derbend, Shemakha, Baku, and Tabriz was short-lived.[17] By the early seventeenth century, the Porte was compelled to abandon this region and its far-reaching plans to expand Ottoman control to the Caspian shores.

The early and failed ambitions of another empire were also visible here in the ruins of the Russian forts of Tersk and Sunzhensk—the former built and abandoned twice throughout the 1560s and 1570s and the latter built and abandoned three times during the seventeenth century. The ruins stood in ominous silence as a monument to Russia's tenacity but also as a reminder that after several centuries of Moscow's intermittent presence in the region, the Caucasus and its peoples continued to defy and elude Russia's imperial designs.

Semën's party crossed the Sunzha at a place named the Ford of Timur. It was a shallow spot with stones placed in the riverbed. Like the road, this ford was attributed to Timur, who had purportedly ordered such crossings built so that his heavily laden camels could cross the river safely. For the next twelve miles the road passed through several Chechen hamlets before it reached the Aksai River. Originating in the mountains of the Salatau range, the waters of Aksai flowed northeast through the inhospitable Nogay steppe, until the river gave up on reaching the wide flow of the Terek and disappeared amidst barren steppe and sand dunes.[18]

Upon crossing the Aksai, the party entered the Kumyk heartland formed by the four principalities: Braguny in the west, Aksai in the northwest, Kostek in the northeast, and Enderi in the southeast. Throughout the centuries, Russian officials considered the inhabitants of these four areas the real Kumyk people, and they referred to other Kumyks farther east as the "Kumyks from beyond the Sulak River." Today the four former principalities compose the district of Khasavyurt, and its local dialect forms a standard Kumyk language.[19]

The Russians persistently used the word "village" (*derevnia*) to describe these settlements even though many of them were fairly large. The town of Kostek, for example, had 650 households, or about 3,500 people, while Aksai with its 800 households had no fewer than 4,000 residents. By contrast, Semën's birthplace of Naurskaia had about 260 households with a population of nearly 2,000. By far the largest and most significant of the Kumyk towns was Enderi, with 1,500 households, or about 7,500 residents. With the exception of Kizliar (population 20,000), it had more residents than any of the large Russian towns in the area, such as Mozdok (4,000) and Stavropol. Nevertheless, the Russians continued to refer to Enderi as a village and corrupted the original Kumyk name ("the place where wheat is threshed") into a similar-sounding Russian name, Andreev.[20]

Enderi

The sixty-mile stretch of road from the banks of the Aksai River to the Kumyk town of Tarki on the coast passed through the Kumyk plain along the edge of the northern slopes of the Salatau mountain range, whose peaks reached eight thousand to nine thousand feet. Here the terrain was less fertile, with fewer woods and more marshlands. Before crossing the Sulak River Semën's party stopped at Enderi. In the past, this thriving Kumyk town had been a major commercial center and an important political player in the North Caucasus.

Like other local people, the rulers of Enderi had an uneasy relationship with the encroaching Russian Empire. They easily swore allegiances and delivered hostages when they sought to profit from military and economic ties with Russia, just as they ambushed and raided the Russians when presented with equally gainful opportunities. The Russian troops did not spare Enderi. They burned it down in 1591 and intermittently laid siege to it throughout the seventeenth century. During Peter I's military campaign in the region in 1722, the Russian army razed Enderi to the ground, thoroughly destroying its three thousand households. Shortly thereafter, Enderi regained some of its commercial importance, but it never fully recovered.[21]

At the time Semën's party entered Enderi, it was still a bustling town and the largest non-Russian market in this corner of the Caucasus. Since the late sixteenth century, it had enjoyed prosperity as the most significant slave market in the region. The local peoples—Kumyks, Chechens, and Avars—came to Enderi to barter slaves for horses, armor, and other valuable items, and many desperately poor families offered their children for sale.

First and foremost, however, Enderi was known as a major international slave market trading in Adyge, Slavic, Georgian, and Armenian captives. Persian merchants purchased slaves whom they later resold in the markets of Derbend and Shemakha. Ottoman and Crimean merchants brought slaves from Enderi to be shipped from the ports of Azak and Kaffa in the Crimea until the bulk of the slave trade shifted to the markets of Anapa and Sukhum-kale on the Black Sea coast. It is likely that the seventeenth-century Ottoman traveler Evliya Chelebi had the market of Enderi in mind when, with his typical flare for exaggeration, he described a regional fair that each spring drew merchants from all over the world and lasted forty days.[22]

Russia's demands to stop slave trading in the region had little effect. In 1763 the government resorted to a new measure and ordered the flogging of those local merchants doing business in Russian towns who were recognized as slave traders. In 1804 it decreed the abolition of the slave trade in the North Caucasus and on the Black Sea coast. Yet none of these measures were successful because slave trading was the region's most profitable business. In the first half of the nineteenth century, the prices for Circassian women varied from 200 to 800 silver rubles, while attractive young women could fetch as much as 800 to 1,500 rubles and boys between 200 and 500 rubles.

Russian attempts to ban the slave trade became more effective only with Russian military expansion in the region. Thus Enderi remained a major slave market until 1819, when the proximity of the newly built Fort Vnezapnaia (Sudden) allowed the Russian military authorities to enforce the ban. Of course, Russian commanders were mostly concerned with the fate of Christian slaves sold into the hands of non-Christians. Russian authorities turned a blind eye to, and often openly encouraged, the sale of non-Christian captives to Russians. The Russian antislavery policy was more a product of the concern for fellow Christians than the result of a broader moral sentiment.[23]

SEMËN'S party spent a night at one of Enderi's numerous karavan-sarays, an inn designed for merchants traveling with a large number of beasts of burden. The next morning they rose early to attend a morning prayer at a local mosque and make a brief visit to a busy bazaar. Here they purchased some Russian-made textiles, rolls of coarse silk cloth manufactured at the Cossack village of Shelkovskaia (Silktown), and a few chests, mirrors, scissors, pig-iron pots, and other items valued in the native villages.[24]

They were now ready for a short journey to Tarki. From Enderi the travelers followed the curving road along the Caucasus mountain range until at last they reached the town of Tarki, principal residence of the *shamkhal*, a Kumyk ruler.

Tarki

Tarki was founded in the fourteenth century on the same site, it is believed, where had once stood the city of Semender, the early capital of the Khazars, who dominated this region between the sixth and tenth centuries. The town had been constructed to take full advantage of its natural defenses.[25] The main part of it had been built in a circle on the steep mountain slope overlooking the Caspian Sea. Semën and his party passed through the only gate into town and found themselves in the narrow streets leading up the mountain. The streets, in fact, were so narrow that two horsemen could not ride side by side. As they passed through the town, they saw a great abundance of mills built at the numerous springs and streams that cascaded down the mountain.

The town's 1,500 houses were built out of rock and were well suited to defend the occupants against intruders. Tarki's defenses were virtually impregnable until the arrival of Ottoman and Russian artillery. The outskirts of Tarki were turned into sprawling cemeteries, where unassuming slabs of stone announced the names of the deceased.

Leaving behind the mosque and residential houses, the party continued to make its way uphill until the men spotted a watchtower and a large house on top of the mountain. This was the residence of the shamkhal. In the sixteenth century, a shamkhal was still a typical medieval overlord. He lived in a large walled compound with houses of stone and wood. The tower and the compound dominated the settlement below, where residents farmed the nearby valleys in exchange for the shamkhal's protection. In the late 1500s, a shamkhal's personal retinue numbered about two hundred horsemen. When he was successful in rallying around him the chiefs of neighboring towns and villages, he could field a formidable force of as many as five thousand cavalrymen.[26]

For centuries the shamkhals took advantage of their geographic location, which placed them at the northern periphery of the Persian realm and the eastern edge of the Crimean-Ottoman area of influence. Skillfully playing off the conflicting interests of the two empires allowed the shamkhals to maintain their political independence, while control of the vital land passage along the narrow plain of the Caspian Sea provided them with sizable revenue. The arrival of the Muscovites in the late sixteenth century threatened to disturb this equilibrium.

In 1589, alarmed by Moscow's rapid expansion in the region, the shamkhal Surkhai wrote to the Protector of all Muslims, the Ottoman sultan Murad III. In his dramatic appeal Surkhai described how the Muscovites had seized his river, built a fort, and prepared to send a large army against him. He warned that they would soon take his land and convert his people to Christianity, and "then the cities that you took from Persia—Derbent, Shemakha, Shirvan, and Ganja—will not be able to defend themselves; and the Muscovites will unite with the shah of Persia and the king of Georgia, and then they will march on Istanbul from here and the French and Spanish kings from the other side and you yourself will not survive in Istanbul, and you will be captured and the Muslims will become Christians, and our faith will come to an end, if you do not intercede."[27]

But the Ottoman Empire was entering its slow and irreversible decline. In the wake of the internal social upheavals and the consuming war with Safavid Persia, the sultan had priorities other than sustaining control of the distant region in the northeast Caucasus. It took two hundred years for Surkhai's prophecies to come true. By the early nineteenth century Russia was in indisputable control of the region, and the shamkhals turned into loyal servants of the empire on the Russian payroll.

The present shamkhal, Mehti, had been placed on his throne by the Russian authorities, and in May of 1797 he swore his allegiance to the emperor, Paul I. Unlike his many predecessors who swore and abandoned allegiances with equal frequency, Mehti was left with little choice but to cooperate closely with Russia. With the proximity of Russian military forts and the increasingly attractive rewards and opportunities, it became harder for local chiefs to avoid the Russian stick or refuse the Russian carrot.

In 1797 the Russian authorities declared Mehti the ruler of Daghestan and gave him a cash annuity of 6,000 rubles and the title of privy councilor. Three years later he was promoted to the rank of lieutenant general of the army and received generous gifts. For a short while, after the Russian conquests in the area in 1806, he was also granted the title of the khan of Derbend and Baku.[28] His most apparent reward was to remain in the shamkhal's seat from 1797 to 1833, much longer than any of his immediate predecessors.

Mehti was the last shamkhal to enjoy the full support of the Russian government, with prestige and status rivaled only by the khan of Derbend: each enjoyed a 6,000-ruble annuity and the rank of lieutenant general. The rulers of other Daghestani regions—Kaytag (Dargin), Tabasaran, Kazikumukh (Lak), and Kiurin (Lezgin)—received the rank of major general and annuities between 1,500 and 2000 rubles.

Between the 1830s and 1860s, when Daghestan and Chechnya were embroiled in holy war against Russia, the Russian authorities began to disassemble the traditional political structures in the region. In 1860, shortly after the war in the North Caucasus was over and Russian military rule reasserted, the government adopted Laws concerning the Governing of Daghestan Province. Daghestan was now to be divided into four military districts under Russian control. The position of shamkhal became purely nominal and was finally abolished in 1867 when the last shamkhal, Shamsuddin, was compelled to resign. The principality of Tarki ceased to exist and was transformed into Temir Khan Shura (present-day Buinaksk) district.[29]

In the meantime, Shamkhal Mehti, a well-educated, intelligent man of quiet and sad disposition, understood that, for better or worse, the future of the region and its peoples was inextricably linked to Russia. Perhaps this young boy Semën Atarshchikov would be the best symbol of this new relationship. The boy was Russian-born and Russian-speaking, but his father was doing his best to preserve the ancestral ties with the world of Kumyk customs and traditions. The shamkhal was all too glad to welcome the boy, who was to reside in his lands with Karabudakhkent's beg as his guardian and patron.

An audience with the shamkhal was no doubt both an honor and a matter of great curiosity for the boy. The shamkhal, a middle-aged man dressed in a simple local tunic, welcomed his guests into his courtyard. In the middle of the yard was a well enclosed by a roofed veranda, and in the corner they saw a dilapidated watchtower. From there he led them into the house, a two-story stone structure with smaller gates, and upstairs into his sparsely furnished audience room. The floor was covered with traditional Daghestani carpets. Mats made from expensive cloth had been rolled up and placed on shelves along the walls. Servants unrolled the mats for the guests to sit on, while the shamkhal took a seat in the only armchair in the room.[30]

While the shamkhal and Semën's two guardians were chatting over tea and fruits, Semën stepped out onto the adjacent balcony. Below him was the entire town with its narrow twisted streets and haphazardly built houses dug into the mountain like the footprints of some giant mountain climber. In the north the inhospitable steppe stretched out to the horizon, and in the south the fields and forests appeared to merge magically with the waters of the Caspian Sea.

The audience with the shamkhal was soon over, and the three visitors set out on the last leg of their journey. They traveled for about twenty miles along the narrow land corridor squeezed between the mountains and the Caspian Sea before turning west and moving up the eastern slopes of the Caucasus. After eight more miles, they approached their destination, the village of Karabudakhkent, the main settlement in a cluster of nearby hamlets and auls that formed a single principality. Together with Buinaksk, Erpeli, Jenguti (Mekhtuli), and others, Karabudakhkent was one of the smaller principalities under the shamkhal's rule. At the same time it had the largest number of Kumyk noble families and mosques in northern Daghestan.[31] The boundaries of the shamkhal's lands were in flux, as various villages intermittently accepted or rejected his sovereignty. While Kumyks were the core population of the shamkhal's domain, his subjects also included the Dargin villages in the southwest, the Avar and Chechen villages in the west, and the nomadic Nogays in the north.

After Tarki, Buinaksk was the second-most-significant principality and a seat of the *krym-shamkhal,* the shamkhal's heir apparent. The rulers of other principalities were also members of the shamkhal's dynasty. They owed political loyalty to him but enjoyed complete sovereignty in financial and military matters. It was in the family of the beg of Karabudakhkent that Semën was to reside for the next six years.

Karabudakhkent

Karabudakhkent was a typical Kumyk settlement. It was picturesquely located at a place where the Paraul-Ozen River absorbed the waters of the

Gubden River before continuing toward the Caspian Sea under the new name, the Manas River. Unlike Tarki, with its terraced layout of houses built into the mountainside, Karabudakhkent had a predominantly horizontal plan similar to that of the Kumyk settlements in the plains. Its public square was ringed by houses in one closed circle. Several narrow streets wound their way from the square into a dead end farther up the hill. The town also had several mosques with madrassas (religious primary schools) attached to them. Roughly cut stones and tree trunks were usually placed along the mosque's wall to serve as benches where men could sit to discuss village affairs or chat after prayers.

The village, which included several hundred houses, was divided into several quarters, each compactly settled by the members of the same clan. Whereas typical houses on the plain were made of mud and reeds or bricks of mixed clay and hay, the houses of Karabudakhkent were solidly constructed from stone and readily available wood. In an unmistakable sign of Karabudakhkent prosperity, one could notice a good number of two-storied houses and several compounds among the more typical one-storied, one-room houses.

Like all the settlements in the region, Karabudakhkent had been planned with one paramount concern in mind—security. The village had a watchtower but no defense wall in the traditional sense. Instead, a wall had been formed from an uninterrupted chain of house walls and fences. Many house walls had small openings ordinarily closed with rocks. At the time of hostilities these openings served as embrasures through which the townspeople could shoot at the enemy. Such house-to-house defense was sufficient to fend off the members of a feuding clan or small raiding parties, but it proved useless against the artillery of modern armies.[32]

The beg of Karabudakhkent lived in a large compound consisting of several houses and a large yard fenced off by a stone wall. The main house was a large, two-story building. Most of the first floor was occupied by the harem. Women and children lived here, and men were prohibited from entering this part of the house. A reception room and the men's bedrooms were on the second floor. The rooms were mostly lit through the doors, which were very low and required one to bend in order to enter. The windows were small slits in the wall. Because dining, resting, and other activities took place on the floor, the windows were placed about one foot above floor level. Storage sheds, animal pens, and small houses for the servants and slaves were scattered around the compound. The oven was outside in the shed, where all the cooking and baking took place.[33]

Ordinarily, a welcomed visitor was given one of the rooms in a kunak house, a separate structure built specifically for guests. The idea of a guest room (kunak room)—or a guest house in the case of the more well-to-do—was so central to a life of the peoples of the Caucasus that even the most modest house had one. A kunak was more than just a guest. For instance, two men from different villages could become kunaks, that is, close friends or blood brothers, ready to offer each other help, hospitality, and protection. But a visitor or guest was also considered a kunak while staying in the owner's house, and hospitality demanded that he receive the same protection as would be offered to the closest of kin.

Too young to stay in a kunak house and too old to live on the harem floor, Semën was given a room in the men's quarters on the second floor and was quickly integrated into the beg's household. In time, he became particularly close to the beg's second son, Araslan, who was a year older, and both boys shared the joys and hardships of growing up in a Kumyk village. Like other boys from the families of the Kumyk nobles, Semën and Araslan were expected to acquire the necessary manly qualities: martial skills, physical strength, endurance, and the ability to exercise authority and lead others in battles and raids. The practical demands of being brought up as a warrior merged imperceptibly with leisure time, and their favorite activities predictably included horse racing and arrow shooting. They also trained in shooting from the traditional long-barreled musket, practicing their skills during hunting expeditions.

Of course, the boys also enjoyed other, more innocent games, as well as singing, dancing, and telling stories. They spent countless hours looking after the herds of horses and spending nights in the mountains under the open sky. Like all boys, regardless of social status, they learned from the older men to look upon women as their property, to treat them with contempt, and to expect from them little beyond their usual responsibilities: performing endless daily chores and bearing children.[34]

In addition to learning martial skills, the children of nobles were expected to attend a madrassa, where they studied Arabic and memorized verses from the Quran. Semën, however, occupied a peculiar position in Karabudakhkent. It was assumed that since he had been born and raised in a Christian village, he had been baptized. Yet it was understood that such baptism was often involuntary and remained purely nominal. Though not Muslim enough to attend a madrassa and please a local imam, Semën was also not Christian enough to be despised as an alien and infidel. Thus he continued to stay at the house of his atalyk, informally learning the Kumyk, Chechen, and Arabic languages.[35]

Semën's situation was not at all unusual. The frontier environment increasingly fostered dual identities as more native hostages were sent to St. Petersburg or other Russian cities, where they were educated in Russian schools, converted to Christianity, and enlisted in the Russian military. One of the earliest and best-known examples of such transformation was the Kabardin prince and Russian colonel Ismail Atazhukov (Khatokshoko, in Kabardin), who became the prototype for Mikhail Lermontov's poem "Izmail-bey." During the twenty years after his father surrendered him to the Russians, Atazhukov was raised and educated in the imperial capital, spoke fluent Russian and French, served in the military, reached the rank of a colonel, and received a handsome annuity and decorations. Yet he kept his wife in Kabarda, sent his ten-year-old son to an atalyk there, and was known to take off his cross, medals, and officer's ribbon when visiting his native land.

Until his death in 1812, Ismail Atazhukov continued to search for the shaky middle ground between the inevitable consequences of the Russian conquest and the interests of his own people. By contrast, his cousin, Colonel Roslambek Misostov Atazhukov, who also was brought up and educated in Russia, chose a more decisive course of action when he deserted to the highlanders, launched raids along the frontier, and was finally killed by a relative paid by the Russians to commit the murder. Semën did not know yet that his own life—one that would have passed unnoticed but for a few yellowing pages in a military report preserved in the Russian archive—would so closely come to resemble those of Ismail and Roslambek Atazhukovs.[36]

The years passed quickly for young Semën. As he came of age in the peaceful Kumyk aul of Karabudakhkent, the memory of his childhood in a Cossack village faded. But his Russian past proved to be less distant and Karabudakhkent less peaceful than he thought. In 1816 the Russian government resolved to consolidate and expand its control over the North Caucasus. This task was entrusted to a war hero, General Aleksei Petrovich Ermolov.

Ermolov's policy of ruthless expansion soon turned the region into a cauldron of anti-Russian resistance. The new Russian forts were built on occupied land near local auls. Imams and Sufi sheikhs preached resistance in the name of Islam, denouncing those who accepted Russian rule as collaborators who put their own interests above those of their people. It was in this atmosphere of brewing discontent that the residents of Karabudakhkent rebelled against paying taxes to the shamkhal. Unable to suppress the rebellion on his own, the shamkhal appealed for help to the Russians.

Reminders of the Russian incursions were never far away. One of these was a worn-out stone inscription on the main mosque of Karabudakhkent. Referring to the Persian campaign of Peter the Great in 1722, the inscription read, "In the year 1134…[t]he white tsar burned down Karabudakhkent."[37] Now, in 1818, eleven-year-old Semën watched as Ermolov's troops marched into Karabudakhkent. The intimidated residents were eager to accept Ermolov's offer of a pardon and pledged to resume payments to the shamkhal. To leave no doubt as to what might await the rebels in the future, Ermolov ordered one of the riot instigators executed, his family expelled, and his house razed to the ground.

For a few days Ermolov camped outside the village. Here he received the shamkhal, who was then on his way from Derbent to his residence in Tarki. It was their first meeting. Later, the grateful shamkhal admitted that he had been so shocked by the simplicity of Ermolov's lifestyle in comparison with that of his predecessors that he refused to believe this was indeed the famous Russian commander, convincing himself that Ermolov had sent another general under his name.[38]

In the following years, the residents of Karabudakhkent rebelled several more times, and each time the shamkhal called for the Russian troops to suppress the uprisings and restore the status quo. Although Semën did not yet realize it, the world of his childhood was already on an irreversible collision course with the world of his adolescence.

3

Journey through the Northeast Caucasus

IN 1822 Semën turned fifteen—the age of maturity for boys. Now he was entitled to wear a dagger, participate in men's councils, and marry. After spending seven years in the family of his atalyk in the Kumyk village, Semën was ready to return to Naurskaia. But before that he wanted to travel in the region to observe its variegated human and geographical landscape. In the spring of 1822, Semën, accompanied by two uzdens, departed from Karabudakhkent on a journey through the Northeast Caucasus.

Derbend

His first destination was the magnificent city of Derbend—the oldest, largest, and most sophisticated city in the North Caucasus. A two-day journey along the Caspian coast was unremarkable. The party moved through a semidesert covered with tamarisk shrubs, grass, and bushes. In the afternoons, clouds appeared over the mountains and moved menacingly in their direction. But each time the clouds failed to deliver their precious cargo, and while heavy rain poured over the mountains, the coast remained dry and hot.

The coastal plain was a narrow strip of land never exceeding a width of 12–15 miles and stretching for about 150 miles along the eastern shore of the Caspian. But when the party approached Derbend, the monotonous coastal plain seemed to end, giving way to the intimidating view of a wall that appeared to have risen out of the water, climbed up the mountain for several miles, circled around it, and then turned back east toward the Caspian Sea before disappearing into the water again. It looked as if a giant serpent had ringed this part of the plain and the nearest mountain of the Jalgan Range in one tight loop before becoming forever petrified. In front of Semën and his companions stood the ancient walls of Derbend.

Built in the narrowest place between the mountains and the sea, about 1.5 miles wide, Derbend sat astride the only land passage connecting the Asian lands in the south with the territories north of the Caucasus. The Caspian coastal plain was an ancient route for both trade caravans and invading armies, and the fortifications of Derbend could stop either one dead in their tracks. It was for this reason that the Persians named the city Derbend, "the closed gate" controlling the narrow passage critical to both war and peace.

The earliest known fortifications had existed here since the sixth century BCE. But the rise of present-day Derbend can be traced to the Sassanid rulers of Persia, who in the early sixth century CE erected a citadel to protect Persia from the raids of the various nomadic peoples from the north. Since then the city with its formidable fortifications retained its strategic and commercial importance throughout the centuries. Derbend remained the most northern frontier of Persian civilization, guarding against the invasions of the Khazars in the sixth century, the Turks in the eleventh, the Mongols and the Golden Horde in the thirteenth, the Ottomans in the sixteenth, and finally the Russians in the eighteenth.

Throughout this time Derbend was ruled by different occupying powers, but it also enjoyed long periods of independence. By the time Semën and his party arrived, the city was in decline and rapidly losing its strategic significance as Russia's frontier moved farther south into Azerbaijan. Russian troops were stationed near the city, and the khan of Derbend with the rank of lieutenant general was on the Russian payroll.[1]

They entered Derbend through the main gate in the northern wall, the Kirklar Kapi, literally the Gate of Forty. According to legend, this gate had been named to honor the forty Muslim martyrs who had fallen there in the eighth century while fighting against the Khazars and who were buried at the nearby cemetery. The fact that Arab historians and travelers referred to this gate and later the city itself as Bab al-Abwab (the Gate of Gates) or Bab el-Jihad (the Gate of the Holy War) indicates Derbend's strategic importance on the northern frontier of the Islamic world. The gate was about ten feet wide, and much of its once elaborate architectural ornament had been lost. Only two statues of lions continued to gaze at the passing travelers with the supreme and unperturbed confidence of yesteryear.

The northern wall was a formidable piece of fortification rebuilt and strengthened over the centuries. It was twelve feet thick and rose to an average of forty feet above the ground with towers placed every 200 feet along the wall. The southern wall had been erected later, and its defenses were much less impressive, as if underscoring the obvious fact that Derbend had been built primarily to contain the danger coming from the north.

Kirklar Kapi, which the Russians called the Kizliar Gate since it faced in the direction of the Russian city of the same name, was the main entrance for caravans coming from the north. This explained the nearby presence of a small mosque and public bath, offering tired merchants a chance to cleanse both their souls and bodies. Not far away were a bustling ba-zaar and three caravan-sarays for those who needed rest. Semën and his companions passed through the gate to the outskirts of the city. To their left was a coastal plain full of gardens, orchards, and grazing cattle. Not until the 1860s, when the Russian administration embarked on a major transformation of Derbend, did the orchards give way to a residential neighborhood.

Having passed through the Kirklar Kapi, Semën and his compan-ions turned right into the main street that took them up the hill toward Derbend's fabled Jumma Mosque. They entered the mosque compound through the gates in the eastern wall. Until a few years earlier, the wall of the compound had been a part of the inner wall, which separated the densely populated inner city from its outskirts. Now the wall was gone, and the compound of the mosque appeared in front of them as a large open square amid the twisting lines of the old and narrow streets.

Among the fifteen mosques of Derbend, Jumma was the largest and the oldest. In fact, with a main hall over two hundred feet long and a cupola reaching thirty feet in diameter, it was the largest mosque in Daghestan. The stone over the main gate bore an inscription in Arabic dating the foundation of the mosque to 733 CE. This made it the oldest mosque in the Caucasus, testimony to the significance attributed to Derbend by the early Arab invaders.

As elsewhere in the ancient world, zealous newcomers were quick to destroy the old houses of worship so they could rebuild them in the image of their own God. At first, churches replaced pagan temples, just as mosques would grow later in place of churches. In its architecture the Jumma Mosque was very similar to the Grand Mosque of Damascus in Syria, and like the latter, the Jumma was built on the foundations of the former Christian church.

From the time when Christianity began to spread in the eastern Caucasus in the first half of the fifth century CE until the Arab conquest in the early eighth century, Derbend was an important Christian center and the seat of a patriarch. After the Arab conquest it became a predominantly Muslim city with sizable Jewish and Christian minorities. In the early nineteenth century, Armenians constituted the largest Christian community in a city of 1,600 to 2,000 houses with a total population estimated at between eight and ten thousand people.[2]

Semën had heard many things about the old Jumma Mosque. Now as he walked around the mosque courtyard in the shade of the old plane trees, he must have felt a link with the thousands of worshippers who, throughout the centuries, had come here to pray, learn, and rest.

Adjacent to the mosque was an ancient madrassa with a row of simple eight-by-ten-foot cubicles used for student residences. Semën walked along the arcaded lane of the school observing the young men of his age who lived and studied here, learning Islamic law in preparation for their future roles as imams and qadis (Islamic judges). Under different circumstances he might have been one of them.

Walking farther up the hill, Semën passed the baths, the only remaining part of the once-bustling market center. In the seventeenth century trading rows and caravan-sarays had occupied this spot before the Kirklar Kapi became the main marketplace later on. The street narrowed and changed into a short staircase before it dead-ended at the wall. Behind the wall, occupying the top of the mountain, was a citadel known as Narin Kala, the oldest part of Derbend and the residence of its khan.[3]

The rocky mountainside together with the man-made walls punctuated by watchtowers formed what had formerly been the impregnable defenses of Narin Kala. The citadel had two gates, in the west and the east. Semën and his companions entered through the Narin Kala Kapi, the eastern entrance to the citadel. A barely readable inscription over the gate mentioned the name of Shah Abbas—a clear indication that the gate dated back to the early seventeenth century, when the city had been under Persian control.

The sprawling complex of the khan's palace together with the nearby baths and water reservoir dominated the citadel. The size and sophistication of the palace stood in sharp contrast to the modest abode of the shamkhal in Tarki. The khan's palace dated to the twelfth century but had been thoroughly rebuilt in the 1770s and 1780s after Derbend came under the rule of Feth Ali, the khan of the principality of Kuba some thirty miles south of Derbend in present-day Azerbaijan. Shrewdly combining military conquests and political alliances with the most significant local rulers—the shamkhal of Tarki, the khan of Baku, and above all, the Russian military commanders—Feth Ali lived up to his name (Feth means conquest) and became the region's most powerful overlord. His heirs continued to rule Derbend until the Russian government abolished the title of khan and turned the city into another administrative unit of the Russian Empire.

In the meantime, the khan of Derbend continued to reside in the palace. A contemporary Russian officer left a description of the khan's residence, noting that it contained a beautiful pool as well as several rooms with intricately decorated ceilings and brightly painted walls depicting martial and amorous scenes.

Different occupants of the palace had left their imprint on the city and its architecture. At the time of Semën's visit, the new Russian rulers were busy changing Derbend to fit their own image. Apparently the citadel was deemed the safest part of the city and therefore a suitable place for a Russian garrison. Moreover, the Russians built the *hauptvakhta*, a military prison, in direct proximity to the khan's palace. It was hard to tell whether this, like other Russian actions in the region, had been done out of simple insensitivity or was meant to be a warning or a deliberate insult.

Southern and Central Daghestan

After spending a few days in Derbend, Semën and his companions left through the city's west gate, traveling along the so-called Mountain Wall, the ancient defense fortification line that extended southwest from Derbend into the lands of Tabasaran. Even though the wall had been abandoned for centuries, the remaining parts, including forts and towers, were a vivid testimony to the old days of glory. The Mountain Wall's strategic significance was to serve as a defensive barrier protecting Sassanid Persia and the Arab khaliphate in the south from raids by the Khazars in the north. The wall was intended to stretch from the Caspian Sea to the Great Caucasus mountain range, but only a part of it was completed. A major part had been built in the sixth century CE and stretched for about thirty miles from Derbend to the banks of the Rubas River. With the collapse of the Khazar khaganate in the tenth century, the wall was no longer needed and had fallen into disrepair.[4]

The wall ended in the upper reaches of the Rubas River, in the lands of Tabasaran. Armenian and Arab writers referred to Tabasaran as early as the seventh and eighth centuries. In the 1820s, some thirty thousand residents lived in Tabasaran's seventy auls scattered through the valleys of the Rubas and Chirakh Rivers. These auls were divided between those ruled by a qadi and those ruled by a *maisum* (Arabic for pure, chaste). At the time, both rulers were already on the Russian payroll.

Semën's party crossed the Rubas River on its way to the Tabasaran aul of Khuchni. With more than three hundred houses, Khuchni was one of the largest settlements in southern Daghestan. Approaching the aul, one could observe a row of simple structures with conical roofs. These were *sarays*, or storage places for hay that were usually built on the outskirts of an aul. In the aul, two-storied houses built from local sandstone housed both people and herds under the same roof.

Straddling one of the two roads connecting the auls of southern Daghestan with those farther north, Khuchni had a thriving bazaar and a mosque built in the eighteenth century. Perhaps the most interesting place to visit was the local cemetery. It had numerous ancient funeral stones with strange geometrical ornaments and mausoleums of prominent Muslims, including one to the eighteenth-century Sufi saint (*pir*) Bashly.[5]

Where was Semën to travel from here? South of Derbend, along the Caspian Sea coast were the auls of the Azeris, the old-time subjects of the khan of Derbend. Farther south, the free village societies of the Lezgins dominated the valleys and mountains of southern Daghestan and northern Azerbaijan.[6]

In the middle of Daghestan, just to the north of Tabasaran, were the lands of Kaytag, a powerful principality dominated by the Dargins, one of the largest ethnic groups in the North Caucasus. In the first half of the seventeenth century, according to a contemporary report of the well-informed Kabardin prince, Rüstem-khan, the ruler of Kaytag with the title of *utsmii*, was second to none, a sovereign ruler capable of fielding of up to twelve thousand armed men. Under Rüstem-khan the customary law was codified, and Kaytag reached the height of its power. Rüstem-khan successfully manipulated the regional rivalries between the Russians, Ottomans, and Persians until he was deposed in the 1640s by the invading Persian army of Shah Abbas II. Racked by internal wars, Kaytag was further devastated in the 1740s when the army of another Persian ruler, the famous Nadir Shah, marched through its territory.[7]

By the late eighteenth century, Persian influence was waning, and it was now the Russians who frustrated the utsmii's regional ambitions. One notable incident in 1774 brought the Russian armies into Kaytag. In 1774, Dr. Samuel Gottlieb Gmelin, a member of the Russian Academy of Sciences, was detained by the utsmii Amir-Hamza while returning from his second expedition to Persia to explore the indigenous flora and fauna. The utsmii informed the Russian authorities that Gmelin would be kept as hostage until the utsmii's grievances were addressed. Once again Amir Hamza demanded the return of his subjects—two hundred families of the Terekemens (a Turkic farming community on the Caspian plain) and eighty Jewish families who had fled in the 1740s to the Kumyk towns of Enderi and Kostek. His previous demands to have them returned or to be paid a compensation of 30,000 rubles were denied.

Even as the negotiations were taking place, Gmelin, reportedly kept in harsh conditions, died in captivity. Despite St. Petersburg's desire to avoid any provocation in the region, the death of Gmelin, who had traveled under the protection of Empress Catherine II, could not be left unanswered. In 1775 the Russian government launched a punitive expedition led by General I. F. de Medem.[8]

The Treaty of Gülistan that ended the Russo-Persian war (1804–13) and recognized Russia's control of Daghestan and Azerbaijan simply acknowledged the inevitable fact of Russia's continuous expansion. Some local rulers chose cooperation when offered a salary and the rank of major general in the Russian army, but most notables, ulema, and commoners responded to the growing presence of the Russian military and administration with hostility and resentment. The new Christian authorities introduced limitations and restrictions far more severe than those attempted by the Persians or Ottomans in the past. The Russians interfered in local political struggles by supporting and appointing loyal but unpopular individuals. They imposed strict control on travel, requiring the locals to obtain travel documents from Russian authorities. They controlled regional trade, making it dependent on the population's political loyalty to Russia. Worst of all, they tried to limit and then put a halt to the Muslim pilgrimage to Mecca.[9]

Within a few years complaints to the Russian authorities were followed by armed rebellions, and General Ermolov's scorched-earth policy in dealing with the insurgency only further alienated the local population. In 1818–19, Russian troops marched through Daghestan routing rebellious rulers and burning auls to the ground. Among the defeated was the utsmii of Kaytag, Adil-khan. In the following year, Ermolov abolished the position of utsmii, leaving Kaytag's thirteen districts (*magals*) to be administered by their respective begs, under the control of a Russian military liaison. All the taxes previously collected by the utsmii were to be paid to the Russian treasury.[10]

It was shortly after these events that Semën and his party arrived in Majalis (in Arabic, a meeting place) from Khuchni. A former residence of the utsmii, Majalis was still a prosperous settlement but now only a shadow of its former self. Situated on the plain in the mid-Ullu Chay River, it was an almost idyllic place, sheltered from the wind by the mountains and surrounded by plentiful orchards and vineyards. The main street of Majalis was lined up with giant walnut trees. Several mosques and a market were in the center of town. The ustmii's former residence was on the slope of a mountain, in the upper part of town, and so were most other residences.

In Lower Majalis there was another unmistakable sign of the town's former commercial importance—a synagogue and the residences of several hundred Jews. Known as Mountain Jews, or Jufud to the local peoples, a total of several thousand Jews resided in Daghestan's main commercial centers. In their appearance, everyday life, and language they were quite distinct from their European coreligionists. In fact, they looked like their Daghestani neighbors and spoke Tat, a dialect of an Iranian language. Because they shared a language with the Tats, who were the Iranian residents of Daghestan, in Soviet times the Mountain Jews would be confused with them. At the time, however, the Mountain Jews and the Tat Shiite Muslims were two distinct groups.

Majalis was the last major settlement on the plain before the road disappeared into the mountains. Twenty miles west of Majalis, at a height of 1,500 meters, was the party's next destination, Kubachi, a town of legendary craftsmen and artisans. Even those accustomed to the sight of mountain auls and towns were awed by their first view of Kubachi. Through a thin fog they could see the precipitous mountain slopes with hundreds of houses built compactly on top of each other so that the roof of one house was the floor of the next one. From a distance, the town appeared to be one massive multistory house.

Famed for its metal works, gold and silver jewelry, and stone carving, Kubachi was particularly renowned for manufacturing highly valuable armor and arms. The tradition of making armor was apparently quite old. As early as the sixth century CE the town had been known as Zirikhgeran (in Persian, armor-maker), and its current name had been derived from the Turkic equivalent, *kübeci*. Several competing legends surrounded Kubachi and its residents. Some claimed the Kubachins were of European origin, descended from Genoese, Greeks, and Moravians.

Myths notwithstanding, Kubachi was indeed one of the oldest continuing settlements in Daghestan and the center of ancient Caucasian Albania. Three dilapidated ancient towers and remnants of the defense wall were all that was left of the town's fortifications. Rumor had it that one of the several mosques, had been built on the foundation of a Christian church.[11]

Throughout its history Kubachi remained a self-governed town administered by a council of seven elders elected by the town community. Numerous invading armies had spared the town, allowing it to preserve its unique character. Outsiders preferred to collect tribute in arms and other valuable products manufactured by the town artisans, whose highly prized skills were passed from one generation to another.

To the north of Kubachi lay another important part of the former Kaytag principality—Akusha, a large aul and the residence of a qadi. Like other free societies of Daghestan, Akusha had formed an alliance with the neighboring auls and had only loose ties to the ustmii. By the late eighteenth century, the Akusha alliance consisting of over a hundred auls broke with the utsmii and became one of the most powerful alliances in the region. In 1819, armed militia from Akusha had confronted the invading Russian army of General Ermolov. Even though the Akushins were routed in the ensuing battle near the aul of Levashi, Ermolov and other contemporaries were deeply impressed by their valor and determined resistance.[12]

To the northwest of Kubachi was Kumukh, the former residence of a shamkhal and the center of the Kazikumukh principality. Destroyed by the Mongols in 1240, Kazikumukh had risen again to become the most powerful principality in Daghestan by the early sixteenth century. Situated on the river Kazikumukh Koysu, Kumukh dominated the region populated by a small ethnic group, the Laks, but the shamkhal's control extended far beyond the Lak auls to include numerous neighboring auls of the Avars, Kumyks, Dargins, and Lezgins.

In the late sixteenth century, the Kazikumukh principality split between rival factions: one representing Ottoman and Crimean interests, the other those of Safavid Persia. For a short while, the Ottomans were successful in establishing their supremacy on the Caspian coastal plain and supported the newly emerged splinter rulers in Enderi and Tarki. The Persians maintained their influence among the local rulers in the highlands. But as Ottoman authority in this remote corner of the Caucasus waned in the 1580s, Moscow began to fill the vacuum by projecting its influence in the region from the newly constructed Fort Tersk.[13]

In the early seventeenth century, the Russians were confident enough to intervene directly in the succession struggle between the shamkhal's heirs. With their growing dependence on Moscow, the shamkhals chose to relocate their principal residence to Tarki and use Kumukh as their summer retreat. Yet their close ties with Moscow made them appear to be Russian puppets and in the 1640s provoked a popular uprising in Kumukh. No longer in the shamkhal's domain, Kumukh was now ruled by a local elder who was elected by a popular assembly and bore the title *halklavchi* (representative of the people).[14]

In the following centuries, Kazikumukh suffered from the punishing expeditions of the Persian Nadir Shah in 1740 and General Ermolov in 1820. At the time of Semën's visit in 1822, Kumukh appeared to have been subdued by Ermolov's recent campaign. Yet it took another forty years of bloody wars before Russia could finally crush the resistance in the northeast Caucasus, replace the local rulers with Russian authorities, and integrate Kazikumukh into the imperial administrative system.

After taking one last look at Kumukh with its castle ruins, crumbling defense towers, cemetery, and mosques, Semën and his party began their journey north into the lands of the Avars. Crossing the large plateau, they passed the auls of Megeb and Chokh before reaching Gunib, a significant Avar settlement.[15] The Avars were an ancient people and one of the largest ethnic groups dominating the mountains of western Daghestan. The Avar auls were surrounded by a virtually uninterrupted circle of mountain ranges and occupied most of the plateaus between the tributaries of the Sulak River: Andi Koysu, Avar Koysu and Kara Koysu. This territory was a part of ancient Albania and later, between the fifth and twelfth centuries, the powerful Christian kingdom of Serir. The name Avar is thought to have come from the title of a ruler of Serir (there is no relationship between the Avars, the powerful Hunnic people of antiquity, and the Avars of the Caucasus).

Like other political formations of Daghestan, the Avar khanate was a loosely organized society with its center at Khunzakh. Its ruler, the *nutsal,* claimed control over the subservient Avar auls and the aul alliances of the neighboring Chechens, Kumyks, and Laks. Typically, the aul residents identified themselves with a particular aul or an aul alliance.

The Avar khanate had emerged as a significant regional power under Umma-khan in the early seventeenth century. In a clear indication of the growing central authority, Umma-khan had ordered a compilation of the first law code. Several decades later, in a further sign of centralization, the traditional political succession, where the title of the nutsal was disputed among the senior members of the ruling dynasty, was replaced by primogeniture, in which title passed from father to eldest son. Until the early nineteenth century, the Avar nutsals together with the Kumyk shamkhals presided over the two largest and most influential political entities in the northeast Caucasus.

Traveling through the Avar lands in the early nineteenth century, one could not tell that a millennium earlier the three world religions had met here. Between the eighth and tenth centuries, the Christian rulers of Serir were neighbors of the Khazar Jewish rulers in Semender—where many believe Tarki was founded later—and of the Muslim rulers of Derbend.[16] By Semën's time, however, both Christianity and Judaism were long gone. The northeast Caucasus was firmly ensconced in the Sunni Muslim world until the mid-eighteenth century, when Sufi preachers of the Naqshbandi order began to wrest control of religious life from mainstream Sunni clerics.

Early on, the Avars learned to defend their auls in the rugged mountains against foreign invasions. They built fortifications with towers and defense walls in strategically located auls. The system of mutual defense bound the auls in military alliances. An attack on one would immediately trigger a swift mobilization and deployment of militias from the others. Individuals or auls that failed to help faced hefty fines and disgrace. The system functioned just like the polis system of ancient Greece or similar community alliances elsewhere.

In the early nineteenth century, a new and formidable invader attempted to penetrate Avar lands and destroy traditional power arrangements in the Caucasus. Worse yet, unlike the previous Muslim powers, which had attempted to establish their control in the region, these new intruders were infidels—Russian Orthodox Christians. It was hardly accidental that throughout the first half of the nineteenth century, Avar lands became the epicenter of resistance to Russia and a place where a famed Avar named Shamil founded his Imamate.

As they approached Gunib, Semën and his companions were awed by its extraordinary location. Like an impregnable fortress designed by nature itself, Gunib sat atop a mountain that commanded the surrounding heights. The steep slopes rose half a mile high from the bottom at an angle of forty-five degrees. At the top, the mountain was surrounded by boulders that formed a stone belt, which made Gunib appear to be sitting at the bottom of a cup. The Russian soldiers called Gunib Guitar-Mountain because its terrain was shaped like a guitar without a handle. Only one narrow path squeezing among the hanging cliffs led to Gunib.

Semën and his companions found themselves in Gunib long before it would become legendary in Russia's epic war in the North Caucasus. This was the place of Shamil's last stand against the Russians. It was here at Gunib that Shamil's struggle came to an end on August 25, 1859. Several hundred defenders were completely surrounded by an overwhelming number of Russian troops, who proved to be no less determined and ingenious than their enemy. After two days of bloody battle the Russian troops scaled the mountain and stormed Gunib. Rather than dying a martyr, the aged imam Shamil chose to save his family and surrender himself to the commander of Russian forces, Prince A. I. Bariatinskii. It was the end of Shamil's Imamate and his war against Russia, which had lasted for over a quarter of a century.[17]

A short stop at Gunib followed by a two-day journey brought Semën to his next destination—Khunzakh, the residence of the Avar rulers and, after Derbend, the second-largest town in the North Caucasus. In the late eighteenth century, Khunzakh reportedly had about two thousand houses, which would have put its population at around ten thousand, or two-thirds of contemporaneous Tiflis or Boston.[18] To reach Khunzakh, Semën needed to cross the Karadakh Canyon. At nine miles long, it was the longest canyon in Daghestan. To enter the canyon one had to travel through a narrow passage in the rocks, three hundred meters long and barely two meters wide. It was at places like this that one appreciated the difficulty of conquering and subduing the highlanders.

Halfway between Gunib and Khunzakh was the large aul of Gergebil. It was another twenty-eight miles from this point, across the river Avar Koysu before Semën reached Khunzakh, perched at the very edge of the Tsolotl Canyon and overlooking blossoming orchards and waterfalls. Everything in Khunzakh spoke of its glorious history: the khan's palace, the number of mosques, the nearby ruins of the Fortress Arani, and several Christian tombs—a silent reminder of Khunzakh's Christian past.[19]

As in other settlements in the North Caucasus, the houses of Khunzakh were built so closely together that there were no actual streets. Instead, extremely narrow paths chaotically wound between the houses, often leading into dead ends or turning into underground tunnels. Each house in itself was a stronghold, and the town, composed of houses built on top of one another, was in essence a multistoried fortress.

Security needs dictated that the khan's palace be located in the upper part of town. At the time, its resident was Surkhai, a Russian protégé appointed by General Ermolov in 1819 to replace the rebellious Sultan-Ahmed. Propped up by the Russian administration, Surkhai never gained popularity among his own people. Seeking to find an acceptable compromise, in 1829 the Russian authorities would appoint two khans: Surkhai remained in charge of a small part of the Avar khanate, while the son of the deceased Sultan-Ahmed, the nutsal Abu-Sultan, took residence in Khunzakh and assumed control of a larger part of the khanate. Each one received the rank of colonel and an annuity of 2,000 silver rubles.[20]

From Khunzakh, Semën's itinerary took him northwest into Chechnya and toward his native village of Naurskaia. Before reaching Chechnya, he stopped at one last significant settlement under the control of the Avar rulers, Botlikh, about forty-five miles north of Khunzakh. Because of their traditional political ties with the Avars, the residents of Botlikh and several smaller villages in the area were often assumed to be Avars. In fact, like other small neighboring populations such as the Andi and Akhvakh, they composed a small ethnolinguistic subgroup closely related but separate from the Avars.

Situated in a depression and surrounded by mountain peaks, Botlikh was a prosperous aul of about 350 houses, or 1,400 people. Fields of grain, vineyards, orchards, and gardens dotted the slopes around the town, and travelers were invariably impressed with the very efficient use of land terraces. Irrigation of the terraces was strictly regulated, and fines were imposed on those who used the water before their allocated time.

Botlikh was one of the best-fortified auls in the region. Its three gates controlled access to the aul, which was also guarded by seven towers (*sheba*) connected via underground tunnels. Some families served as advance outposts living in settlements of several houses and scattered around the aul to watch for the approach of outsiders and raise the alarm. Unlike most auls in the region, Botlikh was initially settled by independent clans, each possessing self-rule and territory with a tower, mosque, and cemetery. By the nineteenth century, this clan-territorial structure had already been absorbed into the territorial-administrative units with no extended family ties.

Given its prosperity and location, Botlikh evolved into an important commercial hub in western Daghestan and was involved in vigorous trade with the neighboring auls and peoples in Daghestan, Chechnya, Derbend, Georgia, and the Persian provinces. The role of Botlikh in regional trade was severely undermined only with the arrival of the Russians in the early 1800s and particularly by Russia's ban on Botlikh trade with Georgia.

One evening, when Semën stopped by a local tea house where men were chatting over tea and a game of backgammon, it did not take him long to understand that the locals deeply resented the Russians, whose policies were blamed for all their recent misfortunes: preventing merchants from traveling to Georgian or Persian cities, controlling the prices of commodities, installing puppet rulers, and all in all, bringing changes to the region that greatly reduced Botlikh's influence and prosperity. It is hardly surprising that a decade later the residents would enthusiastically join Shamil in his war against Russia and continue to rise periodically against the authorities.[21]

The Chechens

After a few days at Botlikh and its bazaars, Semën was ready to depart for the lands of the most numerous and, by all accounts, the most bellicose people of the North Caucasus, the Chechens. The road from Botlikh led north into the uplands. The travelers soon left behind the meadows of blossoming flowers and a large lake popularly known as Trout Lake. Beyond the high pass of Kharamia at 2,200 meters were the highlands of the upper Aksai River, the lands of Ichkeria. This was the southeast corner of Greater Chechnya bounded by the Aksai River in the east and the Argun River in the west. Across the Argun as far west as the Assa River were the lands of Lesser Chechnya.The first reports about the Chechens reached Moscow in 1587, when Muscovite envoys passing through the highlands on their way to Georgia mentioned the Michkiz (Michik), Indili (on the Ingilik River), and Shubut (in the upper reaches of the Argun River) clans. Typical in a region with poorly consolidated political entities, the same people were often known to their neighbors under different names. The Chechens, for instance, were known as the Shashan or Chechen (the name of the village) to the Kabardins, as the Michik (the name of the river) to the Kumyks, and as Kisty to the Georgians. Though they initially used all these names, by the early eighteenth century the Russians had adopted the aggregate term "Chechen." When dealing with outsiders, the Chechens called themselves the Nakhchi, or "the people," but they identified one another through their membership in a certain kinship group.

The fact that the Chechens lived in free societies—a cluster of clan-based auls united by kinship, territory, and a mutual oath—was an open secret, but the Russians preferred to see others in the mirror of their own society and had difficulty imagining a people without a state and single ruler. This situation came as something of a revelation to the governor-general of the Caucasus, P. S. Potemkin, who in the late eighteenth century observed that "the peoples referred to as the Chechens and Kumyks do not comprise real nations [natsii] under such names, but every village has its own chief [vladelets] and is governed by its own laws."[22]

Semën's first destination was Veden (Vedeno), an aul of 260 houses perched on the banks of the Khulkhulau River. Though four decades later it lay in ruins, razed by the Russians in their crucial victory over Shamil, at the time of his visit Veden was no different from many auls in the region. A one-day journey beyond Veden brought Semën to the largest settlement in Greater Chechnya, the aul of Shali with 780 houses and about four thousand residents. The road to Shali wound down along the mountain slopes toward the plains formed by the Terek and Sunzha Rivers. Here at midstream the rivers became calmer, and the ominous mountain gorges were left behind. But the feeling of safety, whether from the forces of nature or human predations, was only illusory. For one now entered the dense primordial forests of Chechnya, where more than one traveling party had been robbed and kidnapped by roving bands.[23]

Situated on the banks of the Bass River, one of the Sunzha's many tributaries, Shali was a prosperous aul connecting the trade routes from the mountains to the plains. It was surrounded by orchards and fields and was a well-known marketplace where the animal products of the mountains were exchanged and traded for the agricultural products of the plains. The nearby forests supplied another great source of revenue: honey, wax, and, most important, logs, which were shipped lashed together.

By the time of Semën's travel in the region, Shali, like other auls of significance in Daghestan and Chechnya, was undergoing a dramatic change prompted by the growing Russian presence. The main source of discontent was the continuing flow of Slavic migrants to the North Caucasus. The Russian population in the North Caucasus was around 20,000 in 1762, but thirty years later it had grown to 111,400 Russians in addition to 38,500 Ukrainians and 14,500 Christians of other ethnic groups. The migrants settled along the Terek River, displacing the Nogays from their traditional pasturelands. The numbers spoke for themselves: between 1762 and 1795, the Nogay population declined from 109,000 to 44,000.[24]

The arrival of the Slavic population and other newcomers (Armenians, Germans, and Greeks) undermined the traditional social and commercial relations in the region. The sudden advance of the Russian military from its positions along the Terek to the Sunzha River in 1818–20 and the construction of new forts in immediate proximity to the Chechen auls were only the latest developments in Russia's relentless expansion in the Caucasus. The discontent in Shali was as obvious as it was in other Chechen auls. Throughout the nineteenth century Shali became one of the epicenters of anti-Russian and Sufi activity—the two were largely synonymous.[25]

At Shali, Semën discovered that the Russian frontier was much closer than he had imagined. The landscape of the North Caucasus had visibly changed in the eight years since his departure from Naurskaia in 1814. As the frontier advanced from the Terek toward the Sunzha River, his home village of Naurskaia was no longer a quintessential Cossack frontier settlement. Just north of Shali, the new frontier line separated the indigenous from the Russian North Caucasus.

The footprints of Ermolov's conquest were everywhere. In June 1818 he had founded a fort on the left bank of the lower Sunzha River and named it Groznyi (Menacing). The location had been chosen for its strategic importance in enabling the Russians to control the approach to the mountains via the Khankal Gorge. Its name and location should have left no doubt of Ermolov's intentions—"to impose upon the Chechens the rules and duties that will impress upon them that they are the subjects of His Imperial Majesty and not allies as they hitherto imagined."[26] Within the next two years, Ermolov built two other strategic forts: Vnezapnaia near Enderi and Burnaia (Stormy) near Tarki. The initial three forts and those that followed were intended to project Russian control over the plains and the foothills of the Caucasus before Russia's further advance into the mountains.

In his 1817 report to the authorities in St. Petersburg, Ermolov argued that advancing the Russian frontier and building a new fortification line on the Sunzha River would permit the conquest of the North Caucasus and thereby achieve the empire's strategic objectives: protecting Russian interests in Georgia and elsewhere in the Transcaucasus region. In the meantime, the new forts would project Russia's influence in the immediate surroundings. Forts Vnezapnaia and Burnaia were to prop up the loyal shamkhal against the recalcitrant Kumyk nobles, while Groznyi would secure the wilderness between the Terek and Sunzha Rivers, a traditional safe haven for brigands.

Unavoidably, the issue of security could not be separated from the issue of land. Ermolov made clear his intention to redistribute the fertile lands along the Sunhza River among the Cossacks and some loyal Nogays, leaving the Chechens only "enough lands for their needs." Any resistance by the Chechens would lead to their expulsion, and "all their lands would come into our possession."[27]

Ermolov's land policies were not new; they faithfully followed Russia's established practices of the late eighteenth century. By seizing the traditional pasturelands, the Russian authorities were successful in displacing various pastoralist peoples: the Kalmyks from the banks of the Volga and the Nogays and Kabardins from the Kuban and Terek Rivers, respectively. The pastoralists were replaced by Cossacks and the Russian, Ukrainian, and German peasants who had transformed the former pastures into rich agricultural land, and by the Armenian, Georgian, and Greek merchants who had founded prosperous commercial enterprises. The lands along the Sunzha held the same promise for Ermolov.

During four months in the summer and fall of 1818, Ermolov personally supervised the construction of Groznyi. As long as Russian intentions were not immediately clear, the local Chechen villagers hesitated in their response. But when the Russian commanders demanded hostages from the nearby Chechen auls and compelled the residents to deliver timber for the construction of the fort, it became apparent that the Russians had come to stay. Several Chechen auls joined by their neighbors from Daghestan launched major attacks. But the local militia force was no match for the devastating power of the Russian artillery, the tactical knowledge of the Russian officers, the strict discipline of the Russian army, and its ability to sustain long-term operations. Not least important was Russia's reliance on native informers and guides, who kept the Russians abreast of the Chechens' intentions and the local topography.[28]

With the rise of Fort Groznyi, the residents of Shali found themselves in uncomfortable proximity to the new frontier. Only dense forest and the rapid waters of the Argun separated Shali from the Russian garrison. Semën knew he was halfway between Shali and Groznyi when he crossed the Argun near the Chechen hamlet of Beglekoy. Another eight miles through the forest and he approached Fort Groznyi. From a distance the Russian fort must have resembled a typical Muslim town. This was only an illusion, of course, created by the four nearby Chechen villages whose minarets dominated the landscape. As Groznyi itself began to emerge in plain view, it looked anything but menacing. Semën could see the wooden fort, its earthen ramparts six feet high and fortified with palisades, two deep moats, a watchtower, and even the mouths of the cannons visible through the portholes. Like many similar Russian forts, Groznyi was built as a regular hexagon, each corner of which was a bastion armed with two cannons.

After crossing the Sunzha on a narrow wooden bridge, Semën's party entered the fort through its southeastern gates. It was a hot summer day, and except for a few soldiers on guard duty and those working around arms depots, most of the garrison was resting inside their barracks. Outside the fort walls stood a modest compound for married soldiers and other service personnel. It consisted of small wooden houses, a chapel, a bathhouse, horse stables, a kitchen, and other sundry buildings. By the 1830s and 1840s the compound would also become the residence of many artisans and traders, including a small colony of Mountain Jews. Near the compound was a cemetery that seemed to have too many graves for a fort constructed only a few years earlier. Semën was soon to learn that many more Russian soldiers had died from yellow fever than from hostile fire.[29]

In reaching Groznyi, Semën crossed not only the geographical frontier separating the Russian military from the indigenous population of the North Caucasus but also cultural and psychological frontiers that, as he would later find, were not easily negotiated. During the eight formative years that he was away from his birthplace, the valleys and the mountains of the Caucasus had become his second home. The languages of the Caucasus sounded more natural to his ears than the sounds of Russian. Despite all that the Russians had borrowed from the very people they came to conquer—clothing, customs, weapons, domestic architecture, and economy—they remained unmistakably different from their neighbors in the Caucasus. Semën was returning to the world of his early childhood, a world that, at the moment, must have seemed distant and strange. Within a few short years the Russian and the native worlds would collide with greater force than ever before, and so would the inner worlds of Semën Atarshchikov.

Return to Russia

Groznyi provided the first culture shock that awaited Semën upon crossing the frontier. After he had traveled through prosperous native auls surrounded by blooming orchards and lush pastures, Groznyi appeared austere and uninviting. As was typical of Russian forts, the garrison lived in wretched conditions, with large numbers stricken by diseases and completely dependent on the neighboring Chechen auls for food and other supplies.

Semën's party left the fort through the main gate to take the only road that connected Groznyi with the rest of the Russian Empire. From Groznyi the road passed to the Cossack village of Chervlennaia on the Terek River and then farther north, toward the towns of Kizliar and Astrakhan. The Groznyi-Chervlennaia stretch of road was new and served as an important symbol of the changes wrought in the landscape by the Russian presence. The road cut through Chechnya's primeval forests and was critical to the Russian conquest of the region. Such roads were vital routes for supplying the growing number of Russian forts. Cutting through the dense forest required nothing short of a full-scale military expedition, and more than one Russian soldier was ambushed and killed while laying the roads through the region.[30]

The only settlement between Groznyi and Chervlennaia was the Chechen village of Staryi Yurt (later renamed Tolstoy Yurt). Six hours after he had departed from Groznyi, Semën approached Chervlennaia. Here the Terek was wider, forming one of the most heavily trafficked river crossings in the region; it was used equally by peaceful parties, brigands, and armies. Originally, the Cossack settlements had been founded right on the banks of the river, but in time the bank had washed away, and now only ruins remained, hidden amid orchards and wild blackberries.

Chervlennaia had been founded at a former Nogay camp known as Oraz Kala, and like other Cossack settlements along the Terek was a part of the the river's defense line: a series of Cossack villages, outposts, and towers guarding the Russian frontier. But it also became an important economic hub because of the nearby flour mills and its location on the road from Kizliar to Groznyi. In the early 1850s, the young officer and future Russian writer Leo Tolstoy was stationed at Chervlennaia, which later became the setting for his famous story "The Cossacks" (Tolstoy named it Novomlinskaia, or the New Mills).

After having crossed the Terek, Semën rode for about three miles through a dense forest before reaching Chervlennaia. The village was surrounded by an earthen rampart and a forest of blackthorn. The village gates through which he entered were covered with a reed roof. Next to the gates was a gun carriage with a rusty cannon, which seemed to have seen little if any use. An armed Cossack guard was supposed to be standing watch, but more typically the gates were left unguarded, as was the case now. A sign below the roof of the gates announced the population of the village: 266 houses, 897 men, and 1,012 women.

Even at first glance, the contrast between the world he had left behind in the mountains and the world he was returning to was starkly apparent. The stone houses, curvy streets, and tall minarets of a typical haphazardly built mountain village had been replaced by the long rows of clean wooden houses with windows and high decorated porches of the typical Cossack village. The Cossack houses were built on beams twenty-eight inches above the ground and stood comfortably apart from each other forming wide lanes. Behind the houses were blossoming bushes of acacia and lilac, bright yellow sunflowers, grape vines, and cultivated gardens. But this lush vegetation occupied a fairly thin stretch of land, about six hundred meters wide. Beyond it to the north were the sandy dunes of the arid Nogay steppe. This was the southern tip of the enormous Eurasian steppe that stretched from southeastern Europe across the deserts and steppe of Central Asia toward the shores of the Pacific Ocean.

In the main square of the village Semën noticed three small shops selling sundry things. Behind the high fence in the shade of several large trees stood the largest house in the village, the residence of the regimental commander. Except on Sundays, the streets of the Cossack village were empty. The Cossacks were performing their military duties on patrols or expeditions. The old men were busy hunting, fishing, and helping the women in the orchards and gardens. Only the very old, the very young, and the sick stayed home.

The road from Chervlennaia to Naurskaia stretched along the Terek River connecting the Cossack villages and outposts into a fifty-six-mile-long defense line. After a four-hour journey through familiar terrain, Semën arrived at Naurskaia shortly before sunset. At this time the residents were returning home after a day of work. The usually empty roads and streets of the village were coming to life. Shepherds herded cows and buffalo, Nogay laborers spurred oxen pulling carriages, men returned from the river with fresh-caught fish, women carried firewood on their backs, and boys played in the dusty streets. Smoke rising from the chimneys carried the aroma of sun-dried animal manure (*kiziak*).

This was the village where Semën had grown up. Once again he was struck by the close links between the Cossacks and their non-Christian neighbors across the Terek. Of course, they all shared the same values— the desire to be free from the authorities and pride in their martial skills. The Cossacks were proud of being able to converse in Tatar, which they often used even among themselves, and many had friends in neighboring

Chechen villages. Some married Chechen women and forged close ties with the bride's kin.

It was deeply ironic that the Cossacks had far more liking for the neighboring Chechens who periodically raided, robbed, and even killed them than for the Russian soldiers who were there to protect them from these raids. The Cossacks despised the Russian troops who were billeted in their villages and to whom they disparagingly referred as *moskali* (Muscovites). They reserved an almost equal scorn for Ukrainian settlers, known as *khokhly* (tufts of hair)—a reference to the haircut characteristic of the Zaporozhian Cossacks. Whereas the Ukrainians were outsiders who competed with the Cossacks for land and trade, the presence of the Russian troops threatened their very lifestyle. The Russians limited Cossack traditional freedoms and, in order to steer them from the Old Belief, forced Russian priests upon them.[31]

Life in the Cossack village had its own rhythm: for women it meant endless domestic duties and for men military service, and all villagers spent most of their time working the land. At first Semën's life took a predictable turn. In the spring of the following year, he was summoned to pledge an oath. Several hundred young Cossacks gathered in the village square in front of the church. After the priest finished reading the oath, each one approached to kiss the cross. From now on, they were no longer young village lads but Cossacks in the service of the tsar and defenders of the Russian Empire.[32]

In the summer Semën left for a camp where local Cossacks gathered for their annual training and military exercises. A month later he joined his fellow Cossacks on daily military patrols along the Terek. But soon Semën's unique linguistic skills and his intimate knowledge of the peoples across the frontier were urgently needed elsewhere. Chechnya and northern Daghestan were in revolt, and General Ermolov once again intended to pacify the region. In 1823, at the age of sixteen, Semën enlisted as an interpreter with the Mozdok Cossack Regiment.

4

Inside Ermolov's
"Iron Fist"

The General

In the wake of Russia's military victory over Napoleon and the empire's enhanced role in European politics, St. Petersburg decided that the time had come to pacify the North Caucasus. Several tactical and strategic reasons dominated the thinking of the Russian government: preventing brigandage along the frontier, seizing the lands that could be used for farming and commerce, bringing the natives into submission, and securing Russia's expanding control of Transcaucasia: the Georgian, Armenian, and Azeri lands.

The task of pacifying the North Caucasus fell to the commander of the Russian troops in the Caucasus, General A. P. Ermolov, whose long tenure in the region (1816–27) would leave a controversial legacy. To some he was a legendary general whose bravery and determination had finally brought the natives of the North Caucasus to their knees. To others he was a ruthless and shortsighted conqueror whose policies unnecessarily turned the natives into Russia's permanent antagonists.

In May 1816 Ermolov arrived in Tiflis to assume command of the Georgian Corps, which four years later was renamed the Caucasian Corps. A man of war, he found himself in an atypical role a year later, when he was entrusted with a delicate peace mission to Iran. His task was to mollify the Iranian court into acquiescing to Russia's annexation of Azerbaijan and accepting the Russian border along the Kura and Araks Rivers. The Iranians had been forced to cede control of most Azeri provinces to Russia in the Treaty of Gülistan in 1813, but now, encouraged by Britain, they were pushing to revisit the conditions of the treaty. Ermolov was instructed

A portrait of General A. P. Ermolov by P. Z. Zakharov—Chechenets, 1843

to reject the Iranian demand for Russia's withdrawal north of the Terek River but to do so without provoking a military confrontation with Iran, whose army had been newly supplied and trained by the British East India Company officers.

Ermolov was the wrong man for a sensitive diplomatic mission. His reputation for honesty, simplicity of lifestyle, intolerance of corruption, and concern for his soldiers was well deserved and ensured the respect and fear of the troops. But he was also a self-centered man of great ambition and vanity, dangerous qualities that were carefully noted and reported by the head of Russia's secret police, M. Ia. von Fok.[1]

Ermolov's tough, direct, and uncomplicated approach combined with a derisive and condescending attitude toward "Asiatic customs" was both confrontational and offensive to his Iranian hosts. Arrogant and cocky, Ermolov behaved like so many Russian envoys before and after him who balked at following the customs of various royal courts lest the dignity of the Russian envoys and the sovereign they represented be compromised. Defying custom, Ermolov refused to take off his boots and put on red socks before entering the royal quarters. In return, he was not allowed inside the palace and was received in the courtyard.[2]

During his brief ambassadorial mission Ermolov displayed the righteousness, conceit, and disdain that characterized his attitude toward "the oriental other." Relying on contemporary clichés that viewed the Orient as a place of corrupt, immoral, treacherous, and cruel despotism, he ignored St. Petersburg's instructions to spend the large sum allocated for gifts for the Iranian court and instead directed most of the embassy funds toward the construction of a Russian military hospital in Tiflis.

Ermolov also believed that the "Asiatics" were guided by different moral standards where notions of truth and honor need not apply. At one point during the negotiations, he proclaimed himself a descendant of the Chinggis khan and mused unabashedly about his destiny of representing the country that had long been ruled by his ancestors. To convince their incredulous hosts, the Russians produced Ermolov's cousin, who at the time was serving in the Russian consulate in Tabriz and whose high cheekbones indeed made him look Asian. This was a grand and daring lie! In the world of Asian politics, the claim of Chinggisid heritage meant that one had a legitimate right to the throne; this therefore implied that the "Chinggisid" general in command of the large army across the border was a serious threat to Iran's ruling dynasty. Whether this absurd claim was taken as seriously as Ermolov believed it was we do not know.[3]

What we do know is that in an attempt to forge his image as a local potentate, Ermolov went beyond mere rhetoric. During his ten-year stay in the Caucasus, he acquired a harem of his own, a little-known fact that Ermolov and those who subsequently wrote about him studiously suppressed. Every marriage was certified by the local mullahs as a *kabin,* a formal marriage that could be dissolved at any time upon the full payment of a dowry. This and other forms of marriage involving payments for the bride were widespread in the region. Ermolov's three wives bore him four sons and one daughter. The sons were sent to Russia, were educated in military schools, and became army officers. Long after his departure from the Caucasus, Ermolov sent money to one of his former wives and a daughter on several occasions and expressed continuing interest in the well-being of his sons.[4] It turns out that the famous Russian general, revered as "a hero of the Caucasus," was also an Oriental satrap.

Like many European government officials who found themselves in a colonial environment elsewhere, Ermolov was confronted by an uncomfortable reality that did not easily fit into his well-established beliefs and values. A typical product of the Enlightenment untempered by self-doubt or empathy, he strongly believed in the superiority of European Christian civilization represented by Russia. But how was he "to spread the Christian faith which was so necessary for softening the barbarity of indigenous peoples" in a region where Islam was already deeply entrenched?[5] How was he to impose imperial rule on peoples who had little taste for central authority? How could he transform the cultures whose traditional practices were outside the imperial legal norms and were fundamentally different from those of the Russians?

Ermolov's answer was the uncompromising pursuit of Russia's interests through violence, fear, and intimidation. He was convinced that the power to inflict violence would command the respect and obedience of the local population, whether they saw him as the awe-inspiring Russian general Ermolov or the omnipotent local ruler to whom they referred as the *serdar* (in Persian, commander) Ermol-oglu.

Numerous contemporaries observed Ermolov's natural ability to inspire respect and admiration. Even such sworn enemies of autocracy as Russia's great poets Alexander Pushkin and Alexander Griboedov were strong believers in Russia's civilizing mission and great admirers of Ermolov. After all, "he was in Asia, and here even a child reaches for a knife," exclaimed Griboedov, who, like so many contemporary Russian writers and poets, romanticized, feminized, and orientalized the Caucasus.[6]

There were a few, however, who saw things differently. One of them was General M. F. Orlov, a member of the Decembrists, a group of Russian officers so named for their unsuccessful revolt against autocracy in December 1825. Orlov was skeptical of the wisdom and efficacy of Ermolov's policies as well as of Russia's entire imperial enterprise: "It is as difficult to subdue the Chechens as it is to erase the Caucasus [Mountains]. This is done not with bayonets but with time and enlightenment, which we, ourselves, do not possess in abundance."[7] At the time, Orlov's criticisms fell on deaf ears, and Ermolov's conquest of the Caucasus proceeded apace.

"The Village Was Razed to the Ground"

While Chechnya and Daghestan remained the focus of Ermolov's activity, the Russian front line advanced into the indigenous territories along the entire stretch of the northeast and central Caucasus: in 1817, in the upper reaches of the Sunzha River, the Russians built Fort Nazran, the present capital of Ingushetiia, and a year later, Fort Nalchik, the present capital of Kabarda. Both forts were intended to provide security along the strategic road connecting Russia with Georgia, the Georgian Military Highway.

The advance of the Russian army south of the Terek River, the rapid establishment of the new Russian forts in the plains of the North Caucasus, and Ermolov's punitive expeditions deeply unsettled the balance of power among the various local societies. Russia increasingly faced a popular resistance movement that combined anti-Russian resentment with a struggle against pro-Russian local elites. By the early 1820s, brooding hostility toward the invading army turned into a series of rebellions: among Kabardins in 1820–21, Avars in 1821, Chechens in 1822, Kumyks and Avars in 1823, in Tabasaran in 1825, in southern Daghestan in 1826, and in Chechnya in 1825–26.

The first wave of widespread resistance occurred in 1818 with the revolt in northern Daghestan and increased raiding activity by Kabardin and Chechen war parties. Despite the annuities and titles recently bestowed by St. Petersburg, most of the local rulers took arms against the Russians as they penetrated deeply inside Daghestan. The combined force of the Avar khan, the Dargins, the alliance of the Akusha auls, and the Kumyks—all together an army of thirty thousand strong by Ermolov's own count— besieged Bashly, an utsmii's residence occupied at the time by Russian troops. Facing overwhelming numbers and suffering serious casualties, Major General Pestel, the Russian commander in Daghestan, was forced to retreat but not before seizing children as hostages.[8]

The defeat of the Russian troops near Bashly was an important victory for the local leaders, but it proved short-lived. Ermolov quickly marched to Pestel's assistance, sowing a path of destruction along the way. Some local residents chose to flee, as was the case in the Kumyk settlement of

Paraul, while others, as in the aul of Great Jangutai, resolved to fight. The battles were bloody and usually ended with the same result: those who resisted were killed in battle or massacred later, and their aul was burned to the ground. At Great Jangutai all six hundred of the aul's houses were ordered to be burned; only a few were left for destitute residents who had no place to go in the approaching winter. Ermolov ordered Pestel to return to Bashly and raze the town.[9]

In the past, the North Caucasus had periodically been subjected to the scorched-earth policy of various conquerors. The notoriously brutal Nadir Shah of Persia employed this tactic in the 1740s, and the ruthless Russian commanders Prince V. Potemkin in the 1780s and General S. A. Bulgakov in the early 1800s did so as well. But Ermolov's tenure was marked by a deployment of more systematic violence through virtually nonstop military campaigns, punitive expeditions, and admonitory destruction of native settlements.

In 1819, after subduing the Kumyk rebels, Ermolov decided to turn attention to the rebellious qadi of Akusha, the utsmii, and the Chechen auls along the Aksai River. The latter were a continuous source of horse rustling and brigandage and posed a threat to the Russian fort under construction near Enderi. To set an example to others, Ermolov ordered his troops to surround the Chechen aul of Dadan-Yurt and demanded that the residents vacate and move elsewhere. Previous experience had taught him that if the residents evacuated their wives and children, there was a chance of their surrender; otherwise they would fight to the end to protect their families. In this case the wives and children stayed, and Ermolov anticipated fierce resistance.

The Chechen men were massacred in the ensuing bloodbath but not before they had killed and wounded more than two hundred Russians and put their own wives to death in order to prevent them from falling into the hands of the infidels. Once again, Ermolov's strategy of spreading fear and intimidation had dictated a necessary outcome: Dadan-Yurt was looted and razed to the ground, about 140 women and children were taken prisoner, and many more were slaughtered or died in artillery bombardments and fires.[10]

The usual fate befell the captive women and children: they were sold as serfs into Russian households, baptized, and given Russian names. Among the Chechen children who survived the slaughter at Dadan-Yurt was a three-year-old orphan. He was brought to St. Petersburg, was baptized Petr Zakharov, and became one of Russia's celebrated painters. He painted the portraits of well-known Russian public figures and, in a stunning irony, was elected in 1842 a member of the Russian Academy of Arts for his portrait of

General Ermolov. Yet Zakharov's self-portrait, depicting a typical Chechen dressed in the garb of his native Caucasus, and the fact that he chose to add the qualifier "Chechen" to his last name clearly reveal a keen awareness of his own background. One can only imagine the mixed feelings of Petr Zakharov-Chechenets as he painted a picture of the General Ermolov, the man equally responsible for the slaughter of his parents and his transformation from a Chechen boy in a distant aul to one of Russia's leading portraitists.[11]

In December 1819, en route to Akusha, Ermolov continued to put the native settlements to fire and sword. But in one case at least he showed

A Chechen-born Russian painter, P. Z. Zakharov-Chechenets, *Self-portrait*, 1842. In Groznyi Art Museum, Groznyi, Chechen Republic, Russia.

uncharacteristic pity. He noted with some regret the destruction of the beautiful small town of Ullu-Aya, whose eight hundred houses had been set on fire and whose residents had fled in such haste that they even left some babies behind. Yet, as if fearing that his empathy signaled weakness, Ermolov offered an immediate justification: "Destruction was necessary as an example of punishment of the proud people who until now submitted to no one; [it was] needed as an instruction to other peoples, who can be tamed only through the lessons of terror."[12]

In the summer of 1820, Russian punitive expeditions continued to suppress the insurgency among Kumyks and Chechens with predictable results—the auls that offered the slightest resistance were razed to the ground and their population slaughtered. Even those who chose to co-operate were not spared, as the inevitable logic of occupation often led to unintended consequences. Ermolov recalled one incident when after a two-week absence from Groznyi, he returned to find out that the nearby Chechen aul that provided supplies for the fort had been plundered by his troops. It turned out that a local Chechen had shot a soldier in an argument over an ox that the Chechen claimed to be his own, whereas the soldier insisted it had been purchased for the Russian military. When the Russians demanded that the villagers surrender the offender, the men sent their families to the safety of the nearby forest and resolved to defend their aul. Eventually the residents fled, and the aul was looted for several days. After this event, all the Chechen auls on the Sunzha's left bank near Groznyi were abandoned, and their residents fled across the river. Regretting the consequences, Ermolov nonetheless blamed the Chechens, reasoning that their social organization precluded any strong authority and that their religion did not allow surrendering Muslims into the hands of the Christian infidels.[13]

Although Ermolov was convinced that his uncompromising approach was succeeding in pacifying the Caucasus, his policies instead proved a ticking time bomb. The destruction and punishment of entire settlements and communities were turning more villagers into rebels armed with the new ideology of resistance, Sufi Islam. It was not surprising that by the late 1820s the initial wave of revolts had escalated into a holy war against the Russians. The so-called Caucasus War would continue until 1859.

Semën's First Doubts

In 1823 Semën was pulled into the whirlwind of the events in the North Caucasus. Ermolov's rule had left behind a wide swath of destruction: auls razed to the ground, crops burned, captives and cattle seized, forests cut down, and pastureland taken away. Semën had learned about the terrible Serdar Ermol-oglu when he lived in Karabudakhkent and when he saw the destruction wrought by the Russian troops. On the other side of the frontier, however, in his native Naurskaia, he heard the Cossacks' admiring talk of the just and fearsome Russian general. Now dispatched to join Ermolov's campaign, Semën was about to have a close-up view of his policies.

As one of the few competent interpreters of Chechen and Kumyk, Semën was immediately dispatched to the region's hot spot. In 1823 he arrived at Fort Burnaia in time to join the fort's commander, Lieutenant Colonel Evreinov, on his march to quell the uprising in several neighboring Kumyk villages. Uncertain whether Evreinov's contingent of one infantry battalion and four cannons would be sufficient, the Russian commander in Daghestan, Major General K. K. von Krabbe, ordered Colonel Verkhovskoi with six infantry companies, six cannons, and the Tatar cavalry to march from the Derbend garrison.

The threat of uprising had been exaggerated, and the appearance of Evreinov's contingent was enough to pacify the villages. Colonel Verkhovskoi was still on the march toward the rebellious villages when Semën Atarshchikov was dispatched to inform him that order had been restored and that the colonel could therefore turn back to Derbend. In yet another irony that would mark his career, Semën caught up with Verkhovskoi in Karabudakhkent. Two years earlier, Semën had appeared indistinguishable from other local young men, but now he was riding into town in a Cossack uniform. He understood both worlds well: the local people with their concerns and complaints against the Russians and the Russians with their uncompromising demand for loyalty and submission. Yet as an interpreter for the Cossack regiment, he unquestionably represented the Russian world. Or at least he was supposed to: for his first encounter with the reality of war proved that the conflict between the Russians and the locals defied simple characterization and promised to confuse further his already tangled identity.

Semën could not have been entirely comfortable with his own dramatic transformation. The sight of the hundreds of Russian soldiers billeted around the town—their bayonets glittering in the sun, their drums and loud songs filling the air—must have seemed a blight on the familiar landscape of the local houses and minarets, green fields, and bountiful orchards. Yet Semën enjoyed playing a host of sorts, mediating between the Russian commander Verkhovskoi and the local beg, who treated his guests to a feast accompanied with traditional horse races, sharpshooting, and wrestling.

During his short stay at Karabudakhkent Colonel Verkhovskoi was accompanied by a young and handsome Kumyk noble named Ammalat, the son-in-law and nephew of the shamkhal. They had met three years earlier and ever since had continued to enjoy each other's company: Ammalat intrigued by things Russian and foreign and the colonel enchanted by the highlander's austere charisma and superb martial skills. What followed, however, proved how fragile a relationship between the Russians and the locals really was.

After three days at Karabudakhkent, Colonel Verkhovskoi and his troops departed for Derbend. Ammalat accompanied the colonel, as he often did. Somewhere along the way, while the two were separated from the rest of the troops for a moment, Ammalat shot Verkhovskoi, killing him and escaping to the mountains.[14] To the Russians, this was clear proof of the natives' treachery, confirming that they could not be trusted.

What exactly provoked Ammalat to act so dramatically is not clear. However, the scope of the rebellion that followed the colonel's assassination indicates that this was hardly an isolated incident. Immediately thereafter, several Kumyk auls rose up in arms. The rebellion engulfed even the shamkhal's residence, Tarki, where the rebels killed a Russian district superintendent (*pristav*) and two Cossacks. At the same time, the Avar khan, Ahmed, also rallied his people against the Russians. It thus appears that the plan for the uprising may have been hatched by Ahmed and Ammalat, the latter probably hoping to ride the crest of the anti-Russian wave into the shamkhal's palace to replace his uncle at Tarki.

Ermolov responded with typically swift and punitive retribution. Semën was ordered to join the expeditionary force of General von Krabbe, who marched against the rebellious Kumyk auls of Karanay and Erpeli. At Karanay, for the first time, Semën witnessed the Russian campaign in action. The villagers resisted but were quickly overwhelmed by the Russian artillery. As the Russian troops pillaged their way through the aul, smoke billowed from stacks of hay, roofs collapsed as houses were set ablaze, and wandering cattle bellowed in desperation. The soldiers carried out carpets, house utensils, and food. One killed a goat while another drank fresh milk from a big pot. A few old men whose age made them indifferent to their own fate were taken out of the houses and helped onto Russian carts. After hours of pillage the entire village was set on fire. This was the picture hidden behind the phrase that so often concluded Russian military reports: "The village was razed to the ground."[15]

The ruins of the large Kumyk village of Karanay must have left a deep impression on the young Semën Atarshchikov. In more than one way, Semën belonged to this people and shared their way of life. To realize that he was a participant in the destruction of the people and places he knew so well must have been deeply unsettling. Was it possible that Ammalat's sudden change of loyalties not only had been motivated by personal gain but was also an act of retribution against the Russians? Were the first seeds of the doubt that would lead to Semën's own defection planted at this time?

Russia's firepower and military superiority seemed overwhelming, yet several encounters showed that the tsar's army was not invincible. Shortly after the destruction of Karanay, the Russian troops moved to subdue Erpeli, another large Kumyk settlement. Here they encountered stiff resistance from residents who skillfully took advantage of their natural defenses. Heavily wooded terrain prevented the Russians from effective use of the artillery they usually deployed with such devastating success. After suffering heavy casualties, the troops were forced to retreat, pursued by the triumphant rebels.[16]

News of the Russian defeat at Erpeli spread quickly throughout the region and inspired others to take their chances against the invaders. The largest and best-organized uprising took place in Chechnya in 1825–26, soon joined by the neighboring Ingush, Karabulaks, Kumyks, Ossetians, and Kabardins. Its leader, Beg-Bulat (Taimazov), was a renowned Chechen warrior who had just returned from Daghestan in the company of the prominent mullah Muhammad. Beg-Bulat was among an increasing number of Chechen leaders who had traveled to Daghestan to learn about the new Sufi teachings. In the spring of 1825 the northeast and central Caucasus were in revolt. While Muhammad provided a spiritual rallying point and was regarded as "a prophet chosen by God to liberate [the Muslims] from the Russians," Beg-Bulat's demands were very specific: abandon Fort Groznyi and the Sunzha River fortifications and return to the Terek.[17]

In the summer of 1825 a large force marched against Groznyi. The Russian garrison chose to avoid a pitched battle and decided to wait it out. But instead of storming Groznyi, a well-defended major fort in the region, Beg-Bulat decided to move toward the lesser forts on the Kumyk plain and unexpectedly stormed and successfully captured Amir Haji Yurt, a small but strategic Russian fort. Ermolov blamed the rebels' success on the careless commander of the fort, which was poorly fortified and relied exclusively on its artillery for defense. When the rebels sneaked into the fort from the nearby forest on a dark and windy night, the cannons proved of little use.

The news of the Russian debacle and the fate of the fort's garrison (out of 181 defenders, 98 were killed and 13 captured) reached Ermolov at his headquarters in Tiflis. Shocked and infuriated, he quickly realized the danger if the revolt spread throughout Daghestan. Indeed, the number of rebels was growing rapidly as news of their victories traveled around the region. Because the number of Russian troops was inadequate and thinly stretched, Ermolov ordered the local Russian commanders to gather the available troops and march against the rebels without delay. Two Russian generals, Nikolai Grekov and Dmitri Lisanevich, set out immediately and arrived with their troops just in time to relieve the besieged Russian fort at Gerzel-aul.

Accompanying Major General Grekov, Semën once again found himself a witness to the cruelties and human drama of war. After the rebels were dispersed, the commander of the Russian force, Lieutenant General Lisanevich, intent on teaching the natives a lesson, ordered that three hundred of the most important men from the neighboring aul of Aksai be punished. Grekov and several local loyalists who were more familiar with native customs advised Lisanevich against such retribution. They explained that the residents of Aksai had already offered their apology for disloyalty and asked forgiveness—detaining and, worse yet, punishing their notables would only create more trouble. But Lisanevich was implacable.

The next morning the three hundred men were brought into the fort. Inexplicably, they were neither searched nor disarmed and were left unguarded while many Russian soldiers were procuring food and firewood outside the fort. Lisanevich, in the company of several senior officers, scolded the Kumyks, rebuked them for their treason, and threatened to kill those found guilty. Two Kumyk men were called in front of Lisanevich, who ordered them arrested and their daggers seized. The third Kumyk refused to come forward, but when forced to do so, he quietly approached Lisanovich and suddenly pulling out a hidden dagger, struck and mortally wounded the general. Before anyone could come to his senses, the Kumyk then rushed at General Grekov and struck him several times with the dagger, killing him instantly. He was able to wound another officer before finally being shot.

All this happened so quickly that for a tense moment both the Russian soldiers and the Kumyk men stared in silence and disbelief. "Bayonet [them]" was the last word of the expiring Lisanovich, which turned the scene into a fearsome bloodbath. The soldiers opened fire on the crowd of Kumyk notables, who were caught between the bullets of the garrison and those of the returning military parties as they tried to escape. Most were shot or bayoneted; only a few found their way back home.

Semën must have found the incident at Gerzel-aul deeply troubling. It revealed once again the seemingly unbridgeable gap between two different cultures and sets of values. For the Russians this was a clear-cut case: an

outrageous act of treason that proved again, if further proof were necessary, the natives' perfidious nature. From the Kumyk point of view, it was
the Russians who had violated the traditional rules of the game: once the
rebels had sued for peace, they expected to be pardoned. Instead, Gerenal
Lisanevich had summoned the Kumyk notables to abuse and disarm them.
Insults and confiscation of daggers were the worst kind of humiliation, and
it was hardly surprising that some chose to fight and die to preserve their
traditional honor.

The event sent shock waves across the region, unleashing a new cycle of
distrust and hatred between the native population and the Russians. The
situation in the northeast Caucasus became more precarious than ever,
as the uprising began to spread farther west, into Kabarda. Two senior
Russian generals were dead, and Ermolov himself rushed to the region to
take control of the situation. Setting out from Tiflis, he marched toward
northern Daghestan via the Russian strongholds at Vladikavkaz, Groznyi,
and Chervlennaia. At each fort Ermolov added several more companies
and cannons to his expeditionary force. In late summer 1825 Ermolov's
force, now consisting of six infantry companies, 300 Don Cossacks,
250 Terek Cossacks, and nine pieces of artillery, crossed the Terek and approached the Kumyk town of Enderi. The arrival of this large and lethal
force had the desired effect: the insurgents fled and the town residents
pledged their loyalty.

Despite several other clashes between the Russian troops and the rebels
in 1825–26, the uprising led by Beg-Bulat was now running out of steam.
In part this was a function of Ermolov's decisive measures. In the fall of
1825, with a renewed sense of urgency, Ermolov embarked on the restruc-
turing of the region's entire system of defenses. The old forts were either
razed or further fortified, and new ones were erected; old roads were rebuilt and new ones constructed. The native population was resettled to
prevent any further uprisings. Such was the fate of the residents of Aksai
after the Gerzel-aul incident. Built in rocky and thickly forested terrain,
Aksai was abandoned on Ermolov's order, and its residents were moved to
a new and less defensible location in the nearby valley. A Russian fort was
also constructed near the new location to keep a close eye on the residents
of the new Aksai.[18]

Even as the new defenses and reinforcements were preventing rebels
from any effective action, their uprising was collapsing from within. Beg-
Bulat began to lose the support of a crucial contingent among the rebels, the Kumyks. Intimidated by Russian arms and fearful of losing their
trade privileges, many Kumyk notables now sought a compromise with the
Russian authorities.

The relative pacification of the Kumyk plain did not spell the end of the uprising, however; in 1826 it flared up anew in Chechnya and Kabarda. Again Ermolov marched into Chechnya; in the spring of 1826 he approached the largest settlement in Lesser Chechnya, Urus-Martan. After the locals refused to surrender hostages and prepared to defend themselves, Ermolov surrounded the aul and ordered an artillery barrage. The residents fled, suffering heavy losses. Ermolov recalled later that on his orders "the village was destroyed and its splendid gardens and orchards cut to the ground."[19] Two more auls were razed on his way back to Groznyi.

Throughout the spring of 1826, Ermolov continued to leave behind a bloody trail of destruction and retribution. The fate of Urus-Martan also befell the largest settlement of Greater Chechnya, Shali, as well as several smaller Chechen auls. The dense forests adjacent to the Chechen auls were cut down, rendering the residents defenseless. New roads were cut through the forests, cultivated fields, and orchards with a single purpose—to address Russia's security concerns. New forts and redoubts were erected to control the trade routes between Chechnya and Daghestan. Taking a cue from his foes, Ermolov dispatched the Terek Cossacks and loyal native cavalry to raid and rustle the cattle from the Chechen auls. By June 1826, he was happy to report that the uprising in the region had been suppressed and that, with the exception of the Chechens on the Michik River, all major Chechen settlements had surrendered hostages.[20]

Ermolov was proud of his military feats and confident that his cruel but decisive measures in the North Caucasus had demonstrated Russian resolve and eliminated sedition. However, St. Petersburg was increasingly concerned that his actions had been excessive and counterproductive. Occasional instructions to Ermolov to show more discretion in his military campaigns had little effect. Violence was an intrinsic part of Ermolov's modus operandi and personality. In his memoirs he recalled with undisguised joy how in 1823 a group of Cossacks had surprised several Nogay villages across the Kuban River, slaughtered 400 men and women of all ages, and captured 566 people and two thousand cattle.[21]

Two years later, the Black Sea Cossacks under the command of Major General Vlasov razed to the ground several auls belonging to the Natukhays, and a troop led by Colonel Bekovich-Cherkasskii massacred three hundred families from another aul. When Ermolov recommended Bekovich-Cherkasskii for the Order of St. George, however, it appears that he crossed the line. An exasperated Emperor Alexander I again expressed his strong disapproval of the bloody retributions that only increased the resentment and resistance of the local population. The emperor flatly rejected Ermolov's recommendation, admonishing him that the slaughter of innocent civilians, mostly women and children, was a disgrace to Russian troops, who should be showing courage in battle and mercy to the defeated, not revenge against an unarmed population. In July 1826, the new Russian emperor, Nicholas I, addressing the actions of Major General Vlasov in the previous year, went beyond the moral exhortations of his predecessor and ordered Vlasov court-martialed. Eight months later, suspicious of sedition, wary of Ermolov's Napoleonic proclivities, and unhappy with the state of affairs in the Caucasus, Nicholas I dismissed Ermolov and sent him into retirement.[22]

Semën Atarshchikov must have been deeply skeptical of Ermolov's achievements. He knew the people of the North Caucasus far better than any Russian commander did and understood that reliance on military means alone was unlikely to pacify the region. The rebels might be dispersed and their leader, Beg-Bulat, gone, but the main issues underlying the revolt remained. The Russian seizure and colonization of the indigenous land did not stop. Neither did the coercive practice of demanding hostages and a pledge of allegiance to the tsar. The Russian reprisals only generated a thirst for revenge and further escalated violence. In addition, the Russian authorities banned the lucrative slave trade, forced the natives to trade only at Russian markets, and used mosques as storage places. In short, a refusal to make concessions to local sensibilities and the belief in Russia's innate superiority vis-à-vis the local peoples promised to provoke further conflicts.

At every turn Atarshchikov confronted the deep differences and misunderstandings between the Russian authorities and the indigenous elites. Where the locals sought compromises, multiple political alliances, and preservation of traditional freedoms, the Russians demanded unquestioning submission and allegiance to the tsar. In essence these were two different worlds: that of the empire-state with a centralized bureaucracy and that of highly fragmented societies with their traditional kinship structures.

By the late 1820s new winds were sweeping through the valleys and mountains of the North Caucasus. The disparate societies and peoples of the region began to share a common cause and ideology: anti-Russian uprisings were increasingly taking place under the banners of Islam. Whereas earlier rebellions had focused primarily on pragmatic demands in a futile effort to win some concessions from the Russians, the leaders of the new movement were first and foremost warriors in a holy war against the Russians and their collaborators. The teachings of one mullah, a respected religious scholar from Gimry, the Avar aul in Daghestan, called for ghazawat, or holy war, against the Russians. This mullah, appropriately named Ghazi Muhammad, became the first imam and the founder of the Imamate, an Islamic state in Daghestan and Chechnya that existed for thirty years (1829–59).

While Ghazi Muhammad and his followers were preparing for holy war in the North Caucasus, an uprising in another faraway corner of the empire caused great anxiety in the Russian capital. Inspired by the European revolutions of 1830, the Poles rose up in arms against Russian rule. Unexpectedly, Semën Atarshchikov found himself a witness to the Polish insurrection. In 1830 he was ordered to St. Petersburg to become an interpreter in a cavalry unit newly formed from the North Caucasus elite. A year later his unit became a part of Russia's military campaign in insurgent Poland.

5

St. Petersburg
and Poland

IN May 1830, Semën Atarshchikov arrived in St. Petersburg. The journey was long and arduous. Russian roads were notoriously bad, particularly during the spring rains. It took Semën about two weeks in the postal service carriages to reach the imperial capital.[1] It was his first trip outside the North Caucasus, and demanding and tiring as it might have been, it also held the promise of new and exciting experiences along the route that traversed much of European Russia.

Semën's journey began in Kizliar, where the road bent northeast along the Caspian lowland before reaching Astrakhan, Russia's major port on the Caspian Sea. Astrakhan had been a city of great economic and strategic importance until the middle of the eighteenth century, when Russia's advanced frontier, newly constructed towns, and shift in traditional trade routes relegated it to a decidedly provincial position. One of the oldest cities in the region, it still retained some of the old splendor, visible in the once-formidable city fortifications, majestic cathedrals, and public buildings.

Atarshchikov's journey took him farther north along the west bank of the Volga. The melancholy landscape was interrupted only by groups of fishermen busily pulling their nets out of the water and exhausted barge haulers dragging up the river barges full of exotic products from warmer climes. At a distance one could see clouds of dust stirred up by herds of Kalmyk horses and sheep grazing in the steppe. In a few months the steppe would turn into a sun-baked dusty plain, but now, in the spring, it looked like a spectacular, colorful blanket full of blossoming tulips and smelling of fresh wormwood.

A two-day journey brought Atarshchikov to Tsaritsyn (today Volgograd), a city situated at the bend in the Volga where the two mighty rivers of

European Russia, the Don and Volga, came closest to each other. Built in the seventeenth century as a military fort, Tsaritsyn was now a bustling and rapidly growing city capitalizing on the agricultural and industrial developments of the region. Two roads led from Tsaritsyn to Moscow. The older road went north along the Volga River to Saratov and then turned northwest to Moscow via Borisoglebsk, Tambov, and Kashira. This was a centuries-old route taken by various nomadic merchant parties bringing their horses to sell at the Moscow horse market. The newer and shorter road cut through the central Russian plain directly toward Tambov, Kashira, and Moscow. Atarshchikov chose a shorter route.

Traveling for six days before reaching the walls of Moscow offered a typical landscape of the Russian plain: scattered villages, herds of live-stock, several mid-sized towns, and fields of rye and wheat where be-draggled peasants labored for their landlords. No longer the capital of the empire, Moscow continued to be a symbol of Russia. Glittering in the bright sun were the gilded cupolas of the city's numerous churches and cathedrals—clear evidence of its past and present glory. From Moscow it was another three days along the well-traveled road before Atarshchikov reached St. Petersburg.

Atarshchikov was mesmerized by Russia's greatness—the sheer geographical expanse of the empire, its roads and rivers, industries and markets, towns and buildings. But nothing had prepared him for St. Petersburg, an imperial city that was unlike any other place in Russia and that left many a traveler, Russian and foreign alike, to wonder and marvel in disbelief. In the 1830s Petersburg was a city of about 420,000 people, two-thirds of them men, including nearly 60,000 military personnel. It had been conceived by Peter the Great, an admirer of all things Dutch, to be another Amsterdam, and its many canals and bridges indeed bore a close resemblance to the great Dutch city. Yet Petersburg grew to be very different, developing into a pompous imperial city, eschewing the democratic and commercial nature of its Dutch counterpart.

Petersburg's wide avenues lined with neoclassic public and private architecture were more akin to the streets of London and Rome. The city center consisted almost entirely of the splendid palaces of the imperial family, the Russian nobles, and government offices. The city was so thoroughly highbrow that it was not unusual for traveling foreigners to ask where the common people lived. In short, with its blend of different Western influences, the new imperial capital was in a category of its own, just like the empire it was eager to represent.

Arriving from the south, Atarshchikov passed through the Moscow checkpoint, one of three that guarded the southern approaches to the city.

It did not take long to reach the center of the city, Palace Square, where the Winter Palace, adjacent Hermitage buildings, and elegant buildings of the general staff formed an impressive architectural ensemble. Just west of Palace Square was the admiralty, the first public building erected by Peter and the city's architectural center of gravity. From here several major boulevards radiated down through Petersburg, including Nevsky Avenue, the city's most famous promenade. By 1830 some of the grand public buildings—the Academy of Sciences and the Stock Exchange across the Neva River, the Kazan Cathedral, the Old Hermitage, and the Smolny Institute, as well as many private palaces—were already in place. Yet Petersburg was also a gigantic construction site. The imposing column, a monument to Alexander I, was being erected in the middle of Palace Square. The former Peter Square, now the Senate Square, was being redesigned and built around the Bronze Horseman, the famed statue of Peter the Great. The present senate and synod buildings and the towering St. Isaac's Cathedral were only half built.

Atarshchikov was to spend the next seven months in the imperial capital. The novelty of life in the great city—the new places and acquaintances—must have thrilled the young man, who was discovering the city's seasonal cycles. During the short summer season, the city streets and palaces were emptied as the local gentry departed for their summer estates or traveled in Western Europe. By the end of the summer the city had returned to life, and Nevsky Avenue was again full of the impatient cries of cab drivers and the motley crowds of pedestrians. But now the heavy fog and rain had begun to set in, foretelling the winter to come. Atarshchikov probably preferred the peaceful and cool summer days, the blue skies of the famous White Nights, and the rich foliage of the city's parks to the noisy commotion of Petersburg's streets during the dark and damp days of fall.[2]

In time, Atarshchikov's life in the imperial capital settled into a routine. He was attached to the Personal Guard of His Imperial Majesty as part of the special cavalry unit from the North Caucasus, formally known as the Caucasus-Mountain Cavalry half-squadron, popularly referred to as the Circassian Guard. The unit was part of the imperial household and thus fell under the command of Count Alexander von Benckendorff, the notorious head of the Russian gendarmes.

Semën soon learned that, initially, the Russian authorities had hoped to form a squadron of cavalry guards that was to include one hundred horsemen selected from among Kabardin princes and nobles. The guards were to be replaced every three to five years. In January 1812 Alexander I issued instructions to this effect, assuring the Kabardin nobles that the newly formed guard would enjoy all the privileges given to other imperial guards.[3] But despite the government's attempt to portray service in the imperial guard as a distinct privilege, most members of the Kabardin elite were loath to leave their own society for military service in the distant capital of the Christian emperor. For them, the "privilege" bestowed by the Russian government was barely distinguishable from Russia's traditional demand for hostages.

Indeed, in the early nineteenth century, the traditional hostage practice was being increasingly transformed. The same young men who in the past would have become hostages destined to live in oblivion in provincial Russian towns were now taken to the capital, educated at the top cadet schools, and groomed to become a new imperial elite that could plant the Russian imperial order in their native lands.

The formation of a special cavalry guard had to wait until 1828, when, after realizing that it would be impossible to field one hundred Kabardin nobles, the government decided to expand the unit by including other peoples of the North Caucasus: Kumyks, Chechens, Adyges (Circassians and Kabardins), Ossetians, and Nogays. Even then the government could muster no more than fifty or so young men representing the social elite of their respective societies. Thus the idea for a new cavalry unit of the imperial guards materialized as the Caucasus-Mountain half-squadron. As part of the emperor's personal guard, it was expected to take part in the frequent military parades that Nicholas I loved so much. Dressed in their traditional colorful uniforms, the Circassian Guards together with similarly formed non-Russian units were supposed to display the exotic diversity of the Russian Empire.[4]

In 1830, when Atarshchikov joined the Circassian Guard, two other famous sons of the North Caucasus had just begun their military service in the same unit. They were young Adyge men—the Circassian Khan Giray and the Kabardin Shora Nogma—who would be the founding fathers of the modern Adyge historical and literary tradition. It did not take long for Semën to get to know the young Shora and to learn his life story.

Shora Bek-Mirza Nogma (Nogmov) was born in 1794 in a small Kabardin aul near Piatigorsk (Beshtau). He was schooled to be a mullah, and after studying at a local *mekteb* (Islamic elementary school), he was sent to pursue religious learning at the prestigious madrassa in the Daghestani town of Enderi. After graduating in 1813, he had begun to work as a village mullah when the Russian commanders noted his scholarly proclivities and interest in Russia. Several influential Kabardin nobles suggested that he be appointed a secretary and interpreter at the Kabardin Provisional Court, which was responsible for mediating everyday relations between Kabardins and Russians. Instead, the Russian authorities decided to use

Members of the Circassian Guard

Nogma as an intermediary to help facilitate the conquest of the region. At first an unofficial interpreter in the Russian army, by 1825 he had become the official scribe and interpreter of the First Volga Cossack Regiment. At this time, he already had a good command of five languages apart from his native Kabardin—Arabic, Kumyk, Abaza, Persian, and Russian—and was working to create an alphabet for the Kabardin language.

Eager to reach the imperial capital, where he could expand his interests in languages and history, in 1828 Nogma petitioned to join the newly formed Circassian Guard. His plans were thwarted when his village was relocated farther south to make room for Russian towns and spas (today this is the district of Mineralnye Vody [Mineral Waters]). In 1829, after setting up a household in a new settlement on the Malka River, Nogma was appointed a teacher at a school for native hostages at Fort Nalchik. In 1830 a new opportunity came along when several members of the Circassian Guard returned to the region to recruit young local nobles. Nogma received an invitation from the commander of the Circassian Guard, S. A. Mukhanov, to come to teach the members of the unit to read and write in several languages. The imperial authorities, however, preferred to staff the guard with horsemen who excelled in martial arts rather than with a literary figure such as Nogma. Determined to come to the imperial capital, in April 1830, Shora Nogma departed for St. Petersburg at his own expense to become an arms bearer, the rank and file in the Circassian Guard.

As new members of the guard, Semën Atarshchikov and Shora Nogma found themselves under the command of a prominent Adyge prince, Khan-Giray. He was a descendant of an illustrious lineage, the Giray ruling house of the Crimean khans, as was well attested by his full name, Krym-Giray-Muhammed Giray Khan-Giray. Throughout the centuries, the Crimean khans had sent their princes to collect slave tribute and to rule the Adyges of the northwest Caucasus. Some of these princes settled there, assimilated, and became a part of the Adyge complex social structure. Indeed, Khan-Giray's father was one of the chiefs of the Khamysh (Khmish) clan of the Bzhedug tribe, a subdivision of the Adyge people residing on the left bank of the Kuban River east of the newly founded Russian fort of Ekaterinodar (presently Krasnodar).

Some time in the early 1800s, Khan-Giray's father, Muhammed-Giray, attracted by offers from the Russian authorities, decided to cross the Kuban, which separated the Ottoman and Russian borderlands, and settle on the Russian side. To protect Muhammad-Giray from the retaliatory raids of his compatriots, the authorities sent him farther away from the frontier to settle near the Cossack village of Pavlovskaia, about 75 miles northeast of Ekaterinodar. In 1816, Muhammed-Giray was rewarded for his loyalty to Russia: he was formally enlisted in the Black Sea Cossack Host and given one of the highest ranks, the *voiskovoi starshina*.

At the time, Khan-Giray was eight years old, growing up in circumstances very similar to Atarshchikov's. Following the established practice among the peoples of the North Caucasus, Khan-Giray too was sent away to spend his adolescent years in the family of his atalyk, an old and distinguished notable of the Shapsug tribe of the Adyge. There, in a mountain aul, Khan-Giray was groomed to be a leader; studied Arabic and the Quran; and imbibed the martial spirit of his people. After his father's death, the young Khan-Giray came to the attention of General Ermolov, who dispatched him to St. Petersburg to study at the prestigious Cadet Corps. In January 1830, Khan-Giray joined the Circassian Guard as a highly decorated lieutenant of the Russian army who had already distinguished himself in Russia's wars against the Persian and Ottoman Empires between 1826 and 1829.[5]

The two young guardsmen, Atarshchikov and Khan-Giray, followed in the footsteps of their fathers, the former becoming a military interpreter and the latter a career officer in the Russian army. Yet most members of the Circassian Guard, like Shora Nogma, were newly recruited from among the indigenous elite. The guards spent most of their days in routine activities: military drilling, horse riding, shows at the parade grounds, horse races, and studying Russian. One of the most important events was the imperial parade. Nicolas I, like Russian emperors before and after him, loved military parades. Such parades were often staged to impress visiting dignitaries with the imperial military might. At the same time, they showcased the multifaceted nature of the Russian Empire, as the different ethnic groups put their loyalty and devotion to the emperor on magnificent display. By all accounts, the performance of the Circassian Guards was the most spectacular part of the parade: their dazzling uniforms and extraordinary horsemanship invariably left witnesses, Russian and foreign alike, spellbound.

The large parades and exercises took place on the Field of Mars, near Palace Square or in the square itself. Nearby were the imperial stables and the Mikhailovskii Manège, the riding school of the imperial cavalry guard. The highlight of these military ceremonies was the Sunday review of the cavalry guard. It was an entertaining show during which each unit tried to outdo the other by impressing the emperor with the smartness of its uniforms and its superior skills. It was also, as some contemporaries recalled, a kind of social club, where the officers mingled with their superiors and enjoyed the proximity to His Imperial Majesty, who knew many of them individually.[6]

The emperor's passion for parades and military reviews was not the only reason for the formation of the Circassian Guard. More important, membership in the guard was meant to bind the indigenous members to the emperor and the court, thereby creating a loyal, privileged, and assimilated non-Russian elite that would later serve imperial interests in the guard's native lands.

Assimilation, of course, began with language. Learning Russian was an indispensable step in this process. The members of the Circassian Guard regularly attended Russian classes taught by I. Gratsilevskii, an instructor at St. Petersburg University with a good command of Persian and Arabic. Gratsilevskii's experience in teaching members of the guard led him to create the first Circassian alphabet based on the Russian script.

Apart from such formal studies of Russian, Atarshchikov was the main facilitator in the daily life of the Circassian Guards as the only native speaker of Russian among them. Eventually, most of the former guards would become perfectly fluent in Russian, and one of them, Khan-Giray's younger brother, Sultan Kazy-Giray, become an important figure on the Russian literary landscape.[7]

Amid the routine military drills, parades, and imperial reviews, Atarshchikov must have missed the wide steppe and the rugged mountains of the Caucasus. The notorious Petersburg weather would no doubt have contributed to his nostalgia. After the short summer, the damp chill of the air seemed to get into one's bones, and trying to stay warm in the poorly heated guard barracks at night had always been a challenge. The dark and dreary days invariably put many a city resident and visitor into a gloomy mood.

In his social life Atarshchikov found himself ill at ease, more so than Khan-Giray, Nogma, or some of his other peers. Khan-Giray was already an officer, and as such was entitled to rent an apartment instead of living in the barracks. Impeccably dressed and well educated, Khan-Giray was a charming socialite who was welcomed into the literary salons of the capital and enjoyed a personal acquaintance with many Russian men of letters, including Pushkin. Shora Nogma had vigorously pursued intellectual interests, establishing close ties with several university professors, studying languages, and devoting much of his time to writing the first Kabardin grammar.

Atarshchikov, on the other hand, seemed to have fallen into the netherworld. He was too lacking in the glamour and exoticism of his Circassian peers to be of interest to the Russians and was too much of a Russian commoner to be included in the Circassian social elite. In a sense, his was the classic predicament of an interpreter, a traditional intermediary between two cultures who was equally at ease in both while never fully belonging to either.

Moreover, whereas Atarshchikov was a Christian, the other members of the Circassian Guard formed a tight Muslim community, though preserving their religious identity in the capital's Christian environment proved difficult. In 1798 the five hundred Muslim members of the Russian military stationed in St. Petersburg had submitted the first petition asking that they be granted land for a house of prayer and a cemetery. It was rejected. In 1826 the government granted a plot of land for the cemetery but no money; two years later the Muslim community still could not afford to fence it in. In 1822 the Muslim merchant community of St. Petersburg had succeeded in convincing the authorities to appoint "the imam-hatip of the grand mosque." The problem was that there was no mosque, and rented apartments would serve as the gathering place for Muslim prayer until the construction of the St. Petersburg Grand Mosque in 1913.[8]

Atarshchikov's life in the imperial capital would have continued apace had it not been for a sudden new development. The revolutionary winds blowing through Europe had reached Poland, where in November 1830 the long-brewing political crisis broke into a full-scale uprising against Russia. The two distant parts of the Russian Empire, the North Caucasus and Poland, different as they were in almost every respect, erupted in violence at the same time and for the same reasons. Having come under the Russian sway only recently, both regions continued to resist St. Petersburg's attempts to incorporate them into the administrative and political structures of the empire.

Poland and the Caucasus presented different challenges and cast the Russians in opposite roles. In Poland, Russia worked to stop modern reforms and unravel existing political institutions. From the Polish perspective, Russia was a despotic and oppressive half-Asiatic power representing a nation and culture much less advanced than their own. In the North Caucasus, by contrast, in its attempts to change the traditional social norms, Russia embodied modern European values vis-à-vis a thoroughly premodern world. In both cases religion—Catholicism and Islam—played an important role in uniting the local population against the Russian outsiders. Eventually both uprisings shared the same sad fate of bloody suppression, deportations, and mass emigration.[9]

In the meantime, in December 1830 the emperor ordered Field-Marshal Dybich to assemble an army to crush the Polish uprising. Within a month, an army of 127,000 men with 348 guns was prepared to march on Warsaw. Confident that the Circassian Guard would be more than a match for the famed Polish cavalry, the emperor ordered the guard to join the invading army. After initial mishaps by its commanders, the Russian army crossed into Poland in early February 1831. Despite the brave resistance of the Polish troops, the Russians entered Warsaw in September 1831 and brought an end to the Polish uprising.[10]

On February 28, 1832, the Circassian Guard rode into St. Petersburg to parade in front of the emperor. Nicholas I personally commended the guards for the bravery they had shown in the Polish campaign and ordered that they be generously rewarded with honorable mention, medals, and promotions. Shortly thereafter, Khan-Giray was promoted from a lieutenant to a captain and was appointed the commander of the Circassian Guard. Semën Atarshchikov was promoted to the rank of cornet and received two Marks of Distinction, that of St. George and the Polish Order of the Fifth degree. The Order of St. George was the most prestigious military decoration, and its variant, the Mark of Distinction—which consisted of a silver cross and the St. George band—was intended for soldiers and low-ranking officers in recognition of outstanding acts of bravery. The St. George Mark of Distinction was accompanied by an automatic promotion, salary raise, and exemption from corporal punishment and taxes.[11]

The year of the Polish campaign proved to be an important experience for Atarshchikov and his comrades in the Circassian Guard. Their valor on the battlefield and the misfortunes they had shared in the course of the campaign created a new sense of camaraderie among them. In the summer of 1831 Atarshchikov, Shora Nogma, and three other guards, struck down by a cholera epidemic, spent six weeks convalescing together at the hospital in Vilno.[12] Together they shared their first experience of life in eastern Europe outside Russia: more prosperous villages, better roads, more churches, and ethnically diverse towns. Vilno in particular, with its mingling of different peoples and classes, presented a great contrast with the contrived self-importance of the Russian imperial capital. Upon his return to St. Petersburg in February 1832, the imperial city must have looked different to Atarshchikov. Impressive as it was, it clearly lacked the more human and natural scale of Warsaw, Riga, and Vilno, and it must have appeared artificial, even if it was a grand model erected to fulfill the dreams of its founder.

Atarshchikov's promotion to officer's rank entitled him to rent an apartment in the city, but as fate would have it, he had no time to settle in St. Petersburg. In the summer of 1832, after two years as an interpreter for the elite military unit at the tsar's headquarters, he was ordered back to the North Caucasus, where his services were urgently needed in the region set ablaze by a new uprising against Russia.

6

Return to the
North Caucasus

The Naqshbandi Tariqat

By the late 1820s the northeast Caucasus had been pacified. Or at least it appeared so to a Russian government convinced that Ermolov's brutal campaigns, excessive as they might have been, had had the desired effect. Not until 1831 did it become abundantly clear that in fact Ermolov's policies had produced the opposite effect—driving the antagonized and embittered local population toward further resistance. Moreover, the previously disparate uprisings and revolts against Russian rule were now coordinated into a larger religious war, the ghazawat, while the teachings of the Sufi order of the Naqshbandi'ya had spread through the auls of Daghestan and Chechnya like wildfire.

Historically the North Caucasus had been Islamized unevenly. Whereas Islam had deep roots in the northeast, it was largely nominal in the northwest. After the initial Arab conquests, the long and haphazard process of Islamization of the region had received a strong impetus from the Ottoman and Persian influences during the sixteenth and seventeenth centuries. Most of the indigenous population fell under the sway of the Sunni Islam practiced by the Ottomans, while smaller numbers in the area adjacent to the Persian Empire adhered to Shi'a Islam.

As elsewhere, Islam had to compete with earlier established practices. The common law, adat, and the religious law, sharia, were often at odds, just as their respective practitioners, the khans and begs on the one hand and the mullahs on the other, competed for power and influence among their own people.

By the early nineteenth century, both secular and religious elites found themselves on the defensive against the rapidly growing ranks of the mystical Sufi orders, in particular Naqshbandi'ya. The Sufi orders were quite different from one another, and each followed its own path (*tariqa*). The Naqshbandi'ya distinguished itself by an iron discipline, the disciples' unquestioned obedience to the teachers (sheikhs), social egalitarianism, and the duty of the faithful to take part in ghazawat.

When and how the Naqshbandis established themselves in the Caucasus remains unclear. There is, however, enough evidence to suggest that the order, founded in the Central Asian khanate of Bukhara in the fourteenth century, had reached the Caucasus long before the nineteenth century. By the late eighteenth century, Shirvan, the region in northern Azerbaijan on the Caspian coast, had become the epicenter of Naqshbandi activity. One of the sheikhs from Shirvan was declared to be a *qutb*, the leader of Naqshbandi followers across the Muslim world. It was from Shirvan that Naqshbandi teachings spread into the adjacent region of southern Daghestan.[1]

Shortly after Shirvan was annexed to the Russian Empire in 1820, tsarist authorities deported two qutb deputies to Siberia while strongly "advising" the kutb, Khadji-Ismail, to leave for the Ottoman territories. Before his forced departure, however, Khadji-Ismail established close contacts with two leading Daghestani sheikhs: Kuraly Magoma in the village of Yarag in Tabasaran and Jemal ad-Din, a secretary to the khan of Kazikumukh. In 1823 Kuraly Magoma was initiated as a *murshid,* or a leader of the Naqshbandis in Daghestan.

Determined to counteract the spread of the militant Naqshbandi teachings, General Ermolov courted moderate Sufi sheikhs and relied on Aslan, the khan of Kazikumukh, to exercise his influence over Kuraly Magoma. By 1825 it was clear that all efforts to curtail Naqshbandi influence had failed, and Ermolov ordered the arrest of Kuraly Magoma. Detained by Aslan, Kuraly Magoma was dispatched to Ermolov's headquarters in Tiflis but under mysterious circumstances escaped his captors and fled to Tabasaran. Facing repression from the Russian authorities, other Sufi leaders, including Jemal ad-Din, were forced to leave the lands of Kazikumukh.

Yet Russia's initial success in halting the spread of Naqshbandi teachings proved short-lived. The emergence of Ghazi Muhammad, a more militant Muslim preacher, forced the Russians to recognize that Kuraly Magoma and Jemal ad-Din were in fact more moderate than they had thought. Born in the Avar village of Gimry, part of the Koisubuly alliance of free societies, Ghazi Muhammad embraced a more militant interpretation of the tariqat: spreading the teachings by word alone was not enough; one must also employ the sword. Not all Naqshbandis shared the view that war against the infidels and their collaborators was essential to the spread of their teachings, however. Jemal-ad-Din objected to the idea of ghazawat, and even the future imam, Shamil, remained unconvinced by his best friend and aul compatriot, Ghazi Muhammad. Only after the leader of the Naqshbandis, Kuraly Magoma, had sided with Ghazi Muhammad did the idea of ghazawat became inseparable from Naqshbandi teachings.

By 1829 the internal disputes within the Naqshbandi were finally resolved, and Ghazi Muhammad began his incendiary preaching throughout Daghestan and Chechnya. The idea of ghazawat spread rapidly among the various peoples in this corner of the northeast Caucasus. In January 1830 the representatives of the region's various communities met in Gimry to embrace the idea of war against all those who opposed their interpretation of sharia. The meeting declared the formation of the Imamate, the Islamic state in the Caucasus, and Ghazi Muhammad was named its first imam.[2]

Russian authorities were slow to recognize the new threat. In 1830 Ghazi Muhammad with six thousand armed men marched on Khunzakh, the residence of the Avar khans, who supported Russian rule in the region. Having failed to take Khunzakh, in the spring of 1831 Ghazi Muhammad launched a campaign against another Russian ally, the Kumyk shamkhal. Joined by the thousands of Kumyks who had become disaffected by the shamkhal's collaboration with Russian authorities, Ghazi Muhammad achieved his first success by seizing the shamkhal's residence, Tarki.

Even though the subsequent siege of the Russian forts Burnaia and Vnezapnaia proved unsuccessful, the uprising against the Russians and their local allies spread rapidly throughout Chechnya and Daghestan. In the summer of 1831 the army of the imam marched through Chechnya and laid siege to Kizliar and later to Derbend. Ghazi Muhammad's message of Islamic justice and equality was directed against the local social elites and proved effective in recruiting large numbers of commoners to his cause.

By this time, the fact that the ghazawat presented a direct threat to Russian interests was no longer in doubt. Troops were sent to reinforce the existing garrisons, and an expeditionary force was assembled to confront Ghazi Muhammad. By 1832, after having suffered several defeats, Ghazi Muhammad's movement had begun to run out of steam. With his influence among the Kumyks diminished, he was forced to retreat into the highlands of Chechnya and Daghestan.

The Return to the North Caucasus

It was at this time, late in the summer of 1832, that Atarshchikov arrived in the Caucasus to be assigned as a translator to the headquarters of the Mozdok Cossack Regiment commanded by Major Grigorii Khristoforovich von Zass. The Mozdok regiment was part of a large expeditionary force led by Lieutenant General Aleksei Veliaminov into the mountainous auls, the heartland of Ghazi Muhammad's resistance.[3]

Having served in the Caucasus for many years, Veliaminov shared Ermolov's view of the local peoples and his aggressive tactics of bringing the war into the rebels' mountainous hideouts. The plan was to march through Chechnya, demolishing the auls and burning the crops, so as to prevent the Chechens from launching raids against the Russian frontier. On August 6, 1832, the Russian expeditionary force, nine thousand strong, set out from Fort Nazran. Leaving a bloody trail of destruction behind them, the Russian troops two weeks later approached a large Chechen aul, Germenchug (Germchiga, Kermenchik), 3.7 miles north of Shali. Here Ghazi Muhammad awaited the Russians with his militia of three thousand Chechens and eight hundred Avar horsemen. In the battle that followed Ghazi Muhammad's fighters were badly outnumbered and outgunned. Many of them died in battle, including the remaining seventy-two defenders who refused to surrender and were burned alive in a house set ablaze by Russian troops. Others, including Ghazi Muhammad himself, were able to escape.[4]

The Battle of Germenchug was a bloody spectacle and must have left Atarshchikov deeply unsettled. An eerily empty village lay in ruins, with black smoke coming from the spots where houses and cattle sheds had once stood. Hundreds of dead bodies, Chechen and Russian, were scattered around. If anything, the battle proved that Russia's barbarously brutal approach was equally matched by the rebels' fierce determination to kill or die. If Atarshchikov was distressed by the grim and bloody scenes of Russian conquest, he was not alone. A young Russian officer, Fedor Tornau, who, like Atarshchikov, arrived in the Caucasus in 1832, described "the last act of the bloody drama" in his memoir: "Each performed his duties conscientiously. The main actors departed for eternity; other participants and the spectators after them began to leave for their tents with a stone on their hearts; and it is possible that more than one reached deep into his soul to ask a question: What is this all for? Is there not enough room on earth for all, regardless of their tongue and faith?"[5]

Yet as in all wars, the recurring sight of bloody slaughter dulled the first shock and disbelief at the human capacity for cruelty. After Germenchug, Russian expeditionary forces continued to move south into the mountains of Chechnya. Three weeks later, the Russians sacked and destroyed one of Ghazi Muhammad's residences, the mountainous aul of Dargo (Diarga) near Vedeno. Because of the aul's well-defended position on the steep bank of the river Yassy and its tradition of arms manufacturing, both Ghazi

Storming of the aul Gimry

Muhammad and later Shamil had chosen Dargo as their residence. In both cases, as often happened in mountain warfare, capturing Dargo proved a trap for Russian forces. The Chechens blocked the road back with huge slabs of rock, and the only way out was return via a different and less secure road. Retreating through the dense forests and mountain paths, the Russians were incessantly harassed and ambushed by the Chechens, suffering heavy casualties. Fedor Tornau was one of them, shot and seriously wounded by a Chechen hiding behind a tree stump.[6]

Despite its initial successes, by the fall of 1832 the uprising of the first imam was nearly over. Russia's ruthless advance, leaving in its path the smoking ruins of auls and the corpses of slaughtered residents, persuaded many local societies to sue for peace. In October 1832 Ghazi Muhammad and his followers were surrounded in the Avar aul of Gimry, where two years earlier they had proclaimed the ghazawat. When Russian troops stormed the aul and approached the last point of resistance, the aul's tower, Ghazi Muhammad jumped out and tried to flee but was bayoneted by Russian soldiers. A close associate who leaped after him was seriously wounded but almost miraculously managed to escape. His name was Shamil.[7]

The Northwest Caucasus

With the fall of Gimry and the death of Ghazi Muhammad, the northeast Caucasus once again appeared to have been pacified. The Russian commanders could now shift their attention to the right flank of the Caucasus Fortification Line, that is, the northwest Caucasus. Russia had long feared an insurgent movement that would unite the entire North Caucasus, and this concern was hardly unfounded. It was well known that Ghazi Muhammad had sent his envoys to stoke the flames of rebellion in the northwest and that the local peoples had greeted them warmly. Had the insurgents been able to coordinate their efforts, they would have endangered the entire Caucasus Fortification Line and its undermanned Russian garrisons. Furthermore, they could have threatened the Georgian Military Highway, the only and vital link between Russia and Georgia.

Geopolitics provided another reason for Russia's renewed attention to the northwest Caucasus. In the summer of 1828 the last Ottoman strongholds on the east coast of the Black Sea, including the formidable Fort Anapa, fell to the Russians. A year later, in the Treaty of Adrianople, the Ottomans conceded that the east coast of the Black Sea, among other territories, was an integral part of the Russian Empire. The northwest Caucasus was now encircled by the fortification line along the Kuban River in the north and the new Russian forts on the Black Sea coast to the south. Similar military and political circumstances had determined the pacification of the northeast Caucasus when the region became enclosed by Russian forts along the Terek and Sunzha Rivers in the north and Russian control of Georgia in the south. Now was the time to proceed with the conquest of the northwest Caucasus.

This was the homeland of the Adyge people, better known as the Circassians, the region's most numerous and powerful people. There were also Abkhaz and Ubykh peoples who lived along the Black Sea coast; the Abazas (Abazins) in the upper reaches of the Laba River and its tributaries; and the Turkic-speaking Karachays, Balkars, and Nogays in the upper reaches of the Kuban, Kuma, Podkumok, and Malka Rivers. At the time, the estimates of the total indigenous population varied widely from three hundred thousand to over six hundred thousand.[8]

The Upper Kuban River was a major divide that roughly separated the eastern from the western Circassians. The eastern Circassians included the Kabardins, most of whom lived east of the Kuban, and a smaller tribe, the Besleney, west of the Kuban in the upper reaches of the Urup, Laba, and Khodz Rivers. From the late eighteenth century, an increasing number of Kabardins had either fled or been expelled by the Russians, who were rapidly turning the former Kabardin lands into a region of mineral spas, Mineralnye Vody. These Kabardins moved west, crossed the Kuban, and settled along its tributaries, the Greater and Lesser Zelenchuk Rivers.

Apart from these recent Kabardin refugees, the western Circassians were divided into many tribes. The largest among them were the Shapsugs, who lived south of Ekaterinodar between the Kuban's tributaries of Pshada and Shakhe. Their neighbors in the west were the Natukhays (north of Anapa), the Abadzekhs in the east (the southern slopes of the Caucasus range), and the Bzhedukhs and Khatukays in the northeast, near the lower Belaia and Pshisha Rivers. Farther east, the Temirgoys occupied the banks of the Lower Laba River. These were, of course, major tribal units, which in turn were divided into numerous clans.

Russian policies in the northwest Caucasus responded to some of the same concerns and challenges that the Russian empire builders had encountered in the region's northeast. The Kuban Fortification Line and the settlements behind it were under constant assault from raids by the Circassians, Nogays, and other peoples inhabiting the Kuban's left bank—the Russians referred to them broadly as *zakubantsy* (those across the Kuban). To stop such raids and pacify the hostile population, the Russians resorted to a familiar tactic: driving a wedge between different ethnic and social groups, rewarding those who chose to cooperate, and punishing those who resisted.

Yet there were significant differences between the situations in the eastern and western parts of the North Caucasus. In contrast to the northeast, where many peoples had a tradition of centralized political authority (the Avar khans, the Kumyk shamkhals, the Kaytag utsmiis, to mention a few), the western Circassians rarely recognized a single ruler. Some of them were subject to different princely families; others were organized into free societies devoid of social elites. The lack of central authority worked both in Russia's favor and against it. On the one hand it made it easier to sow discord and manipulate local chiefs, but on the other it made it impossible to hold any single ruler accountable for actions hostile to Russia.

One other critical distinction between the two regions concerned land. In the northeast Caucasus the relatively sparse fertile lands were squeezed between the mountains and the arid steppe, whereas in the northwest large tracts of extraordinarily fertile land stretched along the Kuban River. As a result, the Slavic colonization of the region proceeded on a much greater scale than in the northeast. It also meant that the native population had to vacate the land for the new settlers, much as had happened in the New World. It was hardly accidental that the new territories in the south of the Russian Empire received the official name New Russia, reminiscent of New Spain, New France, and New England.[9]

These differences notwithstanding, the Russian commanders saw the entire region of the Caucasus through General Ermolov's prism: the natives were savages and could be impressed and subdued only by brute force. While Ermolov crystallized such views in his relentless and systematic destruction of the region, the great majority of Russian senior commanders shared his approach and vision. In this view, intimidation was an important tactic, and the massacre of the civilian population a legitimate pursuit of war objectives.

The Russian commander in the North Caucasus in the early 1830s, General A. A. Veliaminov, advocated similar tactics in dealing with the native population. In his 1833 memorandum to the minister of war, A. I. Chernyshev, Veliaminov cautioned that even with a larger number of Russian troops in the region, it would take many years to subdue and annex the Caucasus. In the meantime, he believed that the best way to pacify the natives was through preemptive raids, burning down rebellious villages, disarming peaceful ones, and systematically destroying crops and pastures to starve the natives and deprive them of horses. In addition, he recommended continuing the Russian advance into the mountains and bringing in more Cossacks to settle and colonize the region. Until his death in 1838, Veliaminov worked tirelessly to implement his policies, in particular fortifying and expanding the Russian frontier.[10]

Since the early 1790s, when the right bank of the Kuban River had been largely purged of Nogays, the Kuban had become the new Russian frontier in the northwest Caucasus. The Kuban Fortification Line along the river's right bank was a typical system of forts, redoubts, and Cossack frontier settlements. Construction of the fortifications and settlements had taken place in stages over several decades, and thus different parts of the Kuban Line were developed and settled by different social and ethnic groups. The lower part of the Kuban River was settled by the Black Sea Cossacks. These were former Zaporozhian Cossacks who in 1792 received a grant of land on the east coast of the Azov Sea. Thus the Lower Kuban River from its estuary to Fort Ust-Labinsk became known as the Black Sea Fortification Line. The middle Kuban River from Ust-Labinsk to Nevinnomysk was initially settled by the Don Cossacks and later by a motley group from the

Cossacks of the Tersk and Kuban regiments

Russified eastern Ukraine: Cossacks, fugitive peasants, and Old Believers. Finally, in 1823–26, the Khoper Cossack Regiment, a contingent of the thoroughly Russified Cossacks, was transferred to settle the upper reaches of the Kuban, later known as the Batalpashinsk stretch of the line. The disparate Cossack settlements and outposts of the middle and upper Kuban comprised the Kuban Fortification Line. The administrative changes of 1830 created one Caucasus Line stretching across the North Caucasus, with the Kuban Line forming its right flank. Two years later the Cossacks of the Kuban were transformed into a single military-administrative unit—the Cossack Host of the Caucasus Line.[11]

The Confidant of Colonel Zass

In 1833, General Veliaminov put Colonel Zass in charge of Batalpashinsk, the most challenging stretch of the Caucasus Line. Fort Batalpashinsk (present-day Cherkessk) was founded in 1804 on the left bank of the Upper Kuban River to mark a spot where fourteen years earlier thirty thousand Ottoman troops had been routed by a much smaller Russian army. This last Ottoman attempt to assist Sheikh Mansur in his uprising against the Russians failed miserably with the capture of the Ottoman army commander, Battal Hüseyin Pasha, and his many subordinates. Fort Batalpashinsk and a series of smaller fortifications along the Kuban had been built with the strategic objective of containing the Circassians on the Kuban's left bank and severing their ties with the Kabardins and other peoples east of the river. Given the strategic importance and challenges of the terrain in the upper reaches of the Kuban, the Batalpashinsk stretch of the Kuban Line was the focus of the most intense military activity.

The choice of Colonel Zass was no accident. Baron Grigorii Khristoforovich von Zass had been born into a family of the Kurland nobility, received a military education, and spent most of his career in the North Caucasus. Colonel Zass was another typical disciple of Ermolov and Veliaminov. He had distinguished himself in many battles, most recently in the bloodbath of Germenchug, where he was wounded for the second time, received another medal, and was promoted to the rank of colonel. He already had a widespread reputation for supreme valor, daredevil tactics, and effective brutality.

Zass's headquarters was Batalpashinsk—a large Cossack military settlement (about nine hundred men and eight hundred women) surrounded by a moat and an earthen rampart with two cannons.[12] At Zass's personal request, Semën Atarshchikov arrived at his headquarters in the spring of

General Baron G. Kh. von Zass

1833. Clearly, Zass appreciated Atarshchikov's previous service under his command in Chechnya and continued to count on his intimate knowledge of this part of the North Caucasus as well. After all, the colonel much preferred to have at his side a Russian officer who could also counsel him on regional languages, customs, and mores rather than relying on the services of a local interpreter with questionable command of Russian.

The arrival of Colonel Zass at Batalpashinsk meant that previously defensive Russian positions were transformed into a launching pad for aggressive Russian raids deep into enemy territory. In 1833 Zass organized several raids in which he ambushed and routed a large group of Besleneys on the right bank of the Laba River, burning their hay and grain supplies and razing to the ground the aul of the prominent Besleney noble Aitek Kanokov (Konokov, Kanukov).

Apart from further fortifying the frontier defenses, preemption was Zass's key strategy. He destroyed the native auls in the vicinity of the frontier to deny safe haven to raiding parties. He launched surprise raids against the hostile auls deep into the mountains, capturing and destroying them. Zass learned that a speedy retreat was as crucial to successful raiding campaigns as surprise approach. Surprise robbed residents of other auls of the time needed to come to the defense of their neighbors or block the road and ambush the troops on their way back.

In 1834 Zass personally led expeditionary forces across the Kuban virtually every two months. He and his troops seemingly knew no rest, achieving their goals with brutal efficiency. Zass's ability to find out about the impending raids seemed almost mysterious, and he acted quickly by attacking the places where small Circassian bands were to gather before launching their raids. In short, he used the natives' own traditional tactics, speed and surprise, against them. No wonder that some around him believed that Zass had been born to lead guerrilla warfare.[13]

Combining brute force with generous rewards for the collaborators, Zass could boast of a measure of success. Large-scale intrusions across the Russian frontier ceased, while the local population was increasingly divided between those who reconciled themselves to the Russian presence and sought to retain existing privileges and property and those who continued to resist.

Zass's exploits rapidly acquired a mythical quality, not least because he worked tirelessly to create a legend around himself and not only through military feats. Taking advantage of the naïveté and ignorance of the natives, he resorted to various tricks to foster his reputation for magical powers. Using various ruses, he once convinced a group of visiting Circassian nobles that he was invulnerable to their bullets; another time he paid an informer by appearing to turn gunpowder into gold coins. The innocent natives were dumbfounded by musical snuffboxes, sets of mirrors arranged to create illusions, and some electrical devices.

His most impressive ruse was to convince a group of Abadzekhs that he was clairvoyant. When visiting Abadzekhs chiefs informed him that one of the chiefs had stayed home, Zass accused them of lying. Having learned in advance through his intelligence network that this chief was away, Zass assured them that he could read their minds and knew what was going on in their auls. To convince the skeptical chiefs, he took them to a glass door through which one could see a small room. Inside was a large and detailed painting of their aul. The chiefs, who had never seen a painting, believed that they were looking at their actual aul. A translator was hidden behind the painting, and when a question was raised as to whether the missing chief was in the aul, a deep voice replied negatively. Stunned and confused, the Abadzekh chiefs quickly left convinced that Zass was a *shaytan*—a devil, or the Lame Devil, as he became known because of his leg injury. They now understood why they were helpless to protect their auls against Zass's surprise raids.[14]

In October 1834, recognizing Colonel Zass's accomplishments, Veliaminov promoted him to the rank of general and placed him in charge of the entire Kuban Fortification Line, stretching along the river from Fort Ust-Labinsk to the upper reaches of the Kuban. Shortly thereafter, Zass left Batalpashinsk for his new headquarters at Prochnyi Okop (the Steadfast Trench), located at the place where the Urup River discharges into the Kuban.

There is little doubt that Zass owed his success and promotion in part to his quiet and indispensable aide and translator, Semën Atarshchikov. Zass's bravery and determination notwithstanding, it was timely and reliable intelligence that proved critical to his military success. This intelligence came through the network of informants that Atarshchikov helped to cultivate. As was true of many translators of the time, Atarshchikov's real role was that of expert counsel to his commander and liaison with the indigenous peoples. For the next two years he would continue to acquit himself well in these capacities, until a desperate need for a reliable and knowledgeable Russian official to establish Russian authority in the Karachay highlands prompted General Zass to recommend Atarshchikov for this position.

7

Interpreter and Administrator

Tiflis

In May 1836 Atarshchikov was ordered to Tiflis to be interviewed for a position as superintendent of the Karachay people. In 1836 Tiflis (in Georgian, Tbilisi, meaning "warm" in reference to its famous warm mineral springs) was still a typical Asiatic city built on the banks of the Kura River. On the right bank of the river, below the ruins of the fourth-century citadel, was the Old City, a maze of narrow winding streets of two-storied wooden houses with flat roofs, numerous windows, and wide balconies. The haphazardly built and scattered houses gave an impression of chaos, but dozens of Georgian and Armenian churches, together with three mosques, rose majestically above the city, providing its distinct charm.

The Russian presence, which would significantly transform Tiflis by the end of the century, was still minimal. General Ermolov was the first to leave his signature imprint on the city by tearing down the Metekhi Citadel and building barracks in its stead. On the edge of the Old City stood a large two-storied building with arches and columns in front and a large garden. Throughout the nineteenth century, the house served as the residence of the Russian commanders in the Caucasus. Behind the commander's residence, a street led to Erivan Square, the center of the new city built by the Russians. Around the square several new buildings in the Russian style housed military and police headquarters as well as a school (gymnasium).

Across the square a narrow street, called the Armenian Bazaar, wound toward the bridge on the Kura River. If Tiflis was the busiest trading town in the entire Caucasus (nearly a quarter of all houses were occupied

Jean Pierre Moine, street in Tiflis, 1858

by sundry shops and businesses), the Armenian Bazaar was the liveliest among the half dozen in the city. Next to it were several open spaces that served as "unloading docks" for camels carrying various goods, donkeys with large baskets of coal for *mangals* (devices used for both heating and grilling), and buffalo with leather bags filled with wine. Both sides of the street were lined with shops where tailors and shoemakers, smiths and scribes, barbers and bakers were all busily selling their goods and services. Here was a true linguistic babble of Georgian, Armenian, Azeri, Persian, Turkish, and—with increasing frequency—Russian.

At the time there was only one hotel in Tiflis. Whether because of the patriotism implied in its name, "The Just Russia," or a simple lack of competition, the hotel was fully occupied. Atarshchikov therefore chose to rent a room in one of the houses of the German colonists who resided across the river. A small German colony had existed in Tiflis since the days of General Ermolov, who had initiated resettlement of a group of Schwabian Germans in the vicinity of Tiflis.

In its physical appearance and feel, Tiflis would have reminded Atarshchikov of Derbend and other towns in the Caucasus. The blooming orchards of pomegranates, peaches, and almonds grew among the old walnut and poplar trees that appeared to stretch endlessly just outside the city walls. The view of the snow-capped mountains, the blue sky, and the rapid waters of the Kura formed the kind of romantic landscape so familiar to Atarshchikov. And in the Armenian bazaar, the kaleidoscope of national dresses created a most exotic picture.

Even those aspects of the city that so much irritated other Russian residents—the dirt streets, which were made impassable by the lightest of rains and remained unlit at night—must have seemed to Atarshchikov a welcome change from the narrow confines of Russian frontier outposts. The sheer variety and cheapness of food was one undeniable attraction: pheasant, pilaf, fruits, vegetables, and of course wine could be bought for a pittance.

Atarshchikov had a chance to visit Tiflis's famous baths built on hot sulfur springs in the traditional Turkish style. On certain days, two of them were used by women and two by men. Curiously, every Thursday, despite the strict customs forbidding men to be in the proximity of women, part of one bath continued to be used by men while women occupied the rest of it. Only a dark green curtain separated the men's dressing room from the bathing women. Outside, those same Georgian and Armenian women were wrapped in chadors up to their eyebrows, but here they enjoyed themselves with little concern for the bathing men behind the curtain. The Tiflis baths were popular with the Russian officers and were a common meeting place to exchange stories, news, and rumors.

As the headquarters of the commander of the entire Caucasus region, Tiflis served as an assembly point for the various indigenous troops arriving to join the Russian expeditionary force. At this time the city was transformed into an exotic stage for the display of the region's ethnic melange. Every afternoon these troops participated in the traditional show of horsemanship and martial skills (*tamasha* in Georgian or *dzhigitovka* in Russian). Their colorful dress, gleaming weapons, and extraordinary riding and shooting skills impressed many a visitor.[1]

It is no wonder that Tiflis was a magnet for the Russian military elite and the Russified indigenous elite alike. The latter represented the entire gamut of the Caucasus's population: Georgian, Armenian, Azeri, Kumyk, Chechen, Adyge, and others, who despite their religious, linguistic, and cultural differences, had one thing in common—they were officers in the Russian military.

One member of the Adyge elite who happened to be in Tiflis at the time was Shora Nogma, Atarshchikov's old comrade in the Circassian Guard.

In May 1835 after five years of service in the guard, Cornet Shora Nogma had been assigned to the Caucasus Corps in Tiflis. Here he rented a room in the house of Prince Ivan Shakhovskoi, the adjutant of the supreme commander, Baron G. V. Rosen. Well connected and well paid, Nogma might have been content with his new military-administrative responsibilities. But Shora had always remained a scholar, far more interested in linguistics, philology, and literature than in his daily duties. During his stay in the Russian capital, he had become a well-known figure among Russia's Orientalists. His scholarly reputation followed him to Tiflis, where he met the future member of the Russian Academy of Sciences, the Finnish-Swedish philologist and ethnographer A. J. Sjögren, who had come to Tiflis to collect information about local languages. Nogma was a perfect informant, and Sjögren took detailed notes about the Kabardin language and numerous other matters. In return, Sjögren had much to teach Nogma about the general principles of linguistics and science and encouraged Nogma's scholarly pursuits.

Sjögren remained in the region for almost two years. Shortly after his return to St. Petersburg in 1837, he published the first grammar and a dictionary of the Ossetian language and was appointed Academician of Linguistics and Ethnography of Finnic and Caucasian peoples. That same year Nogma, too, was transferred from Tiflis to his native Kabarda. Perhaps, like his former commander in the Circassian Guard, Khan-Giray, he was dispatched to rally the Kabardins in a show of loyalty to the traveling emperor, Nicholas I. If so, he too could boast of little success. The next year he was appointed secretary of the Kabardin Provisional Court in Nalchik, resigning from this position shortly before his death in 1844.[2]

About the same time as Shora Nogma left Tiflis, another prominent Russian exile arrived in town. Mikhail Lermontov was a famous Russian poet who, along with Alexander Bestuzhev-Marlinskii, forged the romantic image of the Caucasus that would shape the Russian view of the region. Lermontov, who had previously dabbled in the study of Oriental languages in St. Petersburg, resolved to learn the regional lingua franca, the local Turkish dialect, generally known as Turki. In Tiflis Lermontov, like Bestuzhev-Marlinkskii, took lessons from a translator at the headquarters of the supreme commander, Mirza Fath Ali Akhundzadeh, better known under his Russified name, Fatali Akhundov.

Akhundov was yet another remarkable member of the Russified indigenous elite. A native of Iranian Azerbaijan, Akhundov joined the Russian service in 1834, combining the duties of translator at the commander's headquarters with those of instructor of Oriental languages at the Tiflis school. He offered private lessons to interested Russian officers. In the

1850s Akhundov would write the comedies and plays that made him one of the founders of the Azeri secular literary tradition.[3]

During his short stay in Tiflis, Atarshchikov renewed his acquaintance with a young Russian officer who also happened to be staying with the German colonists. His name was Fedor Tornau. They had met before, in 1832, when both had taken part in punitive expeditions, first against the rebellious Ingush who had killed the Russian superintendent and two Russian missionaries stationed among them, and later that summer in a notoriously brutal campaign against the Chechen auls. Both witnessed the senseless destruction of the auls and massacre of their residents, most infamously at Germenchug and Dargo.[4]

The two men quickly developed a bond. Both shared a strong empathy for the natives whose way of life and customs they had come to know so well. Tornau had spent a year among the Adyges collecting intelligence about the northwest Caucasus and its inhabitants and had just returned from this secret mission. Over several evenings he shared with Atarshchikov his recent experience and adventures. Later, in 1864, in the comfort of the office he occupied as a military attaché at the Russian embassy in Vienna, Tornau would recount these events in his extraordinary memoir, known for its wealth of geographic and ethnographic information as much as for its author's literary skills.

By June of 1836 it was time for Atarshchikov and Tornau to leave Tiflis. Tornau was instructed to spend another summer at Mineralnye Vody, resting and growing a beard for his next secret assignment. Atarshchikov received permission to visit his family at Naurskaia before assuming the new post of superintendent among the Karachays.

A Superintendent of the Karachays, 1836–1841

During Russia's relentless expansion into Asia, the Russian government traditionally divided the indigenous peoples on the frontier into two stark categories: friend and foe. The former were expected to pledge formal allegiance to Russia and thus became known as "peaceful," whereas those who refused were deemed "hostile." Of course, the submission of the peaceful peoples remained largely nominal. They did not pay tax or provide military service—the standard prerequisites of a subordinate status—and their principal obligation was to remain at peace with Russia. In reality their allegiance was a mutual nonaggression treaty, and their status was that of an ally. In time, however, as the frontier advanced farther, such peaceful populations increasingly came under the rule of the imperial administration. In the 1830s the Karachays were in the process of such transition, slowly but inexorably pulled into Russia's political and administrative orbit.

To maintain relations with the peaceful peoples, the Russian authorities relied on a *pristav,* a specially appointed liaison officer. Initially pristavs were akin to the British official residents appointed to the court of a native prince. They were expected to represent the Russian government and attend to the issues involving Russian interests. As Russian control of the region increased, however, the position of pristav evolved into that of district superintendent. The pristav was usually a compromise candidate, a Russified member of the indigenous people who would command authority among the locals while enjoying the trust of the Russian government.

Previous attempts to streamline the system of superintendents had failed, and the tsarist government continued to appoint one superintendent for each specific people. The institution was rife with nepotism, corruption, and venality. Superintendents were virtually compelled to resort to bribery and extortion since many received no pay, as the government shifted the burden for their upkeep to the local population. In addition, the superintendents were expected to maintain a system of spies and their own bodyguards, all of which required no small expenditure. There were few tangible rewards for a life away from home and full of risk.[5]

By the nineteenth century the office of superintendent had evolved into a seat of virtually unlimited power with responsibilities involving taxation, trade, labor services, and extracommunal legal cases among the locals, who invariably saw the office as the source of widespread corruption. Even General Veliaminov had to concede that superintendents' abuses were often the cause of the raids and hostility from the local population. Wistfully he suggested that the corrupt superintendents should be replaced with honest ones, only to bemoan the fact that the latter were nowhere to be found. Revolts against the superintendents and petitions to have them replaced were common, as was outright murder.[6]

It was in these circumstances that in February of 1836 the government began the search for a new superintendent of the Karachay people to replace warrant officer Atazhuko Atazhukin, who had resigned. A descendant of a prominent Kabardin family that several decades earlier had fled the Russians and resettled near the Karachays, Atazhuko had petitioned to be relieved of his duties, claiming that they threatened to ruin him. He explained that he was receiving no pay in his present job, which prevented him from maintaining his own, now rundown estate.

The correspondence between the superior commanders that followed revealed that Atazhukin was an ineffective superintendent who had been appointed only because of his influential uncle, Major Misost Atazhukin.

Not surprisingly, the commander of the Kabardin Fortification Line, General Malinovskii, was glad to accept Atazhukin's resignation and recommended that he be replaced with another offspring of the prominent Kabardin dynasty, the warrant officer Kudenetov, a former member of the Circassian Guard who only recently had returned to the Caucasus. But General Zass had other plans and pushed for his own protégé, the cornet Semën Atarshchikov.

Investigations of the candidates prompted concerns as to whether Kudenetov was related to the Atazhukins and whether Atarshchikov was the subject of a criminal investigation. Addressing the latter concern, Zass explained that Semën Atarshchikov had been confused with his namesake, the captain of the Highland Cossack Regiment. Cornet Semën Atarshchikov, Zass continued, "had never been the subject of any investigation, has excellent conduct, is very capable and could be very useful in the position of superintendent of the Karachay people, especially because he knows their language so well."[7]

While the matter of Semën Atarshchikov's appointment was being decided in Tiflis, Semën was given permission to leave for his home at Naurskaia to arrange family matters and await orders. A few months later, the orders signed by the supreme commander, Baron Rosen, arrived: Atarshchikov was to assume the position as Karachay superintendent. He requested as his deputy his old Chechen friend Mazay Bashaev, who at the time was serving as deputy to a Chechen superintendent. He was given an additional sum of 250 silver rubles "for the entertainment of the highlanders and sundry office expenditures." On November 1, 1836, Atarshchikov left Prochnyi Okop for the Karachays.[8]

Although the vigilant Russian officials had considered the merits of each candidate, apparently no one had bothered to solicit the opinion of the very people whom the new superintendent was to govern. Some reports suggested that the Karachays were quite content with the previous superintendent and suspected that his departure was the result of General Zass's intrigues. They were certainly right to see the new superintendent as Zass's man. When on November 7 Atarshchikov arrived at the Russian frontier fort, he received a less than welcome reception from a group of Karachay notables. Instead of accompanying Atarshchikov to his new residence, they informed him that without the consent of the people they could not accept him as superintendent and asked him to wait at the fort.

The issue was resolved by a combination of pressure from General Zass and assurances from Baron Rosen that their complaints would be addressed. Not surprisingly, the Karachays were nursing grievances that they saw opportune to air again. Among the most urgent concerns were the damaging raids by Nogays from behind the Kuban Line—in which they suspected General Zass's hand—the attempts by the Russian authorities to regulate the application of sharia, and the restrictions on issuing passports for pilgrims who wished to travel to Mecca.

In a detailed letter to the Karachays, Baron Rosen skillfully turned the issue upside down, implying that they themselves were responsible for the slow pace of Russian justice. He explained amicably that until now, in accordance with their wishes, the Karachay superintendents had been chosen from among the Kabardin princes, who knew neither the Russian language and laws nor the government's orders and regulations. "Keeping in mind your well-being," Baron Rosen continued, "I have chosen as your superintendent, cornet Atarshchikov, a very good man in all respects, who knows well the customs and the language of the highlanders, government regulations, your needs, rights, and duties, and who will protect you from any injustice." Promising that the Karachays' concerns would be addressed, Baron Rosen called upon them to assist Atarshchikov in his duties. On March 18, 1837, almost five months after he had departed for the Karachay region, Atarschchikov reported that he had reached his destination, had been well received, and had assumed his responsibilities.[9]

Unlike the more numerous Adyges, who dominated the northwest Caucasus, the Karachays were a smaller, Turkic-speaking people occupying the mountainous region of the Upper Kuban and Teberda Rivers south of Batalpashinsk (the eastern part of the present Karachay-Cherkes republic). Separated from the Adyges by language and custom, the Karachays were most closely related to their neighbors in the east, the Balkars—mountain dwellers of the upper Baksan and Chegem Rivers who occupied the western part of the present-day Kabardin-Balkar Republic.[10] It was Atarshchikov's near-native fluency in Kumyk, which was mutually intelligible to other Turkic-speaking peoples, that made him a perfect choice as Karachay superintendent.

Atarshchikov's appointment took place against the background of the escalating ghazawat. Despite a series of successful Russian military campaigns and the killing of the two previous imams, the ranks of the Islamic Imamate continued to grow, inspired now by the third imam, Shamil. The scenario that most concerned Russian authorities was the possibility of the war's spreading from Shamil's base in the northeast Caucasus to the northwest, engulfing the entire Caucasus range. This would have linked the Ottoman Empire directly with the rebellious peoples of the Caucasus.

The Karachay lands lay at a strategic juncture that connected the western Adyges with the eastern Adyges (Kabardins) and the northwest Caucasus with the kingdom of Georgia on the other side of the mountain range. The government's plans for containing the ghazawat called for the Karachays to form a vital barrier preventing Shamil's recruiting efforts in the north-west Caucasus.

The Conquest of the Karachays

In 1804 the newly built Fort Batalpashinsk had been the easternmost point of the Kuban Fortification Line. Several years later new forts on the Karachay lands farther up the Kuban River effectively gave the Russians control of the mountain passes leading to the major Karachay auls: Kart-Jurt, Uchkulan, Khurzuk, and others. The construction of forts was only a prelude to a major resettlement of the Don and Volga Cossacks, who began to arrive in 1824. By the late 1820s the old forts had consolidated into large Cossack settlements in the upper reaches of the Kuban (Batalpashinsk, Nevinnomysk) and the Kuma (Bekeshevskaia, Karantinnaia) Rivers, while the recently built forts formed a new fortification line along the Greater Zelenchuk River.[11]

Not surprisingly, the Karachays responded to the Russian encroachment into their traditional pasturelands by increasing their raids against the Russian settlements and turning to the Ottoman Porte for aid. In 1826 they cemented their relationship with the Porte by submitting hostages to the commander of the principal Ottoman fort on the Black Sea, Anapa. During the Russo-Ottoman war of 1828–29, the commander of the Caucasus Line, General Georgii Arsen'evich Emmanuel, resolved to elimi-nate the Ottoman beachhead in the northwest Caucasus and launched a major punitive expedition against the Karachays.

Shortly after the fall of Anapa to the Russians in the summer of 1828, a Russian expeditionary force under General Emmanuel set out from Fort Kislovodsk on a march to Mount Elbrus, the highest peak of the Caucasus (5,642m). On October 20, 1828, the Karachays fought a desperate battle at the gorge near the Elbrus pass, but by the end of the day they had been thoroughly routed. General Emmanuel reported that the Thermopylae of the Caucasus had been taken and that the Karachays had been denied a safe haven.

Notwithstanding his legendary courage and military talents, Emmanuel owed his success in reaching the seemingly impregnable Karachay moun-tain auls to the service of several native guides and advisers. They led his troops through forbidding terrain to approach the Elbrus pass in a place where the Karachays did not expect them. Several days after their defeat, a group of Karachay notables led by the Ottoman-appointed governor, the *vali* Islam Krymshamkhal, sued for peace. The Karachay notables pledged cessation of hostilities, the return of Russian captives and cattle, and the surrender of four hostages. In return, the Russians allowed the Karachays to trade at nearby forts to obtain such basic items as flour, iron, salt, and textiles.[12]

For Emmanuel, a military success was also a prelude for a conquest of a different kind. Born and educated in the Hungarian provinces of the Habsburg Empire and fluent in five languages, Emmanuel was familiar with the scientific missions that had followed the colonial conquests of European powers such as Britain and France. In response to his proposal to organize a scientific expedition to Mount Elbrus, the Imperial Academy of Sciences dispatched a group of its prominent members with expertise in physics, botany, zoology, and geology.[13]

In late June 1829, Emmanuel, the scholars, and a detachment of troops set out from Piatigorsk. They sought to explore the region and to set the first European and most likely first human foot atop Mount Elbrus. A month later the expedition returned with both tasks accomplished. The honor of reaching the top of Elbrus fell to a local Kabardin hunter, Kilar Khashirov. Others had been forced to give up the climb four hundred to five hundred yards short of the peak.[14]

The initial euphoria of military and scientific conquest soon gave way to the everyday burden of maintaining the garrison in a hostile environment. The Karachays were left to their own devices and, for all intents and purposes, remained independent. Concern for the well-being of their hostages in Russian hands, the threat of a punitive expedition, and their growing reliance on trade with Russia combined to provide reasonable assurances that the Karachays would remain peaceful.

A favorable end of the Russo-Ottoman war of 1828–29 allowed the Russians to expedite the conquest and colonization of the northwest Caucasus during the 1830s. The Provisional Committee set up by the Foreign Ministry recommended the construction of forts along the Black Sea coast and increased naval patrols to cut off the region from Ottoman and British influence. The Committee also recommended greater reliance on the local elite, the imposition of the Russian administrative system, and access to customs-free trade at Russian towns elsewhere in the empire.

Some of the Committee's suggestions proved impossible to implement. The region first had to be conquered before it could be administered. In 1837 General Zass recommended to his superiors advancing the Russian front line about 62 miles west to build forts on the Urup and Laba Rivers—the Kuban's tributaries flowing from the south to the north. The new fortification line would allow the Russians to separate the local peoples from one another, to control their migratory routes to the pasturelands, and to deal more effectively with the inevitable raids. To make room for Russian forts and to ensure their safety, the neighboring Adyge auls from the Urup and Laba Rivers had to be deported farther east and resettled on the Greater and Lesser Zelenchuk and Teberda Rivers.[15]

By the late 1830s the Karachays and their newly resettled Adyge neighbors found themselves surrounded by Russian forts and Cossack settlements in the north, east, and west. Only the snow-capped mountain peaks and the southern ridges of the Caucasus main range remained free of the Russian presence. Three or four months a year, before the snow made the high passes inaccessible, the Karachays crossed the mountains to exchange their animal products for iron, salt, and fruits in the villages in the Georgian principalities of Svaneti and Imereti. Despite the shortness of the season, this trade was critical in allowing Karachays to preserve their independence from the Adyges and the encroaching Russians.[16] But not for long.

Expedition into the Svaneti Lands

Russia's strategic offensive in the northwest Caucasus required better knowledge of remote areas. In 1838 the government had decided that it was time to explore and map one of the most isolated corners of the Caucasus, the highlands of Free Svaneti. In June a small expedition set out from Fort Nalchik. The leader of the group was Pozdyshev, a former officer in the Russian army who had been found guilty of embezzlement, stripped of his ranks, and exiled to the Caucasus. Other participants were the superintendent of the Karachays, Semën Atarshchikov; his assistant, the Chechen notable Mazay Bashaev; and the Karachay notable Muhammad Dudov.

From Nalchik the road proceeded along the gorge of the Lesser Cherek River, which was populated by the Balkars. Surrounded by mountain peaks over five thousand meters high, they crossed the main Caucasus range through the Katyn-Tau pass and entered Svaneti. At this time of year, the highlands of Svaneti offered views of breathtaking beauty. Above them were magnificent glaciers and snow-capped summits; below were green blankets of tall grass with clusters of rhododendrons and birch groves.

Between the main Caucasus range in the north and the Svaneti range in the south were the lands of the Lower and Upper Svaneti. The Lower Svaneti was located in the valley of the Tskheniskali River and was part of the Mingrelian principality ruled by the Georgian princely dynasty of the Dadianis. The middle of the Inguri River formed the western part of the Upper Svaneti, a principality ruled by the princely dynasty of the Dadeshkilianis. The eastern part of the Upper Svaneti, located in the upper reaches of the Inguri River, was an independent tribal area, known as Free Svaneti. Like other isolated mountain communities, this ancient land had for centuries been cut off from mainstream civilizations and shrouded in mystery and myths that stirred the imagination of its neighbors.[17]

To the ancient Greek geographer Strabo the Svans were known as the Soanes, the warrior people who lived under the great peaks of Elbrus and Shkara. Nineteenth-century ethnographers and travelers saw the Svans as either a primitive and savage people living in the Stone Age or free people who had created an admirably democratic society. Some twentieth-century linguists claimed they were related to the Georgians, whereas others believed them to be unrelated to any neighboring peoples. Some even suggested a connection to the Basque people in Spain, and some claimed ties to the Hittites.[18] With no shortage of myths and fables, in the early nineteenth century the remote and mysterious lands of Free Svaneti gave rise to yet another legend, which the 1838 expedition was supposed to investigate.

In 1708, in the wake of a failed Cossack uprising, a group of the Don Cossack Old Believers had fled to the Caucasus and taken a refuge in the Taman Peninsula. Here they set up a free and prosperous community and became known as Nekrasovites, after the name of their leader, Ignat Nekrasov. A century later, the advance of the Russian troops and settlers forced the Nekrasovites to flee farther: some chose to leave for the Ottoman Empire and eventually settled in the Balkans; others found refuge among the Adyges on the Black Sea coast and in time assimilated among them. For whatever reason, the leader of the 1838 expedition, Pozdyshev, believed that Free Svaneti was the land inhabited by the Nekrasov community.

After two months in these lands, the expedition returned to Nalchik and confirmed the existence of the Nekrasovites. Pozdyshev compiled a map with a topographical description of the route to Free Svaneti. He also described the geography of the region, the seven rugged villages that comprised Free Svaneti, and the primitive life of their residents. Their houses were surrounded by a high stone wall and watchtowers with embrasures. An average village consisted of about sixty households, but even the smallest villages of thirty-five households had a church with fine frescoes, magnificently carved wooden doors, and numerous icons in silver-wrought frames. The isolation of the villages had helped to preserve an early Christian tradition: the churches remained architecturally different from other churches in the region, and the abundant relics and religious art, brought for safekeeping by the Georgian priests, were well preserved.

The richness of the churches and the residents' seemingly earnest Christian faith persuaded Pozdyshev that he was among the Nekrasovites. This was, however, an error, and it was promptly caught and corrected at the Russian headquarters in Tiflis the next year.[19]

Throughout the 1850s several other expeditions led by the Russian colonel and numismatist I. A. Bartolomei and later by the Georgian ethnographer D. Z. Bakradze left a more thorough account of Free Svaneti and its peoples. In contrast to Pozdyshev, both scholars reported the widespread worship of animist gods among the Svans and attributed their debilitating physique to a severe shortage of salt.

At the time, however, Pozdyshev's expedition was deemed a success, and its participants were appropriately rewarded. Pozdyshev was given a lump sum of 150 silver rubles, Atarshchikov received the Order of St. Stanislav III degree, and his two assistants received an annuity of 750 rubles in paper money, which had just been introduced in the region.[20]

During the last decades of the Caucasus War, Free Svaneti continued to be a self-governing tribal area, and together with other parts of Svaneti resisted Russian domination. In 1857, while the war against the Russians in the western Caucasus was still at its height, the commander of the Russian troops, Prince Bariatinskii, ordered Svaneti to be subdued by arms. The ruling prince of western Upper Svaneti, Constantine Dadeshkiani, was to be exiled to Erivan. On his way to exile, Constantine stopped at Kutaisi to pay a visit to the governor-general of western Georgia, Prince Alexander Gagarin. During the meeting Constantine suddenly drew his dagger and stabbed the prince and three members of his staff to death. Instead of being exiled, Constantine was court-martialed and swiftly executed. A year later the whole of Upper Svaneti was annexed to the Russian viceroyalty of the Caucasus.[21]

8

Russian Policies and Alternatives

Semën Atarshchikov's duties as superintendent of the Karachays did not preclude him from accompanying General Zass in his punitive raids across the frontier. During 1837–38, Atarshchikov took part in a different kind of mission—the effort to find and free from captivity the Russian military spy Baron Fedor Tornau, whom he had gotten to know in Tiflis. The emperor himself took a keen interest in Tornau's fate and instructed the Russian authorities throughout the region to work toward his release. General Zass personally led the selected commando units across the Kuban, hoping to secure Tornau's release, but each time without success.

Chained to a wall and closely watched, Tornau was kept in a distant aul of the Abadzekh highlanders, who continued to demand an enormous amount of silver or gold in exchange for the freedom of their prominent captive. When there seemed to be little hope left, Tornau was finally rescued on a dark night in November 1838 by his friend and companion, the Nogay prince Tembulat Karamurzin. His captivity in the mountains of the Caucasus had lasted for exactly two years and two months.

Atarshchikov, who was familiar with the account of Tornau's previous secret expeditions, was also well informed about the circumstances of Tornau's capture related to him by his close friend, the influential Besleney prince Aitek Kanokov. As a confidant of General Zass, he was aware of the larger significance of the Tornau affair, which became one of the episodes in the geopolitical struggle among the Russian, Ottoman, and British Empires, better known as the Great Game.

The Northwest Caucasus in the nineteenth century

Nicholas I Visits the Caucasus

In the spring of 1837 the region was abuzz with news that the emperor himself was to travel through the Caucasus. In early September 1837 Nicholas I arrived in the Crimea, and two weeks later he left for Gelendjik, the starting point for his journey. Several events of the previous year—the capture of the Russian officer Tornau and the confrontation with the British after the Russian navy's seizure of the British merchant vessel *Vixen* off the Circassian coast—had underscored Russia's precarious position in the North Caucasus. The emperor's trip to the region was designed to impress upon the major powers and indigenous peoples alike that the clamor in European capitals and local resistance notwithstanding, Russia had no intention of relinquishing its claims to the region. It was also hoped that the emperor's personal visit, surrounded by the appropriate pomp and preceded by intense diplomatic activity, would induce the recalcitrant local chiefs to cease hostilities and render homage to the emperor.[1]

Nicholas I was the second Russian emperor to set foot in the Caucasus, and his journey took place exactly 115 years after Peter I had landed on the coast of Daghestan. Nicholas was fond of traversing his empire and did so frequently. During such tours he was generally preoccupied with military matters: observing maneuvers and inspecting regiments and fortifications. His 1837 journey to the Caucasus lasted from late July until late October and was the longest he had undertaken.

Nicholas I left St. Petersburg on July 31 and proceeded south along the western borders of the empire. Arriving in Odessa early in September, he left just in time to escape the plague epidemic that later devastated the city. From Odessa the emperor sailed to Sevastopol, where he inspected the Black Sea fleet, paid a visit to Bakhchisaray, the former seat of the Crimean khans, and sailed eastward for a short visit at Gelendjik. During his two-day stay at Gelendjik he visited the mortally wounded Major General Shteibe, witnessed a rapidly spreading fire that threatened the gunpowder stores, and saw plans for a parade of the garrison thwarted by the strong sea wind. Amid the bad omens Nicholas proceeded, tacking south to the Russian fort of Redut-Kale on the Mingrelian coast. The fact that he made no other stops between Gelendjik and Redut-Kale indicates Russia's precarious hold on the Black Sea coast. From Redut-kale the emperor's journey proceeded into recently acquired lands, skirting the Ottoman border via Kutais, Akhalkalaki, Serdar-Abad, Gumry (Nicholas I renamed it Aleksandropol), and Erevan and then turning north to Tiflis, Vladikavkaz, Piatigorsk, Georgievsk, Stavropol, and Novocherkassk.

The imperial journey to the Caucasus had been carefully planned and prepared. In 1836 Count A. Kh. Benckendorff had instructed Khan-Giray, the commander of the Circassian Guard and the emperor's aide-de-camp, to compose an essay acquainting the emperor with the history and customs of the Circassian people. In the spring of 1837 Khan-Giray was chosen to lead a secret mission to the independent Circassian tribes of the Natukhay, Shapsug, and Abadzekh. He was to arrange their formal submission to Russia in time for the emperor's visit and to suggest ways of administering the region. On May 29 Khan-Giray, accompanied by several other members of the Circassian Guard and the war minister's aide-de-camp, Captain Baron P. A. Vrevskii, departed from St. Petersburg, and two weeks later they arrived in Ekaterinodar.

After spending the summer crisscrossing the northwestern Caucasus and meeting with the notables of various Adyge tribes, Khan-Giray reported that he had failed to convince the native chiefs either to accept Russian suzerainty or to appear in person to pay homage to the emperor. He blamed his failure on the anarchic nature of the indigenous societies, the weak authority of the notables among their people, and the work of British agents who had sowed distrust toward Russia. When briefed by Khan-Giray about the failure of his mission, a frustrated Nicholas dispatched Khan-Giray to ransom Baron Tornau from captivity, but the captors demanded a sum so unreasonable that there was no chance of negotiating the baron's freedom.

One consequence of Khan-Giray's mission was a petition submitted on October 18 in Stavropol by a large group of Adyges and Nogays. The petitioners complained bitterly of pervasive corruption and abuse at the hands of the local Russian administration. They explained that the actions of Russian officials had driven them to resistance. Their petition cast a dark shadow over the commander of the Caucasus Line, General Veliaminov. Assuming that Khan-Giray had instigated their complaints, a furious and defensive Veliaminov turned on Khan-Giray, blaming him for failing in his mission among the Adyges.

Abuse of power and corruption were not isolated events and were hardly a surprise to the emperor. During his short stay in Erevan, he was presented with hundreds of complaints from the local population. The result was the dismissal of several Russian officials and exile to Poland of the regional governor, Prince V. O. Bebutov. There were also indications of pervasive graft in Georgia.

In advance of the emperor's visit to the region, the senate had dispatched one of its distinguished members, Baron P. V. Gan, to inspect the situation. Opinions on how to administer the Caucasus differed: in his 1829 report the commander of the Caucasus corps, General I. F. Paskevich, had advocated the region's speedy integration into the imperial administration, while his successor, General Rosen (1831–37) instead suggested a series of incremental steps. In June 1837 Baron Gan arrived in Tiflis to uncover a network of vast corruption and abuse at the center of which was the emperor's aide-de-camp and Baron Rosen's son-in-law, Colonel Prince Alexander Dadiani. Dadiani had allegedly looted Tiflis, misspent the money, and abused soldiers, forcing them, among other things, to perform labor on his estate and those of other nobles.

Nicholas arrived in Tiflis on October 8. Apprised of the Gan report, he publicly stripped Prince Dadiani of his rank and sent him to be court-martialed. The chief of staff of the Caucasus corps, General V. D. Vol'khovskii, was summarily dismissed. General Rosen was faulted for his mistaken policies of relying too much on accommodation with the local population and was replaced by General I. A. Golovin.

Dismissing the commanding officers, however, was no easy fix, and the government continued its search for a workable policy in the years to come. In 1840, following Gan's recommendations, Nicholas ordered an administrative reform to bring the Transcaucasus into a closer imperial embrace: adat and sharia were to be replaced by Russian criminal and civil statutes. Yet the result was a series of uprisings that threatened to add fuel to the war already raging in Chechnya and Daghestan. When another commission was sent to the Caucasus in 1842, it found that the reforms intended to impose Russian administrative structure on the region were a failure. The commission blamed Gan for arrogance and lack of understanding of the local conditions and recommended an immediate reversal of the 1840 reforms, which were indeed scuttled a year later. It took another three years before the appointment of Prince M. S. Vorontsov as viceroy in the Caucasus signaled a return to a more patient approach of seeking incremental change and greater accommodation with the local population.[2]

Intended as a show of the regions' successful subjugation, the 1837 imperial journey soon threatened to become a fiasco. Nicholas was greatly distraught by the situation in the region: Russia's hold over the Black Sea's east coast remained tenuous, resistance in the northwest Caucasus was growing, corruption and mismanagement were rampant, and the northeast Caucasus was still mired in a bloody war of attrition. A positive image of the imperial visit could still be salvaged, however, if Shamil and his followers could be enticed to lay down their arms in exchange for an imperial pardon and generous rewards.

When the negotiations with the Adyges in the northwest failed to bring them into submission, orders were sent to the other end of the Caucasus instructing officials to induce Shamil to meet the emperor and offer his submission. In mid-September a flurry of activity resulted in an exchange of letters between the Russian authorities and Shamil and eventually led to a meeting on September 30 between the Russian general Kluge von Klugenau and Shamil. Klugenau offered Shamil handsome rewards if he agreed to come in person to Tiflis to meet the emperor to ask for a pardon. But neither rewards nor threats were able to convince Shamil, who remained skeptical of the Russian offer and reminded the general of Russia's treacherous behavior in the past. Once again the emperor's presence in the region failed to bring any change to the increasingly unsettled situation.[3]

Nicholas left the Caucasus in a foul mood. As if political setbacks were not enough, the emperor was slightly hurt when his carriage tipped over and crashed on the sharp descent near Tiflis. Upon arriving at Vladikavkaz on October 13, he was greeted by a large group of local deputies eager to submit their petitions. Nicholas received most petitioners warmly and promised to consider their grievances upon his arrival in St. Petersburg. At the same time, he singled out the Chechens as the most disloyal subjects and summarily dismissed their bitter complaints of abuses by the local Russian authorities.[4]

A few days later the emperor arrived at Stavropol. Except for the military headquarters, the town had no industry or trade and few residents. The officers found refuge from everyday boredom in drinking and gambling at the only hotel in town. Nicholas found the place so dreadful that he decided to abolish the town altogether. Only General Veliaminov's assurances that it had good economic potential saved the town from condemnation. Having left Stavropol on October 18, the emperor's cortege reached Moscow eight days later, traveling via Novocherkassk, Voronezh, and Tula.[5]

The imperial journey to the Caucasus had taken over three months, cost 143,438 rubles, and left 170 horses dead from exhaustion. Not only had none of the visit's goals been achieved, but the imperial visit made the situation worse. Nicholas I, whose habitual instinct was to rely on the stick rather than the carrot, had further empowered those who gladly shared his views to conduct violent and brutal campaigns against the recalcitrant natives. At the same time, the majority of the local chiefs and nobles saw no change in their circumstances, as their grievances against local Russian authorities remained unanswered and unresolved. Was it possible that the corrupt and abusive Russian officials actually represented the policies of the emperor himself? Such was the inevitable conclusion that compelled many among the local population to choose resistance over cooperation. Perhaps each side was beginning to realize the illusory nature of its hopes: for the Russians the speedy subjugation of the region now seemed out of reach, and for the locals, there no longer seemed any chance of a benign Russian presence.

General Nikolai Raevsky

It was by no means obvious from the vantage point of the 1830s that the imperial instructions of September 25, 1829, to the commander of the Caucasus Corps, General Paskevich, prescribing pacification or extermination of the indigenous population, would be carried out. Certainly Fedor Tornau, who understood the Caucasus and its inhabitants better than any other Russian officer, did not share the emperor's view. In 1839, after having been rescued from captivity, Tornau was summoned to St. Petersburg to meet Nicholas I. Skeptical of the emperor's confidence that the Caucasus would be subdued in three years, Tornau pointed out during the audience that even three decades might not be enough to achieve this goal.

Others were even more skeptical. Tornau's contemporary, a German explorer and scholar, Moriz Wagner, who traveled extensively both in Algeria and the Caucasus, maintained that it would take a hundred years before the French and the Russians could subdue or exterminate their respective antagonists. If he was wrong about the timing, he was less wrong about the outcome. Writing in 1881, Tornau confessed, "[A]t that time it never occurred to me that this burning issue would be so favorably resolved by exterminating one half and exiling the other half of the Caucasus's indigenous population."[6]

Although the great majority of the Russian commanders in the Caucasus shared the emperor's vision and preferred to rely on Ermolov's methods of ruthless extermination, there were some exceptions. Perhaps the most notable was General Nikolai Raevsky, a commander of the Black Sea Fortification Line between 1837 and 1841. A son of a hero of the Napoleonic Wars, Raevsky early in his career proved to be a brilliant officer and quickly rose to become a distinguished general. He shared the progressive ideas of the Decembrists, many of whom had been stripped of their officer ranks and exiled to the Caucasus, where Raevsky took many of them under his arm. He was an old friend of Alexander Pushkin and employed the poet's younger brother, Lev, as his personal secretary.

Raevsky's initial observations on the nature of Russia's war in the Caucasus were made clear in his report to the war minister, A. I. Chernyshev. Raevsky compared Russia's bloody conquest of the Caucasus to that of the Spanish conquest of the Americas, though it lacked the initial success enjoyed by the conquistadores. He argued that the methods used by Ermolov and other commanders—punitive raids, destruction of crops, pillaging and burning of the auls, capturing children and women, converting the natives to Christianity by force, founding forts at strategic heights and Cossack settlements in the seized plains and valleys—were counterproductive and only pushed the indigenous peoples toward increased resistance.

Reavsky's solution was to offer the local elite an incentive to keep peace by making them dependent on trade with Russia. The primary trading commodity was salt, which was in desperately short supply in the mountains and was bartered for regional products. Furthermore, to discourage the thriving slave trade along the coast, Raevsky suggested helping the locals to meet their needs, thereby devaluing the Ottoman merchandise that the Russians considered contraband. Essentially, Raevsky's was a call for incremental colonization of the Caucasus without unnecessary bloodshed.[7]

Even though the Raevsky approach appeared to be working and brought relative peace to the coast, other Russian military commanders were unsatisfied with the slow progress of conquest and what they believed to be an excessive accommodation of the local population. More concerned with the highlanders' formal oath of allegiance than with actual peace on the ground, they demanded the cessation of trade and the embrace of more aggressive means. The commander of the Caucasus Fortification Line, General P. Kh. von Grabbe, insisted on an increase in punitive campaigns, while Admiral L. M. Serebriakov (born K. M. Artsatagortsian) called for the continuation of crop burning in order to confront the Adyges with the possibility of starvation come winter. Both hoped military force combined with the widespread destruction of Adyge lands would eventually force them either to submit or depart. Raevsky's warnings that Russian actions threatened to turn the northwest Caucasus into another Chechnya went unheeded.

As late as February 1840, Raevsky's eloquent and subtle analysis of the situation persuaded the emperor to overrule General von Grabbe and promote trade with the locals as the best way to bring about their ultimate pacification. Several years of his peaceful approach, Raevsky argued, had brought more success than the previous forty years of Russia's indiscriminate and massive application of force. A year later, however, Raesky was blamed for the humiliating debacle when in the winter of 1840 the combined Adyge forces killed an estimated two thousand Russians, captured four Russian forts, and laid siege to others. In 1841, recognizing his lonely and hopeless stance within the Russian military, Raevsky submitted his resignation. Leaving the region in the same year, he wrote to War Minister

Chernyshev, "Until now I have been the first and only one who protested the adverse effect of the military actions in the Caucasus and because of it I am compelled to leave the region."[8] Raevsky's departure was a victory for the commanders (Serebriakov, Zass, Grabbe, Golovin) who preferred to rely on the long-standing policies of force and extermination that had in fact been responsible for the growing resistance against Russia.

Throughout the 1830s the Black Sea coast between Anapa and Sukhumi had experienced rapid Russian colonization. Coastal lands were conquered, and their native residents were forced to flee. Dozens of new forts sprang up at strategic locations, and thousands of Ukrainian Cossacks and peasants were encouraged to settle the coast. Some settlers were given a twenty-five-year tax exemption; others received generous support from wealthy Armenian merchants. Initially they became known as "the Anapa settlers" because of the fortified agricultural colonies they founded near Anapa. The Russian blockade of the coast, while not entirely efficient, significantly curtailed the Ottoman trade, as more Ottoman merchant vessels were seized before reaching their destination on the Circassian coast. Made fugitive in their own lands, the Adyge peoples were increasingly desperate.

Yet the rapid colonization of the coast had predictable consequences. The military forts were built so hastily that few of them could withstand a serious assault. During his first journey along the coast in 1835 Tornau had observed that Russian forts there were extremely vulnerable and poorly suited for coastal defense. One of the best examples of the Russian inability to control the coast was the expedition that General Veliaminov undertook in 1837 to purge the coast south of Gelendjik of its native population. It took four days and 104 casualties before the troops reached another Russian fort about 12 miles farther south. It took five days and 128 casualties to march another 18 miles. At this point, unable to move either back north or farther south, Veliaminov found himself completely trapped by the combined force of the several Adyge peoples. With their inadequate garrisons and the absence of roads to link them, Russian forts proved useless. Only Veliaminov's duplicity saved his trapped troops: he assured the Adyge chiefs that Russia's war in the Caucasus had ended, and as a result he was allowed safe passage to the Kuban River.[9]

For a short while, convinced by the Ottomans and hopeful of British naval intervention, the Circassians were able to set aside their internal rivalries and field a sizable force against the Russian forts. The most visible symbol of their unity arrived from Istanbul in 1837. It was Sanjak-i Sherif, the green banner of the Prophet Muhammad to be unfurled only for the holy war. Its simple design—three arrows under twelve stars—represented the twelve Adyge tribes united in their war against Russia.[10]

The national flag of the Adyge Republic in Russia today, designed in 1837 by the British diplomat in Istanbul, David Urquhart, to signify the unity of the Circassian people

To no small degree the Circassian success against the Russians in 1840 was due to the encouragement of the British and their delivery of guns and gunpowder. The British point man in the region was Sefer-bey Zanoko, another remarkable example of a Caucasus native son forced to negotiate the cultural boundaries between several different worlds. His story had an already familiar outline. Born into a noble Adyge family near Anapa and given as a hostage to the Russians, he ended up studying at the elite Richelieu lyceum in Odessa. Upon graduation, Sefer-bey was dispatched as a junior officer to join the Russian garrison at Anapa. Soon thereafter, offended by the regimental commander, he deserted and fled to the Ottomans. After joining the Ottoman military, Sefer-bey soon reached the rank of colonel, and in 1828 he found himself again in Anapa but now as deputy commander of the Ottoman garrison. The siege of Anapa lasted for six weeks and pitted against each other two friends and former schoolmates at the Richelieu lyceum: Sefer-bey and the Armenian junior naval officer Serebriakov, the future admiral of the Black Sea fleet. When Anapa fell to the Russians, Sefer-bey was taken prisoner, dispatched to Odessa, and released a year later; in 1830 he returned to the Ottoman Empire to champion the cause of Adyge independence from Russia for the next three decades.[11]

The Circassian success in capturing several Russian coastal forts and their garrisons in the winter of 1840 proved short-lived. In the spring a Russian naval expedition landed more troops on the seashore and easily recaptured the forts. They were later reinforced against the possibility of a siege from the interior, yet the forts remained highly vulnerable to assault from the sea.[12]

The realization that British intervention was a mirage and that they would have to face fresh Russian reinforcements on their own eroded the Circassians' unity. It was not until 1848, when Shamil's deputy, Muhammed Amin, was dispatched to the region, that the Circassians rallied once again to confront the Russians. This time their holy war was on behalf of Shamil and his Islamic state.

Khan-Giray

Unlike his companions who returned to St. Petersburg after their 1837 mission to the region, Khan-Giray was ordered to stay in the Caucasus under the command of General Veliaminov. His new assignment reflected both imperial ire over Khan-Giray's failure to do Russia's bidding and a belief that he could still play an important role. There was some hope that he could serve as an effective counterforce to the British agents in the region, helping to win various Circassian peoples to the Russian side and arranging for Fedor Tornau's release. To finance his activity in the Caucasus, the authorities allotted Khan-Giray 30,000 rubles, a sizable amount of cash that he proved hard-pressed to account for upon his return to St. Petersburg two years later. As far as the government was concerned, Khan-Giray had little to show for his efforts. British-Ottoman influence over the northwest Caucasus had hardly diminished, and when Tornau was finally freed, it was the result of a daring rescue by his friend Tembulat Karamurzin, not of anything Khan-Giray had done.

The charming "Circassian Karamzin," as Nicholas used to refer to Khan-Giray, was rapidly falling into disfavor. His military career in decline and his health failing, he increasingly turned toward literary pursuits. In December 1839, he petitioned War Minister A. I. Chernyshev for the return of his 1836 treatise, *Notes on Circassia*. When Chernyshev declined, Khan-Giray appealed to the emperor, who deemed its publication "inappropriate" and ordered that the manuscript be kept where it was, together with other secret files in the library of the General Staff.[13]

The successive generations of both Russian imperial and Soviet government officials found Khan-Giray's manuscript incendiary enough to keep it off limits to the public. The first three parts of the manuscript were finally published in 1978, but the fourth and most controversial part containing specific recommendations on "the ways of bringing the Circassians into a civilized state" did not appear until 1992, a year after the demise of the Soviet Union.[14]

General Veliaminov had been asked to comment on the *Notes* shortly after they were written. Khan-Giray's practical policy recommendations and Veliaminov's arguments for rejecting them offer a window into the making of Russian policies in the region. Khan-Giray argued that the best way to govern the Circassians was by supporting Islamic institutions. He had come to view the Muslim clergy as the only group capable of bringing peace and stability to the region. Therefore, he insisted, Russian authorities should help to spread Islamic influence in the region and use Islam as an instrument of their policies "so that the people would realize that the Russian government did not intend to eradicate their faith."[15]

Such views embodied the contradictions of Khan-Giray's own personality. As a Muslim and a Circassian, he well understood the fears and anxieties of his people, who saw in Russian expansion not only territorial aggrandizement but also an onslaught on their religion. But as a well-educated Russian officer, he fully understood the limitations of Islam and the "semi-savage" state of his people. Khan-Giray suggested introducing schools that would educate a generation of imams and mullahs loyal to the Russian government. To undermine the political power of the ulema and Ottoman influence, he called for the creation of a Circassian alphabet, which would replace Ottoman Turkish in everyday correspondence and allow the Quran to be translated into the Circassian language.[16]

A legacy of Enlightenment thought, Khan-Giray's eclectic views stemmed from his conviction that his semisavage people could be changed and improved through education, both religious and secular. He thought it useful to establish schools where the children of both local nobles and commoners could be taught, albeit separately. At the same time, he urged that native hostages be sent to Russian schools in Stavropol and Ekaterinodar and called for the appointment of an "overseer of education and enlightenment among the Circassian people." Rumor had it that Khan-Giray wished to see himself in this position.[17]

Nevertheless, supporting and enhancing the institutions of Islam remained the core of his proposal. Hasan Pasha, an Ottoman military commander at Anapa in the 1820s, was Khan-Giray's model of the ideal governor. He had achieved peace with the Circassians through generous payments, rewards, promotion of sharia, and, as a result, control of the ulema.[18] It was the latter that the Russian authorities had failed to secure.

To establish Russia's influence over the ulema, Khan-Giray presented a detailed proposal, which he called "the new governing order." He suggested the creation of two spiritual directorates (*muftiat*) governed by the muftis on the basis of sharia. One muftiat was intended for the indigenous societies ruled by princes and nobles (the Kabardins and Kumyks, for instance), the other for free societies without princely rule (the Chechens, Abadzekhs, and others). The muftis were to supervise the two highest administrators (*valis*) and two courts (*mahkemat*) guided by both sharia and adat.[19]

But General Veliaminov held a different view and had no need for any new order. In his view, allowing the practice of sharia would only enhance the status of the Muslim clergy and ill serve Russian interests. Instead, he suggested following the model of the courts established among the Kumyks and in Greater Kabarda. These courts relied on adat and if necessary on Russian laws, and their decisions could be appealed to the Russian regional commander and then to the supreme commander in the Caucasus. Veliaminov argued against the publication of Khan-Giray's notes because "considerations of how to affect the minds of the semisavage people should not be available to the public." In the end he rejected Khan-Giray's proposal, and his superiors in the imperial capital concurred, citing, in opaque bureaucratic vocabulary, "the difficulties with its implementation (*neudoboispolnitelnost'*)."[20]

Khan-Giray's primary concern was to have the North Caucasus incorporated into the Russian Empire through nonviolent means: trade incentives, generous rewards, education, and the support of Islamic institutions and the legal system of sharia. General Veliaminov, however, believed that Russia's military policies of merciless destruction and punishment were more effective in pacifying the North Caucasus. He argued that Russia's interests were best served by supporting the established elites and their legal practices of adat rather than by supporting the ulema.

Khan-Giray and General Veliaminov represented two very different views of how to pacify and govern the peoples of the North Caucasus. The former favored accommodation with Islam and an incremental civilizing process. Veliaminov preferred a more confrontational approach: relying on the local elites for the swift integration of the region into the empire's political and legal fabric. Both views were typical of the kinds of challenges and dilemmas that Russian policymakers repeatedly had to confront in the North Caucasus and other regions subject to Russian conquest and colonization.

Not surprisingly, General Veliaminov and his superiors in the capital, including the emperor, found Khan-Giray's recommendations unpalatable. They were reminiscent of the policies adopted during the reign of Catherine II—support for and institutionalization of Islam within the Russian Empire in order to better control the Muslim population. But times had changed, and Nicholas I—chastened by the Decembrist revolt, inspired by his special sense of Russian Orthodoxy, and faced with

Shamil's holy war—was in no mood to consider supporting Islam and its institutions. Besides, Nicholas's natural impulses were always toward relying on force rather than seeking accommodation. General Veliaminov's views could not have been closer to the emperor's. The imperial orders instructed military commanders to double their efforts to subdue and pacify the native population.

OF course, supporting the ulema was not the only alternative to Russia's policies of co-opting the elites and intimidating the local population. Among Russian top military commanders and government officials there were always a few advocates for peaceful and incremental conquest. In 1810, reacting to the brutality and repressions of Russian troops, the newly appointed supreme commander in the Caucasus, General A. P. Tormasov, had written to the war minister, Prince Barclay de Tolly, arguing that excessive violence and abuse only further antagonized the local population. He suggested seeking peace and encouraging trade instead. Six years later, the Russian admiral N. S. Mordvinov also advocated the use of trade rather than arms in winning over the natives.[21]

In the late 1820s General F. A. Bekovich-Cherkasskii, a member of the distinguished Kabardin dynasty, which had been converted to Christianity and Russified for several generations, submitted his own project on the best ways to rule the Kabardins. His recommendation was to co-opt the Kabardin nobility by addressing most of their numerous grievances: returning their land and hostages, allowing the return of fugitive nobles, abolishing the Kabardin Provisional Court, allowing the continuous practice of Islam and customary law, and granting them the rights of the Russian nobility.[22]

A year before his departure from the region in 1841, General Nikolai Raevsky bitterly complained that Russian commanders remained ignorant of the indigenous peoples and their social organization. He explained that in the Anapa region, for example, the Russians did not distinguish between the local nobles (the *uzdens*) and the merchants and artisans, who comprised the estate of free commoners (the *tokh*). Under the Ottomans the tokhs had received various trade privileges, and they now expected the same from the Russians. Yet the Russian authorities chose to support the uzdens, ignoring the tokhs and their concerns. The flaws of this policy and Russian ignorance, Raevsky continued, were visible particularly in Daghestan and Chechnya, where the Islamicists were able to rally the free commoners against the uzdens and Russia. Raevsky believed that Russia's support of the uzdens and khans had ignited a religious war and that Russia's interests would be best served by an alliance with the free commoners.[23]

Yet those advocating trade, patience, and accommodation with the local population—including the viceroy of the Caucasus, Prince Mikhail Vorontsov—remained a distinct minority among Russian commanders. The pacification of the Caucasus by sword and fire became the principal Russian policy under Ermolov and was vigorously continued by his successors. In 1828 Veliaminov submitted his proposal "On the Ways to Accelerate the Pacification of the Highlanders." Summarizing the colonial challenges, he admitted that Russian district superintendents (pristavs) were corrupt and that their abuses were the leading cause of raids across the frontier. He further conceded that Russia's efforts to pit "Kumyks against Chechens, Chechens against Kabardins, Kabardins against Kuban Nogays, Nogays against Abadzekhs and Shapsugs" only helped to unite them against Russian rule, and that Russia's Muslim regiments on the frontier were unreliable. He recommended that Russia build more forts at strategic locations, occupy the plains and settle them with Cossack villages, deny the natives the use of pastures for their horses, burn their crops, and destroy the auls that failed to submit.[24]

Ruthless destruction and brutality were indeed the hallmarks of Russia's conquest of the Caucasus. The horrifying atrocities committed by Russian troops—the indiscriminate slaughter of the elderly, women, and children; setting houses on fire with people and animals still inside; raping; pillaging; and capturing children to take to Russia—were described by both Russian and foreign observers. In 1838 a British traveler in the region, Edmund Spencer, called the Circassians "the most cruelly persecuted people at this moment under the heavens." "How is it possible," he continued," that any man, possessed of the slightest feeling of compassion for his fellow-creatures, can contemplate the burning of the villages, the thousands of helpless orphans, the weeping widows, bereft of all they hold dear on earth, without execrating the authors of such misery?"[25]

9

The First Desertion

The Kuban and Laba Fortification Lines

Fort Prochnyi Okop was founded in 1784, but by the 1830s it had long lost its military significance. Yet because of its central location the fort became the headquarters of the commander of the Kuban Fortification Line and a gathering point for Russian expeditionary forces. The fort, built at the highest point on the Kuban's right bank and across the estuary of the Urup River, offered a great view of the plains. The six-foot-high pentagonal wall fenced in the fort's unattractive and dilapidated structures—the barracks and depots for munitions and provisions. One exception to the fort's crowded and unpleasing interior was General Zass's residence, which combined Asian luxury with European comfort and invariably impressed the visiting natives.[1]

The right side of the Kuban River was a wide, open steppe. On the left side the plain stretched to the foothills of the Caucasus. Seventy miles wide and stretching for over 250 miles toward the Black Sea coast, it separated the Kuban River from the mountains. Riddled with ravines and gullies, the plain was a perfect hiding place for the small bands of natives preparing to raid the Russian frontier.

Russia's presence on the plain was limited to two small and remote forts on the Urup and Chanlyk Rivers. To deter raids across the frontier, the Russian military authorities relied on punitive military expeditions, which in essence were little different from the very raids they meant to prevent. The threat of Russian military retribution worked better on the plain, where several Circassian auls had formally renounced their support for the native raiding bands and were thus considered peaceful. It was more difficult to enforce peace in the mountains—where the Abaza-Abkhaz auls of the Bashilbays, Barakays, and others occupied the wooded slopes and narrow canyons of the main mountain range—and farther south, where the auls of the Adyge peoples—the Abadzekhs, Shapsugs, and Natukhays—were hidden deeply in the wooded highlands.

The three Adyge peoples were at open war with Russia. They also provided a safe haven for the runaway Kabardins, Nogays, and others whose lands had been annexed to Russia and who swore to avenge themselves through tireless raiding of the Russian frontier. These refugees, known among the Adyges as *hajrets* (Arabic for emigration) and to the Russians as *abreks* (the Ossetian term for a refugee or outcast who chose a path of war), had committed themselves to seeking glory and vengeance in the war against Russia.

This was the kind of incessant low-grade warfare that required constant vigilance on the Russian frontier. The defense of the frontier had fallen on the Cossacks. The entire right bank of the Kuban was defended by fortified Cossack villages, placed at a distance of 12 miles from each other. Between every two villages there were two outposts with a watchtower and a small group of Cossacks. In the daytime mounted Cossacks patrolled the designated areas and heights. At night they set ambushes at known river crossings while backup groups were stationed at critical road junctions ready to assist if the alarm was raised. In the early mornings, fresh Cossack patrols left their villages to look for possible signs of raiding parties. Despite multiple precautions, raiding parties continued either to sneak through or force their way across the Kuban into the frontier regions of Mineralnye Vody and Stavropol. On one occasion a group of forty mounted raiders crossed the Kuban and reached as far as the Astrakhan steppe, where they robbed fishermen and pillaged fisheries. They spent thirty days within Russian borders and returned to their native auls without being apprehended.

Obviously the existing defense system offered inadequate protection and needed to be supplemented by punitive expeditions. Such was the view of the commander of the Kuban Fortification Line, General Zass, whose military expeditions were known for a particular mix of surprise, cruelty, and destruction. Whatever the short-term gains, Russian military policies under Zass alienated local chiefs and commoners alike.

Indeed if one man surpassed all others in perpetrating atrocities against the indigenous population, it was General Zass. His headquarters at Prochnyi Okop was enveloped in mystery. Nearby, cut-off Circassian heads, with their beards fluttering in the wind, were exhibited on pikes. On one occasion, an invited female guest had insisted that the gruesome heads be removed before her arrival. They were indeed removed, but later, when someone noticed a noxious smell in one of the rooms, Zass pulled out a big chest that contained the heads. He explained that they had been boiled and cleaned in order to be shipped to his friends, professors in Berlin.[2] Reading these accounts of Zass and his compound, one might well conclude that he was a Russian version of Colonel Kurtz, the brilliant and mad butcher of Conrad's *Heart of Darkness*.

Wounded seven times and dubbed by the locals "the lame devil," Zass earned their grudging respect for his bold and relentless raids and a special hatred for his unmatched cruelty. His contemporaries said that for him a military march or raid produced a joy akin to that felt by British gentlemen on the hunt. Zass argued openly that in the conquest of the Caucasus one should rely not on philanthropy but on terror, as had General Ermolov, whose name the awed locals still used to frighten their children. Contemporaries differed as to whether Zass's harsh policies served Russian interests, but his reputation for spreading fear and destruction was beyond dispute. When in the summer of 1838 word of Zass's march toward Anapa reached John Bell, a British resident in Circassia, he noted in his diary that "women and children in that neighborhood must be in danger."[3]

In 1839 Zass took a significant step toward further conquest. Following the broader outlines of Veliaminov's proposal and Russia's general forward policy, he undertook to move the right flank of the Caucasus Line from the Kuban to the Laba River, thereby denying the natives access to the extensive plain between the rivers and pushing the Russian frontier significantly closer to the mountains.

The Russians' rationale for this strategy had not changed since the construction of the first fortification lines in the seventeenth century: to advance the military frontier and gain new arable lands. The regular Russian military stationed in the forts and the irregular Cossack contingents in their fortified villages were to guard the new frontier, enabling peasant and Cossack colonization to transform the former frontier zone into flourishing farmland.

In the first decades of the nineteenth century colonization of the northwest Caucasus proceeded rapidly. As a result of the mass migration of peasants and Cossacks from Ukraine, in 1824 the Black Sea Host could field as many as twenty-five thousand Cossacks. Even more important was the fact that the new migrants were not individual Cossacks but had arrived with their families. This meant that they had come to stay and needed land for their settlements.[4]

Armenians and Georgians were encouraged to settle the Kuban area to cultivate crops and establish new industries. In 1839 Zass founded a special settlement for Armenians who had lived among the Adyges for several hundred years and were known as the Highland or Circassian Armenians. Linguistically and otherwise, they seemed to be completely assimilated into Adyge culture, except for retaining their traditional Armeno-Gregorian Christianity. Zass was able to engineer their exodus from the mountains and settle them in a small aul where the Urup River discharged into the Kuban. In 1848 this settlement was named Armavir, the name of the ancient Armenian capital, and it rapidly grew into a vibrant trade center.[5] In the meantime, fortification of the new frontier along the Laba proceeded apace. By 1841 four major Cossack settlements— Voznesenskaia, Labinskaia, Chamlykskaia, and Urupskaia—formed the Laba Cossack Regiment. In that same year General Zass decided that Semën Atarshchikov's talents could be better used on the new frontier. He therefore arranged his transfer to the Laba Line, where he would serve as translator for the commander of the Laba Cossack Regiment.

Atarshchikov's First Desertion

In October 1841, Major Igelstrom reported shocking news to General Zass: Lieutenant Semën Atarshchikov had deserted and fled to the mountains. General Zass and others who knew Atarshchikov only as a loyal and highly valuable officer must have met the news with disbelief. What might have triggered such a precipitous action? Or was it perhaps less precipitous than it seemed?

In the report that he submitted to his superiors upon returning to Russia four months later, Atarshchikov ascribed his rash action to tragic family circumstances. Before his transfer to the Laba Line, he had been given leave to visit his family and arrange for its resettlement to the Laba. His family resided in the Cossack village of Bekeshevskaia on the Kuma River in the verdant foothills of the Caucasus. It was one of the largest Cossack villages in the region, and its two thousand residents were a mix of Russian and Ukrainian Cossacks plus a number of Russian peasants. When Atarshchikov arrived home, he had found his despondent wife wailing over the dead bodies of their two children. Their sudden death was so overwhelming, he claimed, that his only desire had been to escape to any place where he would not be reminded of his children's cruel fate. It seemed that only a free life among his friends in the mountains could offer refuge from his unbearable emotional pain, and in this confused state of mind he had decided to flee. A day later he had reached the upper reaches of the Gups River, where his friend the Besleney prince Aitek Kanokov had taken refuge among the Barakay clan of the Abazas.

It is of course possible that grief over the death of his children did indeed prompt Atarshchikov to run away. Epidemics of plague, cholera, small-pox, and syphilis frequently swept through the region, decimating the native population in the southern parts of the Russian Empire. The first two decades of the nineteenth century had been particularly disastrous in the North Caucasus, where plague wiped out a great number of Kabardins, Karachays, and western Adyges. The most common epidemic was chol-era, caused by waterborne bacteria. On average, a cholera epidemic killed 20–25 percent of the stricken population: this was the case among the Kabardins in 1806–7 and 1834 and the Chechens in 1841, and these were only some of the better documented instances.[6] Atarshchikov's children could have died in one of these epidemics.

Nevertheless, his account of the circumstances leading to his desertion is not entirely convincing. While characterizing his desertion as an im-pulsive, spontaneous act, Atarshchikov at the same time apparently knew exactly where to find his old friend Aitek Kanokov, who only recently had deserted from Russian service. The two must have kept in touch, and there can be little doubt that before Atarshchikov's tragic family incident, Kanokov was urging his friend to join him in the mountains.

According to another account, Atarshchikov fled to the mountains along with two Circassian uzdens, the Abaza prince Seralip Loo, and two Cossacks from the Khoper Regiment. In his version of the story Atarshchikov main-tained that he fled only to find solitude and refused to take part in raids across the Russian frontier. However, others claimed that within a few days of his defection he led a party of forty horsemen in a raid on the Russian settlements near Kislovodsk.[7]

Atarshchikov and Kanokov were not the only ones to desert the Russian side at this time. In 1840–41 Russian troops suffered a series of pain-ful military defeats throughout the North Caucasus: by the Adyges on the Black Sea coast and by Shamil and his *naibs* (deputy commanders) in Chechnya and Daghestan. The rapid expansion of Shamil's Imamate—it grew threefold within a year—seemed unstoppable in the east, and the suc-cess of the Adyges' British-inspired resistance in the west put a big question mark over Russia's ability to control the region. Desperate to reinforce their defense fortifications, Russian commanders called for additional troops and dispatched alarming reports to their superiors.

In this atmosphere a number of local chiefs, of varying degree of impor-tance, chose to switch sides and join Shamil's ghazawat against Russia. The most renowned of them was the principal Avar noble and war hero Haji-Murat, who would be immortalized in Leo Tolstoy's classic tale of the same name.[8] In 1841, building on his success, Shamil dispatched his naib

Ahverdy Magoma to the Adyges in hopes of expanding the religious war against Russia and creating a united Imamate across the North Caucasus. When news of Shamil's successful resistance reached the peoples of the northwest Caucasus, many who had previously been classified as peaceful fled to the mountains and launched raids against Russia. Among them were the Barakay clan of the Abazas and the Besleney clan of the Adyges.

Atarshchikov's own fortune had always been closely linked with the plight of the indigenous population. In the past, Russian authorities had been suspicious of his close professional and personal ties to the highlanders. In 1832, while stationed in the northeast Caucasus, he had been accused of fraternizing with the Chechens. E. E. Lachinov, an exiled Decembrist and Russian officer, later recalled that even Semën Atarshchikov, who was then a noncommissioned officer in the Mozdok Cossack Regiment and the foremost expert on the Chechen affairs, had not avoided such charges. He had been subjected to the gauntlet, and only the fact that he had earlier earned the Mark of Distinction of the St. George Order saved him from more serious disciplinary measures.[9]

After his transfer to a new outpost on the Kuban River Atarshchikov had continued to maintain close ties with his old friends and associates. When he was named the superintendent of the Karachays, he requested that his old Chechen friend Mazay Bashaev become his deputy. In 1838, Atarshchikov had met the renowned Besleney prince Aitek Kanokov, who was then in Russia's service. The two became close friends, and Atarshchikov later admitted that Kanokov's defection had strongly influenced his own decision to flee.

Whatever the exact circumstances of his decision, one thing was now clear: the Russian officer Semën Atarshchikov was far less Russian than it had seemed. Like so many locals who for various reasons found themselves in Russian service, Atarshchikov lived in a complex psychological world of dual identities and conflicting loyalties. His intimate knowledge of the local languages and cultures and his friendship with many prominent highlanders prevented him from identifying solely with Russian interests. At the same time, his whole life and his long service in the Russian ranks had made him Russian enough to understand that the distance between him and his native friends could not easily be bridged.

Life on this bloody frontier with a dual identity was no doubt a tormenting experience. Almost a century later, T. E. Lawrence (of Arabia) articulated the pain such a dual existence could inflict: "[M]adness was very near, as I believe it would be near the man who could see things through the veils at once of two customs, two educations, two environments."[10]

Such multiple affinities and sympathies generated doubts and ambivalence that could easily become a constant, grating burden.

What might finally have prompted Atarshchikov to desert? Was it an accumulated stock of grievances and resentments? After all, at the age of thirty-four he was still a lieutenant, having last been promoted three years previously. Atarshchikov might have been comparing himself with his former commander at the Circassian Guards and prominent fellow officer Khan-Giray. Both were the same age, but Khan-Giray was already a colonel when Atarshchikov became a lieutenant. At the same time, his other comrade in the guards, Shora Nogma, occupied an important position as secretary of the Kabardin Provisional Court with the rank of captain. The careers of other natives, like that of the well-known Ossetian Musa Kundukh, also seemed to be on a faster track. Eleven years younger than Atarshchikov and with only four years of service, Kundukh had been promoted to the rank of captain in 1841.[11]

If he was searching for the kind of fame and glory that had eluded him thus far, Atarshchikov was not the first to look for it across the frontier. Many Russian servicemen had chosen to desert for various reasons: some were soldiers escaping the brutality of their superior officers, others were exiled Poles who chose to fight against Russia even when far from home, and some were romantic rebels looking for new opportunities and a better life elsewhere. Among the last group was the recent Cossack turncoat Baryshnikov, who had gained fame and the grudging respect of his former comrades for his shrewd tactics and damaging raids.[12] Was Atarshchikov emulating Baryshnikov or other successful runaways?

Was he competing with another Atarshchikov, who also served under Baron Zass in Chechnya and the Kuban? Born into the gentry in the Kuban region in 1814, Georgii Atarshchikov attended a private school until 1832, when he enlisted in the same regiment where Semën served. Both participated in the Chechen campaign in the summer of 1832, were transferred to the northwest Caucasus, and were promoted to lieutenant at about the same time. Was Semën resentful that he and Georgii, who was seven years younger and had considerably fewer years of military service, were marching in lockstep along the same career path? Georgii Atarshchikov would make a different choice and would be rewarded for his loyal service by promotion to the rank of colonel in 1859.[13]

Did Semën feel slighted and unappreciated by his superiors? Indeed, it seems that his long service in the Caucasus had attracted little recognition from the authorities. In 1831, within one year of the Polish campaign, he had received two Marks of Distinction—those of the St. George Order and

Russian general and Ottoman pasha Musa Kundukh (1818–1889) in the Ottoman uniform and with Ottoman and Russian decorations. In Russian Ethnography Museum, St. Petersburg, from B. A. Kaloev, Osetiny. Moscow: Nauka, 2004.

the Polish Order fifth degree. In the summer of 1832, after his return to the Caucasus, Atarshchikov had again distinguished himself in the Chechen campaign and earned imperial praise. Thereafter, his formal military record, which had mentioned Atarshchikov's engagements in great detail, suddenly fell silent for over five years.

In 1839 he was awarded the Order of St. Stanislav third degree for his role in the Russian expedition to explore the Svaneti lands. Whereas the expedition's members received monetary rewards, only Atarshchikov was presented with the Order of St. Stanislav—the lowest in the hierarchy of Russian orders. He received no cash payment, and his annual salary remained unchanged—316 rubles, 30 kopecks.[14] Was he quietly resentful of Pozdyshev, who was awarded 150 silver rubles for his role as the leader of the expedition, despite the fact that Atarshchikov and his two assistants had made the entire project possible?

There are also indications that Atarshchikov's loyalty may have been adversely affected by the extraordinary brutality exhibited by Russian troops and their commanders. During 1825–26, Atarshchikov took part in some of the fiercest fighting in Chechnya: the bloody battle near the aul of Gerzel, the destruction of Chakhkeri, the massacre at Kurchali, the storming of Great Atagi, the burning of Belokai, and the complete destruction of Urus Martan. He obviously acquitted himself well, for in 1827 he was promoted to a noncommissioned officer. For the next three years, however, before his departure for St. Petersburg in 1830, his name is no longer mentioned in any of the documents related to the fighting in the region.

After his return from Poland in the summer of 1832, Atarshchikov again was thrown into the thick of Russian campaigns and reprisals against the resurgent Chechens under Ghazi Muhammad. At the time Russian commanders were concerned that the anti-Russian sentiment emerging across the Caucasus could threaten the vital link to Transcaucasia, the Georgian Military Highway. To prevent any further conflagration in the region, the Russians moved to squash the uprising led by Ghazi Muhammad and his followers. The result was another campaign of odious violence and atrocities. Auls were burned to the ground, women raped, children and the elderly bayoneted, and the survivors taken to Russia to be sold. Assigned to the Mozdok Cossack Regiment under Colonel Zass, Atarshchikov witnessed horrible scenes of destruction perpetrated by his regiment and the rest of the Russian army. In only six days during late July 1832 Russian troops laid waste to eight auls. During four days of August, the inhabitants of Chenar, Engel, and Germenchug auls were massacred and their houses burned. The latter was a particularly large and rich settlement of over six hundred houses.[15]

Yet again, for the three years leading up to his appointment as the Karachay superintendent in 1836, Atarshchikov's military record is a blank spot. Was it a coincidence that the short bouts of active military service were followed by a much longer period of silence? Is it possible that the brutality of the Russian campaigns against the native population so repulsed him that the Russian authorities came to suspect him of sympathy for Russia's adversaries? This would have explained why after 1832 Atarshchikov was no longer found in the battlefields of Chechnya and was eventually transferred away from the region where his linguistic and ethnic ties were the strongest.

Late in 1835 Atarshchikov would make one last appearance in Chechnya. The relative calm in the summer of that year was broken by renewed military activity in the plains of Chechnya and Daghestan, where Haji Tashav (Tashov-Haji, Haji Tashav al-Indiri), a Kumyk from the town of Enderi, organized a large group of insurgents. A respected and ambitious leader, Haji Tashav represented a direct challenge to Shamil, and his initially successful military operations gave him further credence in his bid to become the imam, the leader of the Islamic state in the Caucasus. In time, Shamil and Haji Tashav would reconcile, the latter becoming one of Shamil's most influential naibs. For now, however, Haji Tashav's threat to Russian control of the region provoked a punitive expedition headed by the notoriously brutal commander of the Sunzha River Fortification Line, Colonel A. P. Pullo. Soon to be promoted to the rank of major general, Pullo was to the northeast Caucasus what General Zass was to the northwest. Contemporary Russian officers described him as a figure deeply hated by Chechens for his "extreme cruelty, indiscriminate means, and frequent injustices." In addition, he had a reputation for shameless rapacity, which, in the view of his contemporaries, led to the large Chechen uprising in 1840. It was only then that General Pullo was removed from the command of the Sunzha Line.[16]

In the summer of 1835, Atarshchikov found himself in the expeditionary force that set out from Fort Grozny under Colonel Pullo's command. Given the nature of the campaign against insurgent Kumyks and Chechens, Atarshchikov's presence must have been indispensable. There are no details of his specific activity at this time, but as a translator he was no doubt intimately involved in Russia's efforts to blunt Haji Tashav's appeal among the local population. He was mentioned as a participant in the punitive expedition against Haji Tashav and his followers in late December 1835.[17]

If the ruthless punitive expeditions of General Ermolov and his followers were the hallmark of Russian military activity in Chechnya and Daghestan, they were also a typical modus operandi in the northwest

Caucasus. As a frequent participant in General Zass's raids against local auls, Atarshchikov continued to bear witness to Russian atrocities. When in early 1841 Zass had turned his energies to the creation of the Laba Fortification Line, the residents of auls on the Laba River were deported to make room for Cossack forts. These were the actions that pushed Atarshchikov's close friend, Aitek Kanokov, to abandon his pro-Russian stance and flee to the mountains.

It was at this time in October 1841, when he was about to be transferred to the Laba Line, that Lieutenant Atarshchikov decided to change his life forever. The sudden death of his two children and the recent flight of his friend Kanokov were the last in a series of factors that prompted his action. The surviving evidence does not allow us to weigh the relative importance of his accumulated grievances against Russian policies, his guilt over participating in Russian atrocities, his unfulfilled career expectations, and his search for personal renewal. For whatever reason, Semën Atarshchikov resolved to flee to the mountains, shedding his previous identity of Russian officer and reinventing himself as native son. As he was to find out, such a switch was not a simple matter.

Among the Highlanders, 1841

On October 17, 1841, instead of assuming his new duties as a translator for the commander of the Laba Fortification Line, Atarshchikov deserted and joined Aitek Kanokov. In his own account, Atarshchikov described how he reached Kanokov on the Gups River within one day, which would have involved traversing over 60 miles and crossing several rivers. Kanokov had found refuge among the Barakays, who resided there in three auls with about 1,200 inhabitants. His choice of settling there was no accident: the Barakays traditionally paid tribute to their Besleney neighbors in the northeast, the two princely families of the Kanokovs and Sholokhovs.[18]

Kanokov and his followers greeted Atarshchikov enthusiastically. After all, Atarshchikov was not only a friend but also a Russian officer with an intimate knowledge of local topography and of Russia's military tactics, administrative structures, and vulnerabilities—in short, he was in command of information indispensable for raiding parties. For the time being, Atarshchikov settled in Kanokov's guesthouse and, as his respected guest (*konak*), enjoyed the full protection of the prince. Kanokov's residence stood on the outskirts of the aul in a group of houses built for him and his retinue. The guesthouse where Atarshchikov stayed was a simple dwelling.

Wooden nails for hanging weapons and horse gear dotted the walls. There were a mattress made out of reeds, several woolen pillows, a goatskin for the daily prayers, and a copper ewer for ablutions. The house also sported a few valuable items that betrayed the wealth of the host: a handsome carpet, silver utensils, and musical instruments hung on the walls.

Like other highlanders, the Barakays led an austere life. The thirty-five houses of Kanokov's aul were scattered over a large distance along the Gups' steep bank. The auls were usually built in clusters of houses belonging to one extended family or a larger clan, with additional walls often built around the clan quarter. The houses were poor, with reed roofs and walls built out of straw and clay. The rear of each house was almost attached to the dense forest. With the natural surroundings providing a formidable defense, the aul appeared virtually impregnable.

The inhabitants' main occupation was animal husbandry—cows and horses—and beekeeping, and like many of their neighbors, the Barakays relied heavily on trade to procure two critical items—cereals and salt. The Russian government made a consistent effort to dominate trade with the locals by establishing a series of bartering markets near the forts and settlements at Naurskaia, Prochnyi Okop, Ust-Labinsk, and others. The marketplaces were usually outside the fort's walls and were strictly regulated. The locals were allowed to exchange their animal products, wax, honey, and locally manufactured clothing for salt, grains, and Russian-made household items. Russia's growing control over the region meant that salt, the most critical trade item—which the locals had previously obtained inexpensively from the salt lakes in the region now known as Stavropol—was now a heavily taxed government monopoly.

In addition to strictly controlling the items bartered, the Russian government severely restricted the natives' access to markets. In the early 1800s it had introduced quarantine stations, where a party of natives could be forced to wait for up to forty days until they and their merchandise were deemed safe to proceed to Russian towns. The ostensible purpose of these stations was to prevent the spread of contagious diseases, but the authorities also used them to collect custom duties and as an excuse to delay traders and their merchandise. Together with the forts and other military fortifications, quarantine stations formed a Russian cordon sanitaire in the Caucasus.[19]

No matter how effective the cordon sanitaire might have been in regulating commercial, economic, and political activity, it could not stop raids across the frontier. As always, raiding activity served a mix of social, political, and economic purposes. As pressure from Russian restrictions increased, so did the importance of raids intended to supplement the highlanders' already strained economic circumstances. In the south, the Russian blockade of the Black Sea coast was increasingly effective in cutting them off from traditional Ottoman merchandise (textiles, silks, tobacco, and gunpowder), while in the north, the Russian cordon sanitaire advanced relentlessly toward their last refuge in the mountains. Not surprisingly, raiding activity along the frontier intensified markedly in the 1830–40s.

The success of raiding activity depended on several factors: good intelligence, expedient communication between auls, the speedy assembly of raiders, and above all the prestige and reputation of the leader. Aitek Kanokov was one such leader, revered by highlanders and feared by Russians. When Aitek's envoys arrived at neighboring auls to suggest a gathering place for launching a raid, there was no shortage of volunteers. A raiding party typically was a collaborative enterprise, and Aitek's horsemen came from the Barakay, Besleney, Kabardin, and Abadzekh auls. The bellicose Abadzekhs were the region's indigenous Adyge residents who formed the backbone of the raiding parties.

In his version of events, Atarshchikov claimed that on numerous occasions he had been urged to participate in raids across the frontier but that each time he had refused, asserting his status as a konak of Aitek Kanokov. Coming to the slow realization that he had made a terrible mistake, Atarshchikov resolved to flee back to Russia. It was then that he approached Kanokov, trying to convince him to return and seek an imperial pardon. Aitek was not amused and began to suspect that Atarshchikov was a provocateur sent by the Russians. Their friendship was over.

Hoping to redeem himself in the eyes of the Russian authorities, Atarshchikov tried to organize the escape of Russian deserters who lived in the mountains as destitute vagabonds. Kanokov's suspicion of his intentions grew when he again refused to take part in a large raid aimed at the Black Sea Cossacks along the lower Kuban. When waiting any longer became dangerous, Atarshchikov and a fugitive Cossack, Vasilii Fenev, rode away on the night of January 30, 1842, reaching Fort Makhoshev shortly before dawn.

Given the inconsistencies in earlier parts of Atarshchikov's account, it is hard to take his version of the events at face value. It is clear that he and Kanokov had significant disagreements. Perhaps Atarshchikov's initial hope of assuming a prominent role among the highlanders quickly soured when he realized that he could not step out from the long shadow cast by his friend. But were thwarted ambitions worth the risk of returning to his previous life and submitting himself to the mercy of Russian authorities? It certainly seemed so in the late January 1842 when Atarshchikov left the mountains to seek a pardon from his superior officers.

Obtaining a pardon from his immediate military commanders proved to be easier than convincing imperial authorities in St. Petersburg to grant him one. The escape and return of a decorated Russian lieutenant and former member of the Circassian Guard was unusual enough to attract attention at even the highest levels. Month after month, reports and recommendations were sent up and down the chain of command until the Atarshchikov case reached the desk of Nicholas I.

Did the emperor remember one of the Circassian Guards who exactly a decade before had ridden with his comrades into the capital after the Polish campaign? After all, as the interpreter, Atarshchikov must have been present whenever the emperor wished to communicate with some of the guards. Or was it the personal and passionate intervention of General Zass that saved Atarshchikov from court-martial? In his forceful request for Atarshchikov's pardon, Zass stated that during the ten years that Semën Atarshchikov was under his command, he had always performed his duties admirably and with great dedication. To dispel any further doubt, Zass gave personal assurances of Atarshchikov's future loyalty.[20]

But this Russian emperor was not easily swayed by assurances of loyalty, even if they came from his most zealous general. The ever-cautious and suspicious Nicholas I found a suitable compromise. Atarshchikov was to be pardoned but transferred to join the Don Cossack Regiment stationed in Finland. An imperial pardon looked very much like an internal exile.[21]

10

From Semën Atarshchikov to Hajret Muhammed

Among the Highlanders, 1842–43

In November 1842 Semën Atarshchikov received his final orders to depart for Finland. He collected his travel money—a large sum needed for the long journey—and then, to everyone's great surprise, deserted once again. He must have fully realized the consequences of his decision: there would be no second pardon from St. Petersburg and no return this time. The die was cast. Semën Atarshchikov had resolved to end his life as a military officer and Christian subject of the Russian emperor and create a new life for himself among the highlanders.

Atarshchikov's decision to desert took place in the context of the turbulent developments in the region. The war in the Caucasus was at its most intense, and its outcome was far from certain. Russian troops were sustaining heavy losses in incessant raids and ambushes by Shamil and his new ally, Haji-Murat, whose defection in 1841 had dealt a heavy blow to Russian interests in northern Daghestan. By December 1841 the Russian commander in the northeast Caucasus, General Klugenau, had all but abandoned any attempt to control the region and absolved himself of any responsibility for future failures.[1]

The nearly simultaneous success of the Adyges against Russian troops and garrisons in the northwest convinced Shamil that the time was right to extend the Imamate. In March 1841 Russian spies in Chechnya reported that Shamil had dispatched his loyalist, the Chechen Muhammed Kireev, to the Adyges. Together with ten other people, Kireev was expected to travel through the Karachay lands, where Semën Atarshchikov was then completing his duties as superintendent.[2]

The Russian government was further alarmed the next year when it became known that Shamil had sent his naibs to spread the call for ghazawat among the Kabardins and the western Adyges. The imam's success among the Kabardins would have endangered the only land communication between Russia and Georgia, the Georgian Military Highway. Luckily for the Russians, Shamil's mission failed, reportedly because the Kabardins rebelled against the imposition of an Islamic tax. A different reaction was observed among western Adyges, where Russian commanders reported a noticeable rise in religious fervor and hostility. The most aggressive and numerous people among the Adyges were the Abadzekhs.[3]

It was among Abadzekhs that Semën Atarshchikov chose to settle on his second and final desertion in November 1842. Located west of the neighboring Barakays, where Aitek Kanokov had taken refuge, the Abadzekhs were a powerful Adyge people living in the safety of the mountains and dense forests in the upper reaches of the Laba, Belaia, Kurjips, and several smaller rivers. In 1835 they reportedly numbered 160,000. Atarshchikov settled in the aul on the Kurjips River, where he joined a group of Kabardin and Nogay fugitives.

Here in the high mountains the Abadzekhs welcomed thousands of Kabardins, Besleneys, Nogays, and others who had fled the lands that had been colonized and settled by Russians. The local people referred to such fugitives as *hajrets*, that is, warriors committed to raiding the Russian frontier.[4] In fact, Atarshchikov adopted the term as part of his new name: the former Russian officer Semën Atarshchikov became the highlander Hajret Muhammed.

The decision to take a Muslim name no doubt was part of Atarshchikov's official conversion to Islam. The process of conversion was fairly simple and was limited to the required recitation of the appropriate lines from the Quran. Yet even conversion to Islam could not immediately change his status as an outsider so long as he continued to reside as a konak in the Abadzekh aul. Atarshchikov (we shall continue to use his old name) seems to have realized that to become fully accepted among the locals required more than becoming a Muslim.

He may have concluded this earlier after a short stay with his old friend Aitek Kanokov. Or perhaps he began to realize it after observing the clashes between Shamil's Chechen naib, Haji-Muhammed, and the Abadzekh chiefs. Haji-Muhammed had arrived in May 1842 but was expelled two years later for his attempts to impose sharia among the Abadzekhs.[5]

To complete his transformation, Atarshchikov understood that he had to build new family ties, to plant local roots, as it were. To do so, he chose to marry a daughter of the influential Besleney uzden Misost Enarukov

(Unarukov), another hajret, who had settled among the Abadzekhs some time earlier.[6]

The father and the groom quickly agreed, but there was one problem—the groom was expected to pay the *kalym,* or bride money. Even though the parties often agreed that kalym would ·be paid in several installments, the kalym for a young daughter of a notable commanded no small amount. Traditionally paid in valuable arms such as armor, swords, and muskets, by the nineteenth century the kalym was usually paid in cattle and horses and increasingly in cash. In addition to the kalym, the groom was expected to offer presents—usually horses or oxen—to the bride's father or brother and to the qadi who officiated at the marriage. A recent fugitive, Semën Atarshchikov had little property to offer, and marriage without a kalym would bring dishonor to the bride's father and even more to the groom.[7]

As always, raiding was the best and quickest way to accumulate property. It was also the best way to prove himself to his new and like-minded compatriots. As the first snow began to melt away in the early spring, Atarshchikov began preparations for raids across the frontier. Given his intimate knowledge of Russian frontier defenses, we can easily imagine that he had little difficulty convincing others to join him.

Even as Atarschchikov prepared to lead the Abadzekhs in raids across the frontier, another Abadzekh notable, Omar Bersei, was fighting on the Russian side against his former compatriots. The two had never met, yet in a way Bersei became Atarshchikov's doppelgänger. In February 1843 he was appointed to a position that Atarshchikov had once occupied: translator at the headquarters of the commander of the northwest Caucasus.

Bersei's was another typical frontier story of easily changed loyalties, lifestyles, religions, and identities. Little is known about his early life except that as a child he was sold into slavery, was raised in Egypt, and lived in Paris before arriving in Russia to become a Russian subject in 1842. Fluent in Arabic, Turkish, French, and Russian, Bersei served his new suzerain with distinction both in the staff headquarters and in numerous skirmishes with highlanders.[8]

In the end, Bersei's path proved quite different from Atarshchikov's. In 1850 he was appointed instructor of the Adyge language at the Stavropol gymnasium, which produced the next generation of Russified indigenous elite. Bersei became one of the first Adyge linguists and writers. In the early 1850s he composed the Adyge grammar and alphabet based on the Arabic script, but a decade later, under pressure from the Russian linguist Baron P. K. Uslar, he compiled an Adyge-Russian dictionary and used Russian orthography for Adyge and Kabardin alphabets.[9]

The Russian Deserters

The year 1843 was the low point in the Russian conquest of the North Caucasus. The Russians suffered heavy losses in the northeast of the region, and the local population joined Shamil in increasing numbers. In a display of the sentiment that prevailed among their peoples, a group of Daghestani mullahs wrote to Russian authorities demanding the withdrawal of troops and charging the authorities with lying, destroying their auls, burning property, and seizing notables. The mullahs chose a curious way of expressing their determination to resist the Russian authorities, declaring that they had sworn on the Quran, Bible, Gospels, and catechism to fight the Russians in the name of God.[10]

In the spring of 1843 the Russian positions in the northwest Caucasus had also come under increasing siege. By the end of March, Russian informers warned that ten thousand highlanders—the number was no doubt exaggerated—had gathered in the woods in the upper reaches of the Belaia River and were ready to attack the Laba Fortification Line. In the following months, numerous large raiding parties attacked the Russian fortifications.[11]

On March 23, 1843, Atarshchikov, along with a group of highlanders, approached a Russian outpost, Zhitomirskii. When a group of Cossacks rode out of the fort to confront them, the highlanders quickly vanished into the woods, leaving behind a letter written by Atarshchikov and addressed to the Cossacks. It was an appeal to defect and join him in the mountains.

The letter quickly found its way to the top military commanders, where it provoked a serious concern. In his secret report to War Minister Chernyshev, the commander of the Caucasus Corps, General G. A. Neidgardt, described the circumstances surrounding the letter and assured the minister that he had taken appropriate measures to prevent letters of this sort from reaching the army's lower ranks. A copy of the letter was submitted with the report and read as follows:

> I, Lieutenant Atarshchikov, am now recognized by the Abadzekhs as their first uzden, and they follow my counsel. I invite you, brother-servicemen, whoever wishes, to come and join me. I have secured the right of freedom for all; when [you] cross the Laba and call yourself my guest, no one will detain you. Here is how you can find me: tell anyone that you are a guest of Hajret Muhammed, a Russian officer, and like Hajret, you are on your way to join him on the Kurjips River; no one can detain you [then], for anyone who detains my guest is liable for a penalty of fifteen cows. I invite carpenters, smiths, soldiers with rifles and gunpowder, drummers with drums,

members of the music band; [you] will be recognized as a master like me, [and] whoever brings money [may] keep it as his property, no one can take it away from him. If one wishes, he can leave for Turkey, and from there anywhere else abroad, in short, I will accept everyone: whether Pole, German, or Russian, do not fear for your earned money, hide it before you cross the Laba. I am saying this so that no one can rob you on the way here. Women here are pretty. I ask you to inform others about my letter—good-bye! Hajret Muhammed. Waiting for you.

It does not hurt to bring something for your new residence. I am writing this on the march, sorry.[12]

Atarshchikov's appeal to his former compatriots was a revealing document. Here was a plain, unpretentious letter intended for low-ranking military personnel who could pass the information to the illiterate soldiers and Cossacks. As a model Atarshchikov offered his own successful rise to influence among the Abadzekhs. He understood well the two major aspirations of any potential defector: the search for personal freedom and material well-being. He guaranteed both. He was offering them protection not as a Russian officer but as a local notable. All they had to do was cross the frontier at the Laba, at which point they would cease to be Russian soldiers and become his konaks, his inviolate guests and protected friends. To banished foreigners like the Poles, exiled after the 1830 uprising, he promised an opportunity to start a new life beyond Russia. To others he offered a vision of marriage and a new household. In short, any deserter was welcome.

Desertions, always a serious problem in the Russian military, had become a particularly critical issue in the early 1840s. The locals' military successes and the corresponding low morale of the tsar's army produced a steadily increasing number of Russian captives and deserters. The everyday brutality of life in the Russian military—twenty-five years of compulsory service, routine abuses, cruel drills, hard labor, privation, and corporal punishment—caused hundreds of Cossacks and soldiers to flee across the frontier. No wonder the Russian authorities consistently tried to negotiate the return of Russian prisoners and captives through either categorical demands or offers of ransom.[13]

The deserters came from different social, ethnic, and religious backgrounds. By far the largest group was the Poles, whose annual quota of recruits and thousands of political exiles were routinely sent to serve in the Caucasus. Others included Kazan Tatars, Ukrainians, Cossack Old Believers, and, like Atarshchikov, first-generation Russians with indigenous roots across the frontier. In the late 1850s Colonel Teofil Lapinskii, who led a contingent of Polish volunteers to help the Adyges in their war

Копія съ письма бѣглаго Сотника Атарщикова.

Я Сотникъ Атарщиковъ, нынѣ признанъ Абадзехами за первостепеннаго ихъ Узденя и слѣдуютъ моему совѣту. Приглашаю братцы служивые кому угодно ко мнѣ идите.— Я для всѣхъ выстаралъ право вольности; за Лабу какъ перейдетъ и назоветса моимъ гостемъ, никто не смѣетъ удержать.— Меня вотъ какъ искать: скажи я гость Хаджерета Магомета Русскаго офицера, и самъ какъ Хаджеретъ дискать иду къ нему на Курчупсъ рѣчку, никто не смѣетъ задержать, ибо кто задержитъ моего гостя подвергнетса штрафу 15 коровъ.— Приглашаю плотниковъ, Кузнецовъ, солдатъ съ ружьями и порохомъ, барабанщиковъ, кто съ барабаномъ, музыкантовъ, господинъ будетъ признанъ какъ и я; кто деньги принесетъ это его собственность, никто не смѣетъ отнять.— Кто хочетъ можетъ ѣхать въ Турцію а оттоль куда угодно за границу, словомъ всѣхъ приму: Полякъ ли, Нѣмецъ ли, Русской ли, съ своими, казенными, барскими деньгами неопасайсь, деньги

The letter written in 1843 by Semën Atarshchikov calling on Russian soldiers to desert and join him in the mountains. From *Rossiiskii Gosudarstvennyi Voenno-Istoricheskii Arkhiv* F. 38, op. 7, d. 93, l. 1.

against Russia, estimated that at the time there were no fewer than four thousand Russian deserters in the northwest Caucasus.[14]

Desertions were not a new problem. Throughout the 1820s and 1830s the numerous desertions in the northeast Caucasus resulted in the formation of a special Russian battalion within the Persian army. In 1837 Nicholas I demanded that the Persians disband the 800-strong battalion and return the runaways. In December 1838, 597 men, 206 women, and 281 children were sent back to Russia. Their Persian titles and Russian names said it all: e.g., naib Naumov, sultan Stepanov, beg-zade Lisetskii, and vekil-bashi Ikonnikov.[15]

Yet many would-be deserters were deterred by the fate of their fellow soldiers across the frontier. Such was the case with the mass desertion of Polish exiles during the 1834 Kuban campaign. When it became known that instead of finding liberty among the Shapsugs, they had been mistreated and turned into servants, the number of such desertions declined sharply.

The plight of the Russian deserters attracted attention on both sides. In 1841 Shamil declared that they were to be freed, given land, and allowed to settle down. The commander of the Northeast Caucasus Line, Major General Ol'shevskii, expressed grave concern to his superiors that the news of freedom among the highlanders would encourage more desertions. To deter them he proposed shooting any deserters who were captured.[16]

From the Russian standpoint, the desertions were more than a breakdown in discipline or a mere embarrassment to the Russian military. In addition to an intimate knowledge of Russian frontier defenses, the deserters threatened to level the playing field by instructing the highlanders in the uses of artillery, which offered Russia its most critical military advantage in the Caucasus war. Indeed, some of Shamil's most spectacular victories in the early 1840s would hardly have been possible without the use of captured Russian cannons and personnel. Former Russian prisoners reported that at Dargo alone, Shamil's main residence at the time, they had observed no fewer than five hundred Russian deserters, among whom many were converts to Islam. Some of them served as his personal guard; others serviced his artillery. Shamil's own house was reportedly turned into a small factory where the Russians manufactured cannon balls and shrapnel.[17]

The Russian authorities tried to deal with desertions in different ways. Those soldiers deemed unreliable were kept under a particularly close watch. Local Russian officials were instructed to demand the return of deserters hiding in auls presumed to be at peace with Russia. In exchange for surrendering the deserters, the officials were authorized to offer salt but no cash payments. The most comprehensive way of dealing with the issue was

Cannon captured from Russians during Shamil's War

initiated by the supreme commander in the Caucasus, General Mikhail Vorontsov. In March 1845, two months after his appointment, Vorontsov issued a broad amnesty to all Russian military deserters except for those charged with committing murder or abandoning their watch.[18]

Raiding the Home Village

Given the overall situation in the region and the growing rate of desertions, it is not surprising that the Atarshchikov affair caused significant apprehension among the highest echelons of the Russian military. This was a Russian officer with an intimate knowledge of local topography, languages, Russian military tactics, artillery, and weaknesses in defenses and with an extensive personal network among key highland leaders. His second escape and conversion to Islam ruled out any possibility of return, and his appeal to his fellow soldiers pointed to the advent of an energetic and dangerous foe.

It was not long before the worst fears of the Russian authorities were realized. In late April 1843 a large highlander contingent approached the Laba Fortification Line. Relying on an extensive network of informers, Nogay scouts, and Cossack secret watches, Russian commanders had a good general idea of the impending campaign. But because the highlanders' traditional tactics favored surprise and speed, it was all but impossible to anticipate their movements.

Given the length of the frontier, Russia's insufficient manpower in the region, and the lightning speed of the raids, the commanders' strategic options were limited. Traditional military countermeasures included spreading the available troops across the frontier, sending reinforcements to possible raiding targets, observing the movements of the raiding parties, and promptly moving the reserves to a trouble spot. Once the raiding party was located, special cavalry with mobile light artillery was dispatched to confront the raiders in a pitched battle. Yet most of the time, aware of their great disadvantage against the Russian artillery, the highlanders preferred to melt into the countryside and avoid open battle. In short, the Russians faced classic guerrilla warfare along the frontier.

On April 26 the highlander army split into several raiding parties, crossed the Laba Line, and moved in different directions. Some parties attacked several Russian forts but were beaten back. On May 2 scouts reported that a large group of highlanders had left camp on the Greater Zelenchuk River, crossed the Kuban, and was rapidly approaching the Cossack village of Bekeshevskaia. The raiders' strategy suddenly became apparent. While other raiding parties deployed to draw away Russian troops, their main three thousand-man force would move toward Bekeshevskaia in a daring campaign deep across the Russian frontier.

There is little doubt that Atarshchikov instigated the assault on Bekeshevskaia, a large and prosperous Cossack village with half a dozen merchant stores and a population of over two thousand Cossacks and state-owned peasants. For Atarshchikov the village was much more than a source of rich booty. This was a place of personal memories, where his family had stayed for several years before his children died and where they lay buried at a local cemetery. Bekeshevskaia stood as a symbol of Atarshchikov's tormented life—a past that had to be purged and a present that needed to be affirmed.

Like those of other Cossack villages along the frontier, Bekeshevskaia's fortifications consisted of a moat, a fence with watchtowers, and a cannon. For the raid to succeed, the war party had to overwhelm the village defenses rapidly. There was no time for a protracted siege because Russian reinforcements could be expected to arrive soon. With musket fire and shrapnel, the defenders were able to repel the first assault. After several hours of fighting, the highlanders surrounded the village and attempted to force their way through the Kumyk and Suvorov Gates, which faced northeast. The situation became serious, and without outside help the defenders had no chance of repulsing the overwhelming numbers of highlanders. A detachment of four hundred Cossacks from Batalpashinsk rushed toward Bekeshevskaia but was quickly surrounded and suffered heavy casualties. The tide turned only with the arrival of five hundred more Cossacks and a company of regular cavalry with two cannons, led by Lieutenant Colonel L'vov, commander of the Kislovodsk Line.

Fearful of being surrounded and cut off from the mountains, the raiding party began to retreat toward the Kuma River, thereby allowing the Russian reinforcements to join forces and press harder against it. When the Nogay cavalry arrived to join other Russian units, the orderly retreat became a rout. So desperate was their flight that in violation of custom they fled without collecting their comrades' bodies. With dusk the fleeing highlanders found refuge in the snow-capped mountains of the Upper Kuma River, and the Russian detachment sent in pursuit returned empty-handed. The highlanders were later reported to have crossed the Kuban River into the Karachay lands and dispersed in different directions.[19]

The large raiding campaign of late April and early May thus ended in failure. The Russians suffered minor damage to their forts and villages and lost two dozen men killed and wounded. The highlanders failed to capture any forts or villages and lost nearly two hundred men at Bekeshevskaia.

The War of Attrition

The debacle at Bekeshevskaia placed the changing nature of Caucasus warfare into high relief. Through an effective network of informers, denser frontier settlement, and improved coordination between various frontier units, the Russians were able to neutralize the highlanders' traditional advantages of surprise and speed. In contrast, the highlanders' tactics remained unchanged. Their frontal assaults were ineffective against cannon shrapnel and concentrated musket fire. Their cavalry force remained a collection of local militias in search of booty and led by independent leaders more often competing than collaborating with one another.

The outcome of the Bekeshevskaia raid and many before and after that was yet further proof that local militias with different agendas and rival leaders stood no chance against the Russian military. Only by transforming the militias into a regular standing army under central command, one motivated by something beyond the promise of booty, could one hope to organize a more effective resistance to Russian expansion.

No one understood this better than Shamil. It was the creation of the Imamate with a unified military command, central administration, and uniform law that had allowed him to achieve a measure of military success and turned the Russian conquest into a long-drawn-out war. That is why in May 1842 Shamil had dispatched his naib, Haji-Muhammed, to the Adyges in what became an unsuccessful attempt to extend the Imamate to the northwest Caucasus.

By May 1843, two weeks after the rout at Bekeshevskaia, Atarshchikov was safely back at his new residence on the Kurjips River. The early spring raiding campaign, an ambitious undertaking that involved large numbers of highlanders and a high-profile target, was over, but the results were not encouraging. Despite Atarshchikov's inside knowledge of the Russian frontier, the raiders had not succeeded in capturing a single Russian settlement or seizing any appreciable booty. The initial hopes pinned on this high-profile Russian deserter had been dashed.

Atarshchikov, too, was disappointed. The military weaknesses of the highlanders and their raiding parties were all too apparent to a Russian officer used to more disciplined and better-coordinated military actions. If they had failed to capitalize on his intimate knowledge of Bekeshevskaia, how could they succeed elsewhere? The fragmentary nature of local societies and war parties consisting of local militias were to blame, but changing these circumstances was virtually impossible, as the British had found out throughout the 1830s and Shamil's naibs were to learn in the 1840s and '50s.

While the Russians could boast of some success in the northwest Caucasus, the situation continued to deteriorate in the northeast. Antagonized by Russia's destructive war and its fire-and-sword approach, more native peoples chose to join Shamil. The ulema and leaders of Chechen, Avar, and various other Daghestani communities demanded withdrawal of the Russian troops from Daghestan. They warned that they had joined Shamil and taken an oath to resist the Russians to the end.[20]

In the last months of 1842, Nicholas I, alarmed by the course of the war, decided once again to replace his top commanders in the region— I. A. Golovin, P. Kh. Grabbe, and G. Kh. Zass. In hope of achieving a decisive turnaround, he also dispatched additional troops to the northeast Caucasus, two divisions, or twenty-four battalions, with thirty-two guns—"a force one could not dream of seeing in the Caucasus." Those who resisted were to be annihilated, those who surrendered, spared. Anxious that Russia's war not be seen as a religious conflict, Nicholas instructed his commanders to show particular respect toward mullahs, mosques, and the Muslim faith, while at the same time buying off the influential local leaders. The dispatched troops were to provide a temporary surge—crushing Shamil and his followers and returning home within a year. As in so many other cases, this proved to be wishful thinking.[21]

Raiding was a way of life, not a calculus of success and failure, and forays across the Russian frontier continued unabated. In July 1843 the combined forces of several Adyge peoples made another attempt to attack the forts and settlements along the Laba, but their plans were thwarted by speedily dispatched Russian reinforcements. A year later the Adyges were reported to have assembled an army of over ten thousand men. When the Russians sent a large force of their own to block the crossing at the Laba River, the Adyges were forced to change their raiding targets, move away, and cross the river elsewhere. Once again the Russians arrived on time to prevent the highlanders from crossing. This cat-and-mouse game was repeated several more times until the Adyge army turned back, unable to approach its targets.

Over time, frontier encounters across the northwest Caucasus settled into a familiar pattern. As the Russian defenses continued to improve—more garrisons, better intelligence, and improved tactics—the large highlander armies, which were usually no match for the regular Russian forces, began to lose their critical advantage, the element of surprise. The only effective raids were now conducted by small war parties ranging from several dozen to several hundred horsemen.

Indeed, small raids against the Cossack villages continued, fetching cattle, horses, and occasional captives. To prevent these raids and avenge the losses, the Russian military commanders adopted the mirror tactics of the locals—they conducted their own raids deep across the frontier. For this purpose, the Russians formed rapid-reaction expeditionary forces that could be assembled with speed and secrecy to cross the frontier and approach the auls under cover of darkness. Unless the residents were warned on time or had a chance to flee into the forest, their fate was always the same: women and children would be taken captives, men slaughtered, houses burned, and auls razed to the ground. Such raids and counterraids made low-intensity, guerrilla war an endemic frontier experience.[22]

In 1842, authorities in the capital decided that the punitive raids were becoming counterproductive given the long marches that exhausted the troops and the unavoidable violence and looting that further antagonized the local population. Instead, commanders were directed to rely on better intelligence and frontier monitoring, improved discipline among the troops, beefed-up infantry reserves in the rear, and more Cossack cavalry on the front line.

The emperor recognized that Russian raiding activity was achieving what Shamil could not—uniting the disparate native chiefs in a common cause against Russia. Yet the new approach made exceptions for preemptive raids against highlanders ready to cross the frontier. Since there was never a shortage of war parties ready to launch another raid, local Russian commanders could always find a convenient excuse for their own raids and expeditions inside native territory. Despite the emperor's order forbidding punitive expeditions against the auls and their residents, raiding activity continued on both sides.[23]

The Death of Semën Atarshchikov

Throughout the 1840s the balance sheet of raiding activity turned decidedly in Russia's favor. While Russians systematically laid waste to the indigenous auls, the natives could rarely break through the defenses of Cossack villages or forts. Skirmishes resulted in a casualty rate far greater among locals than among Russians. A typical Russian military report at the time would have a ratio of about one Russian soldier killed for every fifteen to twenty highlanders. Even allowing for exaggeration in the numbers of fallen highlanders, the ratio remained very high.[24]

On September 26, 1844, during one of the typical raids to rustle horses near Fort Zass (the Adyge sources refer to the place as Arzhy or Marjano's aul), several prominent Besleney and Temirgoy raiders were gunned down by Russian bullets. Among them was the legendary Aitek Kanokov, whose name alone could rally thousands of highlanders for a military campaign against Russia. The death of the renowned warrior was a serious blow to the highlanders' struggle.

His death was compounded by utter humiliation when it became known that Kanokov's body had ended up in Russian hands after others fled the battlefield and left the body behind in violation of custom. The image of the fearless Prince Kanokov was preserved in Adyge folklore, where several traditional wailing songs (*gybza*) bemoaned his death and shamed those who had dishonored themselves by failing to recover his body. Sung by Kanokov's atalyk mother from the Yezugo clan of the Temirgoys, the wails rebuked the Besleneys and Temirgoys for their cowardice and blamed several local notables who had accompanied Kanokov.[25]

Despite the setbacks, raiding activity by small war parties continued. In August 1845 Atarshchikov and his servant, the runaway Cossack Foma Golovkin, were proceeding toward their target in Stavropol province. Not far from Prochnyi Okop, Atarshchikov decided to stop and rest in a nearby forest. When he fell asleep, Golovkin shot and seriously wounded him. Then Golovkin took the horses and rode to the nearest Cossack fort, Novogeorgievskoe, on the Urup River. There he informed the Cossacks that he wished to return to Russia and that in order to redeem himself, he had shot and wounded the notorious outlaw Semën Atarshchikov. Led by Golovkin, a group of Cossacks arrived to find Atarshchikov still alive and ready to defend himself. Mortally wounded, he cocked the trigger of the pistol with his teeth and waited for the Cossacks to approach. Warned that he would be shot like an animal if he did not drop his pistol, Atarshchikov chose to surrender. Shortly thereafter, he died from his wounds while being transported to Prochnyi Okop.

This was the final report that described the last moments in the life of the Russian lieutenant Semën Atarshchikov turned free highlander, Hajret Muhammed. Like all military reports, it was self-serving, trying to match the expectations of the higher-ups and win their approval. There is some discrepancy in the details of Atarshchikov's surrender and death. But the main fact remained: he was betrayed and died shortly after being shot by his servant and fellow deserter. If Golovkin had hoped to be generously rewarded for delivering Atarshchikov to the Russian authorities, he was to be bitterly disappointed. His petition for a reward was summarily rejected on the grounds that he had already been rewarded by a pardon for his desertion and could count on nothing more.[26]

Thus ended the short life of one individual who unsuccessfully tried to negotiate two different worlds: those of the Russians and the North Caucasus's indigenous peoples. He was not alone. Dozens of other natives went back and forth in their search for an answer to the same questions: Can one be both a Russian and native and if so, can one reconcile the traditional values of his native land with the modern Russian ones?

Shamil's Failure among the Adyges

To decisively reverse the course of the war in the North Caucasus the emperor appealed for help to his trusted adviser, the famous statesman Count Mikhail Sergeevich Vorontsov. In January 1845, the sixty-two-year-old governor-general of the New Russia and Bessarabia provinces had been declared a viceroy of the Caucasus. With Vorontsov's arrival in Tiflis, the history of the Russian conquest of the region entered a new and different phase. Brought up and educated in England, Vorontsov held liberal views. He understood that military conquest alone was insufficient and that Russia's control of the region would require greater tolerance of native ways of life and the construction of more schools, roads, and industries, which would eventually bring about a desired change. Military conquest was now accompanied by the classic civilizing mission of bringing Europe to Asia. The region was to be integrated into the empire through Russian language, culture, and science. The growing temptations of Russification presented the indigenous elite with the already familiar challenge of forging their identity within the Russian Empire.[27]

In an attempt to regain the initiative, Shamil personally led his army into Kabarda in 1846. Once again he hoped to enlist Kabardins and western Adyges in ghazawat, thereby uniting the entire North Caucasus in common cause against Russia. But the Kabardins were divided. Those who lived in auls not protected by the high mountains and dense forests were fearful of Russian reprisals. Others had already formed cozy ties with the occupying power and, co-opted by military ranks and payments, had become part of the Russian military-administrative system. For these and other nobles whose main concern was to preserve their landed estates and peasants, Shamil's Imamate with its egalitarian Islamic message was a threat far greater than Russian rule.

In 1848 Shamil would make one last attempt to spread his message in the northwest Caucasus. He dispatched his most trusted naib, Muhammed Amin (born Muhammed Asiyalo), who by accommodating some chiefs and coercing others, had had limited success in introducing the principles of the Imamate among the Abadzekhs and other Adyges. In 1856, in recognition of his importance and influence in the region, the Ottoman sultan bestowed upon Muhammed Amin the title of *mir-i miran,* supreme commander in the region.

In the end, however, the plan to extend the Imamate to the Adyges and create a single Islamic state across the North Caucasus did not succeed. The strict demands of the Imamate were often at odds with the interests of the local population: introducing sharia threatened the status of traditional elites whose power was vested in customary law, imposing a universal tax was resisted by peasants and freemen, and banning all trade with Russians threatened to deprive locals of at least one indispensable item, salt.

Not least important was the bitter personal rivalry between Sefer-bey, who was a fervent proponent of the Circassian nation, and Muhammed Amin, champion of an Islamic state. Forced by desperate circumstances, the two rivals finally met at the Abadzekh aul on April 1858 to try to reconcile their differences, but they were unsuccessful.[28]

By this time Shamil's short-lived Imamate had come to an end. The idea of a united Islamic state was not able to overcome the multiplicity of local self-interests, fragmented tribal identities, persistent rivalries, and economic interdependencies. In September 1859, surrounded and confronted by the futility of further resistance, Shamil capitulated to the Russian commanders at the Daghestani aul of Gunib. Two months later, Muhammed Amin followed the imam's example.

In the late 1860s the Russian military conquest of the North Caucasus was complete—the northeast had been pacified by arms, while the northwest had been emptied through the expulsion to the Ottoman Empire of several hundred thousand Adyges and other indigenous peoples. The North Caucasus had become a part of the Russian Empire. Now not only individuals but entire peoples would confront the same dilemma faced by Semën Atarshchikov, with no easy answer in sight.

Conclusion

Two decades after the collapse of the Soviet Union, the North Caucasus remains a violent and volatile region and poses the most serious threat to the political stability of the Russian Federation. The pro-Russian ruling elites of the region's autonomous republics can no longer hold power on their own, while clan and ethnic rivalries, now fused with extreme Islamic ideology and common criminality, have coalesced to form a potent anti-Russian insurgency. Day after day, news dispatches from the North Caucasus tell of ongoing violence.

Moscow's continuing failure to honestly address the history and legacy of conquest only exacerbates anti-Russian sentiment and resentment of Moscow's rule. Like other remote and poorly understood regions of the world, the North Caucasus attracts the attention of the outside world only during periods of mass violence and war. The most recent Chechen wars made headlines in Western media but did little to deepen knowledge of the region.

The Chechen wars of the 1990s and early 2000s of course were only the latest wave of violence to shake the region. Fifty years earlier Stalin had left his customarily brutal mark when in the midst of war he ordered the wholesale deportation to Siberia and Kazakhstan of the indigenous peoples of the central and northeast Caucasus. Tens of thousands died, and the subsequent amnesty and return of the surviving deportees in 1956 did little to address their long-standing grievances.

The Russian Empire spent most of the nineteenth century conquering the North Caucasus and consolidating its rule, at a huge cost in lives and treasure. When the revolutions of 1917 swept away the old imperial structures, the peoples of the region attempted to create a sovereign confederation in the North Caucasus. The new confederation was short-lived, however, and in 1922 the region became a part of the Russian Federation within the Soviet Union. From the point of view of indigenous peoples there was little difference between the old St. Petersburg and the new Moscow.

Why is it that after three centuries of conquest and rule Russia can boast of little success in integrating the North Caucasus into the fabric of its empire-state? Does the answer lie in the peculiarities of local geography and the social and military organization of the highlanders, in the political theology of Islam, or in the empire's structural inability to assimilate others? To address these questions one must revisit the Russian imperial experience in broader historical context.

Moscow's imperial ambitions emerged under Ivan III, but it took another fifty years before his grandson, Ivan the Terrible, was able to put Moscow's imperial conceits on bold public display when in 1547 he was crowned Tsar of All Russia. The Muscovite Empire became a reality when five years later Moscow conquered a neighboring Islamic state, the khanate of Kazan. The nascent empire expanded rapidly into Asia, claiming suzerainty over the indigenous non-Christian population of animists, Muslims, and Buddhists. In the early eighteenth century, Peter the Great consciously transformed the early modern Muscovite empire he had inherited into a modern Russian empire that, through its various mutations (Russian, Soviet, and post-Soviet), continues to the present day.

To build an empire one had to conquer, rule, and conceptualize—three stages that did not always follow in chronological order. The Muscovite Empire, like other early modern empires that were conceived as universal monarchies, often laid claim to sovereignty over peoples and territories it had yet to conquer. Throughout the eighteenth century the Russian Empire was gradually redefined in terms of the prevailing European ideas of mercantilism and Enlightenment. Whereas military and geopolitical considerations had always dominated the rationale for territorial aggrandizement, economic factors were now emphasized as well.

In the nineteenth century Russia's expansionist project was driven by an additional concept—bringing civilization to its non-Christian subjects in the Asiatic lands of the empire. In a pre-modern Russian empire, where civilization was largely equated with Christianity, proselytizing among the indigenous populations had always been an aspect of Russian expansion, but in the nineteenth century the civilizing mission was increasingly articulated in secular terms. In pursuing its *mission civilisatrice* in its Asiatic territories, Russia had become a colonial empire not unlike its European counterparts.

Since the Russian Empire in Asia included a vast expanse of land populated by very different peoples and societies, the dynamics of imperial rule inevitably varied from region to region. In Siberia, for example, the majority of the native population consisted of small and relatively primitive societies that could easily be brushed aside by consecutive waves of Slavic colonists. Siberia became a refuge for those seeking religious or personal freedom and a dumping ground for the empire's political exiles and criminals. As such, it was similar to the British colonies in North America and Australia. No wonder that some nineteenth-century Siberian scholars and intellectuals tried in vain to have Siberia considered a colony of Russia.

The conquest of Central Asia in the second half of the nineteenth century confronted Russian authorities with a different challenge. The arable lands of the region were densely populated, agriculture was highly developed, the population was thoroughly Muslim, and the urban centers were much older than any in Russia itself. Central Asia could not easily be colonized and transformed into an imperial domain, and it had to be administered delicately by a variety of means. The region's first governor-general, General Konstantin von Kaufmann, tried unsuccessfully to convince St. Petersburg that Central Asia, much like British India, was Russia's colony. Instead, the government regarded the region as an inseparable part of the empire, even as it was administered by the Asiatic Department of the Foreign Ministry, Russia's de facto Colonial Office.

The open expanse of the enormous Eurasian steppe from southern Siberia to the Lower Volga basin was the pastureland of various Turko-Mongol nomadic peoples, most significantly the Kazakhs and Kalmyks. The human and physical geography of this region presented a special challenge to the expanding empire. Here there were no urban centers to conquer and no decisive victories to win against people who were perpetually on the move with all their herds and belongings. The region had to be colonized incrementally through the construction of *limes,* the fortification lines that marked Russia's gradual advance into the steppe. By the early 1800s most of the steppe nomads found themselves cut off from vital pastureland, impoverished, and dependent on Russian authorities. In this region, Russia's civilizing mission included settling the nomadic population and transforming nomads into peasants.

Finally, the Caucasus, an area between the Black and Caspian Seas, consisted of two distinct regions divided by high mountains: the South and the North Caucasus. In the south, the mountains, valleys, and fertile plains had long been settled and subjected to the influence of the ancient civilizations of the Greeks and Persians. By the nineteenth century, the towns and agricultural communities of the Christian Armenians and Georgians populated the southwest and central part of the South Caucasus, while the villages and cities of the Muslim Azeris dominated the southeast. The Armenians and Georgians stood out among the peoples of Asiatic Russia both as the only Christians and as the heirs of once-thriving sovereign kingdoms. Here, too, calls throughout the 1820s to treat the region as a colony were rejected in St. Petersburg, and the South Caucasus was placed squarely within the Russian administration.

The political geography of the North Caucasus stood in sharp contrast to that of the South. Exposed to the vagaries of life on the edge of the great Eurasian steppe, the North Caucasus was only intermittently subjected to the influence of great civilizations and monotheistic religions; nor had the region given rise to any sustainable and sovereign state structures. The North embraced several distinct regions: the steppe, occupied primarily by the nomadic Kalmyks and Nogays; the foothills, where the numerous Kumyk, Chechen, and Adyge auls practiced both agriculture and animal husbandry; and the auls and hamlets of the high mountains, which were protected by the forbidding terrain of the Caucasus range. Because of the region's complex fabric, St. Petersburg relied on a panoply of policies in the course of military conquest: construction of fortification lines, seizure of pasturelands, expulsion of villagers, settling Slavic and other Christian colonists, wholesale destruction of mountain auls and crops, and, finally, the massive deportation of natives to the Ottoman Empire.

Whatever the differences between the regions, Russia's Asian territories were distinguished by the absence of large sovereign polities with defined state boundaries. From the seventeenth century on, the imperial authorities spoke in terms that reinforced the divide between the Russian state and these nonstate societies. Thus, what the native peoples believed to be a peace treaty the Russians claimed was an oath of allegiance to the tsar. For the Russians, local settlements were villages, their military activities were raiding, and resistance to Russian invasion was a rebellion against the tsarist state. The Russian authorities preferred to ignore the inconvenient fact that some of the native settlements were larger than neighboring Russian towns, that "raids" could include up to ten thousand horsemen, and that the "rebels" (*miatezhniki*) had first to join the empire before they could rebel against it.

At the same time, Russian authorities referred to their own raids by a small mobile troop as "military expeditions" and cast their military conquest of the region in terms of geopolitics and progress. It was as if Napoleon's invasion of Russia a few decades earlier had been dubbed a march of progress and civilization, while the Russians were deemed ungrateful and wayward rebels. A double standard indeed, but one that was often accepted when applied to disparate non-Christian societies that failed to evolve into sovereign states or produce national historiographies of their own.

Throughout the nineteenth century, the North Caucasus remained a region with deeply fragmented identities defined not by political structures or common ethnicity but by kinship ties within the tribes and clans. In this sense, the Caucasus War was a struggle between two visions of modernity: the Russian Empire, which triggered an evolution of tribal identities into ethnic ones, and Shamil's Imamate, which sought to replace tribal identities with the state, albeit an Islamic one. Shamil's holy war therefore must be seen not only as an anti-Russian campaign but as part of the broader struggle against the traditional elites over control of the local population.

The absence of the European-type sovereign states in Asiatic Russia helped to shape the nature of Russia's civilizing mission, but the question of how to rule these diverse regions, peoples, and religions remained. Russian authorities refused to concede that theirs was a colonial empire. Instead, the Russian imperial mind continued to nurture dreams of a universal monarch and Christian civilization and a belief that one day the non-Russian peoples would become Russian. Myth and reality could not be so easily reconciled, however, and the result was that particular Russian hybrid of hyperaccentuated empire and underarticulated colonialism.

Throughout the eighteenth and nineteenth centuries, the state's overriding ambition was to integrate the empire's diverse humanity into the Russian Christian imperial polity. But the reality on the ground defied this long-term vision, requiring tactics and policies that could be adapted to specific circumstances. With some exceptions, when Russia sought to sow divisions between indigenous elites and commoners, imperial authorities preferred to rely on local secular and, when necessary, religious elites. Economic and political carrots and sticks were manipulated to ensure the cooperation and loyalty of elites, while courts, administration, schools, and missionary work were designed to facilitate the broader integration of non-Russians into the empire.

Policy choices were never easy and often worked at cross-purposes. Enhancing the authority of a single local ruler risked confronting a more powerful enemy should he choose to switch sides. Encouraging rivalries within the ruling elite could fragment a local society, leading to the loss of Russia's effective control. Supporting the local elites against the commoners earned their loyalty, while giving refuge and converting their fugitive peasants to Christianity antagonized the very same elites.

Local legal structures further complicated imperial politics. Wooing the traditional elite obliged the Russians to encourage the use of adat, which they consistently did. Supporting the ulema would have required reliance on sharia, which the Russian authorities generally found unpalatable. The search for an effective legal structure continued throughout the nineteenth century with little success. The local population resented the Russian military-administrative system and regarded Russian experiments with various hybrid courts as a disguise for imperial rule.

Among the policy tools the Russians employed, one remained constant: to govern this multitude of peoples, tongues, and religions, Russia depended on individuals who possessed an intimate knowledge of both Russia and their own society and were thus able to serve as intermediaries. In the Muscovite Empire, such go-betweens were usually employed as interpreters. Some were new converts, but most were former Slavic prisoners of war who claimed to have learned the native language and mores during their long captivity. In fact, almost all of them were illiterate, and they knew little of the language and culture in which they claimed expertise.

As Russia's involvement with the various non-Russian peoples deepened, authorities increasingly relied on locals who, for various reasons, had become exposed to the Russian way of life. Only in the middle of the nineteenth century did a slowly modernizing Russia begin to train its own experts by having them study indigenous languages, societies, and religions. Russia never had an equivalent of the British Colonial Service, which trained future colonial officials in the laws, languages, and religions of their assigned destination. Yet Russian universities offered courses in non-Russian languages and cultures for the benefit of scholars and future government officials alike.

Throughout the entire imperial era, the great majority of Russia's cultural interlocutors came from the indigenous societies. Many of them, like Semën Atarshchikov's father, were surrendered to the Russian authorities as hostages or, like one of Russia's best portrait painters, Petr Zakharov-Chechenets, were seized as captives at a young age. Some left for Russia of their own free will to seek better opportunities and often ended up as converts to Christianity.

From the late eighteenth century on, Russian authorities began to demand that the native elites send their sons to the imperial capital to be educated at the emperor's court or in Russia's prestigious military schools. The formation of the special non-Russian units of the imperial guard in the 1820s sought to serve the same purpose—to educate and acculturate young men from distinguished indigenous families.

In contrast to previous policies of assimilating and turning non-Christians into Russians, the authorities were now satisfied with merely acculturating these indigenous elites. The newcomers were to learn the Russian way of life but at the same time remain sufficiently "native" to command legitimacy among their own peoples. They were expected to return to their kin as cultural interlocutors, projecting Russian influence and representing imperial interests. In other words, the former hostages were to become a freshly minted colonial elite.

This elite lacked a cohesive group identity. It continued to include individuals of different faiths, languages, and customs, who arrived from the different parts of the empire and returned to their own people as different men: in a Russian officer's uniform, with a strange accent, with outlandish ideas in their heads, and often, with a tiny cross around their necks. They occupied the intermediate space between assimilation and foreignness and proved an effective conduit for transferring Russian political culture to the indigenous societies. But if the members of this new elite had thought they could open communication in both directions between Russian authorities and the local peoples, they were deeply mistaken. Their superiors often disregarded their advice, ignoring their analyses of local situations. Gradually they came to realize that the state intended to use them to channel information in one direction only.

In this book readers have encountered a cohort of such intermediaries from the North Caucasus: Shora Nogma among the Kabardins, Khan-Giray and Sefer-bey Zanoko among the western Adyges, Musa Kundukh among the Ossetians, and of course, Semën Atarshchikov. While all of them were educated in Russia and were Russified to some extent, they chose to identify themselves in different ways. Some retained their basic attachment and loyalty to imperial authorities (Khan-Giray and Shora Nogma); others resolved to change sides by joining the Ottomans (Sefer-bey Zanoko and Musa Kundukh) or the highlanders (Semën Atarshchikov). For years to come identities remained fluid in the imperial borderlands. Shora Nogma proved a loyal subject and admirer of many things Russian, but his two sons chose to emigrate to the Ottoman Empire in 1870. Some thirty years later, one of Shora Nogma's grandsons left Ottoman territory and emigrated to Russia.

The life of Semën Atarshchikov is a particular instance of the paths charted by these native interlocutors, who in different ways tried to bridge the space between the world of their homelands and that of imperial Russia. The push and pull between the two was always challenging but no more so than in wartime, which forced them to choose sides and left little room for compromise—whether political or psychological. Even a first-generation Russian such as Semën Atarshchikov could not elude this stark existential dilemma.

The men of Russia's new colonial elite were marginal individuals negotiating their identities between the old and the new, traditional and modern,

Asia and Europe. Perhaps in the end they had something in common with the Russian elites, who had for centuries debated Russia's own place between the national and imperial, modern and traditional, Western paths and Russia's *sonderweg*. It seems that today, in the second decade of the twenty-first century, this debate is far from over.

Notes

Introduction

1. M. O. Kosven, "Delo sotnika Atarshchikova," in *Etnografiia i istoriia Kavkaza: Issledovaniia i materialy* (Moscow: Izdatel'stvo vostochnoi literatury, 1964), pp. 254–58.

2. Susan Layton, *Russian Literature and Empire: Conquest of the Caucasus from Pushkin to Tolstoy* (Cambridge: Cambridge University Press, 1994), p. 229.

3. Iraklii Andronikov, *Lermontov: Issledovaniia i nakhodki* (Moscow: Khudozhestvennaia literatura, 1964), p. 521.

4. "Memuary generala Musa-Pashi Kundukhova (1837–1865)," *Zvezda* 8 (2001): 100–123.

5. Western historiography has touched upon the history of the pre-Soviet North Caucasus, generally within the context of the broader Caucasus. Among most recent works are Charles King, *The Ghost of Freedom: A History of the Caucasus* (Oxford: Oxford University Press, 2008), and Bruce Grant, *The Captive and the Gift: Cultural Histories of Sovereignty in Russia and the Caucasus* (Ithaca: Cornell University Press, 2009). Other works are focused on specific topics: for example, Moshe Gammer, *Muslim Resistance to the Tsar: Shamil and the Conquest of Chechnia and Daghestan* (London: Frank Cass, 1994); Thomas M. Barrett, *At the Edge of Empire: The Terek Cossacks and the North Caucasus Frontier, 1700–1860* (Boulder, CO: Westview, 1999); Austin Jersild, *Orientalism and Empire: North Caucasus Mountain Peoples and the Georgian Frontier, 1845–1917* (Montreal: McGill-Queen's University Press, 2002); Michael Kemper, *Herrschaft, Recht und Islam in Daghestan: Von den Khanaten und Gemeindebunden zum jihad-Staat* (Wiesbaden: Reichert, 2005). The only comprehensive studies of the North Caucasus are in Russian: the two-volume *Istoriia narodov Severnogo Kakvaza* (Moscow: Nauka, 1989)—which cautiously probes the new approaches reflecting the Soviet transition of the late 1980s—and a collective textbook, *Severnyi Kavkaz v sostave Rossiiskoi imperii* (Moscow: Novoe literaturnoe obozrenie, 2007)—which, mirroring the atmosphere of Putin's Russia, shies away from controversial issues.

6. Among the best-known examples are Fernand Braudel, who attributed thoughts to historical characters in *The Mediterranean World in the Age of Philip II*, trans. Sian Reynolds (New York: Harper and Row, 1972), and Natalie Zemon Davis's *The Return of Martin Guerre* (Cambridge: Harvard University Press, 1983) and her *Trickster Travels: A Sixteenth Century Muslim between Worlds* (New York: Wang and Hill, 2006).

1. The Frontiers of the North Caucasus

1. For the Ottoman inroads in the North Caucasus see *Osmanli Devleti ile Azerbaycan Türk Hanliklari arasindaki Münasabetlere dair Arsiv Belgeleri*, vol. 1 (1578–1914) (Ankara: T. C. Basbakanlik, 1992), and M. Sadik Bilge, *Osmanli Devleti ve Kafkasya* (Istanbul: Eren, 2005). For Persian interests in the Caucasus, see F. Kazemzadeh, in *The Cambridge History of Iran, 7 vols.* (Cambridge: Cambridge University Press, 1969–1991), vol. 7, pp. 314–49, and Muriel Atkin, *Russia and Iran, 1780–1828* (Minneapolis: University of Minnesota Press, 1980). For Russia's initial policies in the region, see Michael Khodarkovsky, "Of Christianity, Enlightenment and Colonialism: Russia in the North Caucasus, 1550–1800," *Journal of Modern History* 71, no. 2 (1999): 394–430.

2. V. D. Smirnov, *Krymskoe khanstvo pod verkhovenstvom Otomanskoi Porty do nachala 18 veka* (St. Petersburg: Univ. tip. Kazani, 1887), pp. 441–43; A. A. Novosel'skii, *Bor'ba Moskovskogo gosudarstva s tatarami v pervoi polovine 17 veka.* (Moscow-Leningrad: AN SSSR, 1948), p. 35.

3. Valerii Sokurov, "Institut vyezda na sluzhbu u cherkesov," *Elbrus*, no. 1 (1999): 123–25. In 1700 the Cherkasskiis were listed as the wealthiest landholders in Russia, with 12,032 peasant households. K. F. Dzamikhov, *Adygi v politike Rossii na Kavkaze (1550–nachalo 1770-kh godov)* (Nalchik: El-Fa, 2001), p. 147.

4. *Kabardino-russkie otnosheniia v 16–18 vv.: Dokumenty i materialy* (Moscow: AN SSSR, 1957), 1:1–20.

5. For more on Naqshbandi'ya see chapter 6. For an overview of the Sufi orders in the Caucasus, see Alexander Knysh, *Islamic Mysticism: A Short History* (Leiden: Brill, 2000), pp. 289–300.

6. N. I. Pokrovskii, *Kavkazskie voiny i imamat Shamilia* (Moscow: Rosspen, 2000), pp. 165–94, and Kemper, *Herrschaft, Recht und Islam in Daghestan.*

7. For the Russian conquest and Shamil's resistance, see Gammer, *Muslim Resistance to the Tsar.*

8. Vladimir Lapin, *Armiia Rossii v Kavkazskoi voine 18–19 vv.* (St. Petersburg: Evropeiskii Dom, 2008), pp. 46–48.

9. For a detailed discussion of these issues, see Michael Khodarkovsky, *Russia's Steppe Frontier: The Making of a Colonial Empire, 1500–1800* (Bloomington: Indiana University Press, 2002), chap. 2.

10. Dzamikhov, *Adygi v politike Rossii na Kavkaze*, pp. 337–42.

11. Sokurov, "Institut vyezda," pp. 116–17.

12. *Akty sobrannye Kavkazskoiu arkheograficheskoiu komissieiu (AKAK)*, vol. 4 (Tiflis: Tip. Glavnogo upravleniia namestnika Kavkazskogo, 1866–1904), p. 340 (no. 1272).

13. Lapin, *Armiia Rossii*, pp. 257–58.

14. V. K. Gardanov, *Obshchestvennyi stroi adygskikh narodov: XVIII–pervaia polovina XIX v.* (Moscow: Nauka, 1967), pp. 180–82. The original social categories were often rendered incorrectly; see G. M.-P. Orazaev, "Tiurkoiazychnye dokumenty iz arkhiva Kizliarskogo komendanta—Istochnik po sotsial'no-ekonomicheskoi istorii narodov Severnogo Kavkaza," in *Istochnikovedenie i tekstologiia Blizhenego i Srednego Vostoka* (Moscow: Vostochnaia literatura, 1984), p. 182.

15. Gardanov, *Obshchestvennyi stroi adygskikh narodov*, pp. 254–61; Mokhmad Mamakaev, Chechenskii taip v period ego razlozheniia (Groznyi: Checheno-Ingushskoe knizhnoe izd-vo), 1973.

16. Ibid., pp. 249–50; Khan-Girei, "Beslnii Abat," in *Izbrannye proizvedeniia* (Nalchik: Elbrus, 1974), pp. 232–40.

17. *Entsiklopedicheskii slovar' po istorii Kubani* (Krasnodar: Edvi, 1997), p. 266.

18. More information on these and other indigenous institutions is found in the chapters below and in F. I. Leontovich, *Adaty Kavkazskikh gortsev. Materialy po obychnomu pravu Severnogo i Vostochnogo Kavkaza*, vol. 1 (Odessa: Tip. P. A. Zelenago, 1882, repr., Nalchik: El-Fa, 2002); Kosven, *Etnografiia i istoriia Kavkaza;* and Gardanov, *Obshchestvennyi stroi adygskikh narodov.*

19. G. N. Malakhova, *Stanovlenie i razvitie Rossiiskogo gosudarstvennogo upravleniia na Severnom Kavkaze v kontse 18–19vv.* (Rostov-na-Donu: SKAGS, 2001), p. 147; A. N. Maremkulov, *Osnovy geopolitiki Rossiiskogo gosudarstva na Severnom Kavkaze v 18–nachale 19 veka* (Nalchik: Elbrus, 2003), p. 110. See also various essays in *Rechtspluralismus in der Islamischen Welt. Gewohnheitsrecht zwischen Staat und Gesellschaft*, ed. Michael Kemper and Marius Reinkowski (Berlin: Walter de Gruyter, 2005).

20. *AKAK*, 4:341 (no. 1272).

21. Maremkulov, *Osnovy geopolitiki*, pp. 108–30; Malakhova, *Stanovlenie i razvitie*, pp. 148–61; Kosven, *Etnografiia i istoriia Kavkaza*, p. 133.

22. Leontovich, *Adaty Kavkazskikh gortsev*, pp. 73–94.

23. *AKAK*, 4:860 (no. 1304), 866 (no. 1312).

2. Atarshchikov's Childhood

1. E. N. Kusheva, comp., *Russko-chechenskie otnosheniia: Vtoraia polovina 16–17 vv. Sbornik dokumentov* (Moscow: Vostochnaia literatura, 1997), pp. 39 (no. 13), 276. S. N. Beituganov, *Kabardinskie familii: Istoki i sud'by* (Nalchik: Elbrus, 1990), pp. 15–16.

2. For more on hostages, see Khodarkovsky, *Russia's Steppe Frontier*, pp. 56–60.

3. *Kabardino-russkie otnosheniia*, 2:316 (no. 220).

4. On schools in the nineteenth-century Daghestan see G. Sh. Kaimarazov, *Ocherki istorii kultury narodov Dagestana* (Moscow: Nauka, 1971), pp. 64–80, 114–18. In 1770 a school for natives in Kizliar offered both Russian and Tatar languages. P. G. Butkov, *Materialy dlia novoi istorii Kavkaza s 1722 po 1803 god.* (St. Petersburg: Tip. Imp. Akademii Nauk, 1869), 1:268.

5. Located just west of Braguny, the former Chechen hamlet of Otar is known today as the New Braguny. Akhmad Suleimanov, *Toponimiia Chechni* (Nalchik: El-Fa, 1997), p. 579. *Otar* originally meant a pastureland in various Turkic languages and later connoted a hamlet. The word *otara* migrated into the Russian language with the meaning "a herd of sheep," while *atarshchik* was commonly used in the steppe to denote a cowboy watching horses. See Mikhail Sholokhov, *Sobranie sochinenii*, vols. 2–5, *Tikhii Don* (Moscow: Khudozhestvennaia literatura, 1966), 4:63–64.

6. *Kabardino-russkie otnosheniia*, 1:256–57 (no. 159), 215 (no. 142), 302 (no. 193).

7. S. M. Bronevskii, *Istoricheskiia vypiski o snosheniiakh Rossii s Persieiu, Gruzieiu i voobshche s gorskimi narodami v Kavkaze obitaiushchimi, so vremen Ivana Vasilievicha donyne*, edited by I. K. Pavlova (St. Petersburg: Peterburgskoe vostokovedenie" 1996), p. 103.

8. In 1785 Naurskaia again stood firm against a large group of Kabardins, Chechens, and Kumyks ravaging the Russian frontier during the Mansur uprising. Ibid., pp. 114, 127–28; F. F. Tornau, "Vospominaniia o Kavkaze i Gruzii," in *Vospominaniia russkogo ofitsera* (Moscow: AIRO—XX, 2002), p. 288.

9. *Istoriia narodov Severnogo Kavkaza, konets 18v.–1917* (Moscow: Nauka, 1988), pp. 75, 79–85.

10. Kosven, "Opisanie grebenskikh kazakov 18 veka," in *Etnografiia i istoriia Kavkaza*, pp. 246–47.

11. V. N. Gamrekeli, comp., *Dokumenty po vzaimosviaziam Gruzii s Severnym Kavkazom v 18 veke* (Tbilisi: AN Gruzinskoi SSR, 1968), p. 202 (no. 57); Butkov, *Materialy*, 2:112.

12. For more on the Terek Cossacks, see L. B. Zasedateleva, *Terskie kazaki. Istoriko-etnograficheskie ocherki* (Moscow: MGU, 1974); Barrett, *At the Edge of Empire*.

13. Kosven, "Atalychestvo," in *Etnografiia i istoriia Kavkaza*, pp. 104–25. It seems that an atalyk could sometimes be a Christian, as in a case of the Armenian atalyk. See J. S. Bell, *Journal of a Residence in Circassia during the Years 1837, 1838, and 1839.* (London: E. Moxon, 1840), 1:288.

14. Suleimanov, *Toponimiia Chechni*, pp. 613–24.

15. Barrett, *At the Edge of Empire*, pp. 31, 61.

16. Suleimanov, *Toponimiia Chechni*, pp. 579–80, 613–15.

17. *Kabardino-russkie otnosheniia*, 1:89 (no. 56).

18. Suleimanov, *Toponimiia Chechni*, pp. 571–90; Butkov, *Materialy*, 1:129.

19. V. G. Gadzhiev, ed., *Russko-dagestanskie otnosheniia v 18–nachale 19 v.: Sbornik dokumentov* (Moscow: Nauka, 1988), p. 223; "Kumyki," in *Narody Kavkaza*, ed. M. O. Kosven, vol. 1 (Moscow: AN SSSR, 1960), p. 421.

20. N. G. Volkova, *Etnicheskii sostav naseleniia Severnogo Kavkaza v 18–nachale 19 vekov* (Moscow: Nauka, 1974), p. 270; V. M. Kabuzan, *Narody Rossii v 18 veke. Chislennost i etnicheskii sostav* (Moscow: Nauka, 1990), p. 74. By comparison, the population of Tiflis, the residence of the Georgian king, was estimated at three thousand households, or fifteen thousand residents in 1803 (Butkov, *Materialy*, 2:340n 1); A. P. Berzhe, *Chechnya i chechentsy* (Tiflis, 1859; repr. Groznyi: Kniga, 1991), p. 100.

21. In 1741 Enderi was thought to number between three hundred and four hundred households. John Cook, M.D. *Voyages and Travels through the Russian Empire, Tartary, and Part of the Kingdom of Persia*, (Edinburgh, 1770, repr. Oriental Research Partners, 1997), 2:260; E. N. Kusheva, *Narody Severnogo Kavkaza i ikh sviazi s Rossiei: Vtoraia polovina 16–30-e gody 17 veka* (Moscow: Izd-vo An SSSR, 1963), pp. 278, 287; Butkov, *Materialy*, 1:21–23, 129; Bronevskii, *Istoricheskie vypiski*, pp. 42, 67.

22. Butkov, *Materialy*, 1:166. Kusheva, *Narody Severnogo Kavkaza*, p. 106. For a discussion of the Ottoman slave trade, see Ehud R Toledano, *The Ottoman Slave Trade and Its Suppression, 1840–1890* (Princeton: Princeton University Press, 1982).

23. *Istoriia narodov Severnogo Kavkaza*, pp. 38, 39, 78, 79, 109; Khodarkovsky, *Russia's Steppe Frontier*, pp. 207–8. By contrast, Anglo-American abolitionism was driven by general moral and religious concerns. For a discussion of Russia's role in the abolition of slavery in the Caucasus, see Liubov Kurtynova-D'Herlugnan, *The Tsar's Abolitionists: The Slave Trade in the Caucasus and Its Suppression* (New York: Brill Academic Publishers, 2010).

24. *Kabardino-russkie v 16–18vv.*, 2:245–48 (no. 181).

25. It is clearly identified on fourteenth-century maps. V. L. Egorov, *Istoricheskaia geografiia Zolotoi Ordy v 13–14 vv.* (Moscow: Nauka, 1985), pp. 121, 137.

26. The description of Tarki is based on several mutually confirming accounts. S. L. Belokurov, comp., *Snosheniia Rossii s Kavkazom. Materialy izvlechennye iz Moskovskogo Ministerstva Inostrannykh del, 1578–1613* (Moscow, Universitetskaia tip. 1889), pp. 404–5; Butkov, *Materialy*, 2:567–70 (attachments); Kusheva, *Narody Severnogo Kavkaza*, pp. 44–45. The etymology of the term *shamkhal* is uncertain.

27. Belokurov, *Snosheniia Rossii*, p. 203 (no. 12).

28. Gadzhiev, *Russko-dagestanskie otnosheniia v 18–nachale 19 v.*, pp. 240–49 (no. 323–36).

29. *Istoriia narodov Severnogo Kavkaza*, pp. 136, 278.

30. Description based on Butkov, *Materialy*, 1:568–69.

31. Kusheva, *Narody Severenogo Kavkaza*, p. 44; *Istoriia narodov Severnogo Kavkaza*, pp. 293, 398. In 1871 the population of Karabudakhkent boasted ninety-nine men and seventy-one women of the beg families and eleven mosques. *Dvizhenie gortsev severo-vostochnogo Kavkaza v 20–50 gg. 19 veka: Sbornik dokumentov* (Makhachkala: Dagestanskoe knizhnoe izd-vo, 1959), p. 696).

32. S. Sh. Gadzhieva, *Kumyki: Istoriko-etnograficheskoe issledovanie* (Moscow: AN SSSR, 1961), pp. 197–202; A. I. Islammagomedov and G. A. Sergeeva, eds., *Traditsionnoe i novoe v sovremennom byte i kul'ture dagestantsev pereselentsev* (Moscow: Nauka, 1988), pp. 41–46.

33. Gadzhieva, *Kumyki*, pp. 204–215.

34. Ibid., 262–67.

35. The 1839 report about Semën Atarshchikov's military service referred to Semën's full literacy in Russian, in contrast to his "familiarity" with Arabic, Chechen, and Kumyk. Rossiiskii Gosudarstvennyi Voenno-Istoricheskii Arkhiv (RGVIA) f. 395, op. 145, d. 205, l. 7 ob.

36. M. O. Kosven, "Kabardinskii patriot Izmail Atazhukov," in *Etnografiia i istoriia Kavkaza*, pp. 130–49.

37. *Epigraficheskie pamiatniki Severnogo Kavkaza na arabskom, persidskom i turetskom iazykakh,* edited by L. I. Lavrov, vol. 2 (Moscow: Nauka, 1966–1980), pp. 51, 126.

38. *Zapiski A. P. Ermolova, 1798–1826,* edited by V. A. Fedorov (Moscow: Vysshaia shkola, 1991), pp. 320–21, 341; V. G. Gadzhiev, *Rol' Rossii v istorii Dagestana* (Moscow: Nauka, 1965), pp. 21, 22.

3. Journey through the Northeast Caucasus

1. V. V. Bartold, "Derbend," in *Raboty po istoricheskoi geografii* (Moscow: Vostochnaia literatura, 2002), pp. 419–30; A. A. Kudriavtsev, *Feodal'nyi Derbent* (Moscow: Nauka, 1993); I. Gurlev et al., *Derbent: Putevoditel' po gorodu i okrestnostiam* (Makhachkala: Dagknigoizdat, 1976).

2. B. G. Aliev and M-S. K. Umakhanov, *Istoricheskaia geografiia Dagestana 18–nach. 19 v.,* vol. 2, *Iuzhnyi Dagestan* (Makhachkala: Institut istorii, arkheologii i etnografii, 2001), pp. 62–63.

3. V. V. Bartold, "Mesto prikaspiiskikh oblastei v istorii musul'manskogo mira," in *Sochineniia,* vol. 2, pt. 1 (Moscow: Izd-vo vostochnoi literatury, 1965), pp. 670–72, 786–96; S. Khan-Magomedov, *Derbent. Gornaia Stena. Auly Tabasarana* ((Moscow: Iskusstvo, 1979); A. A. Kudriavtsev, *Feodal'nyi Derbent* (Moscow: Nauka, 1993); Butkov, *Materialy,* 2:580–83.

4. Khan-Magomedov, *Derbend,* pp. 207–26.

5. Ibid., pp. 231–69; Aliev and Umakhanov, *Istoricheskaia geografiia Dagestana,* 2:62, 131–48. Bronevskii, *Istoricheskie vypiski,* 177–78.

6. The Lezgins had no tradition of centralized political power until 1812, when the Russian government decided to intervene in a local power struggle and created the Kiurin khanate on the lands between the Rubas and Samur Rivers; see Aliev and Umakhanov, *Istoricheskaia geografiia Dagestana,* 2:131–92; *Istoriia Dagestana,* vol. 2 (Moscow: Vostochnaiia literatura, 1968), pp. 65–68.

7. *Istoriia narodov Severnogo kavkaza,* vol. 1, 1988, pp. 241, 293, 323, 344, 345, 420; Gadzhiev, *Russko-dagestanskie otnosheniia v 18–nachale 19 v.,* pp. 63–67 (no. 17).

8. Butkov, *Materialy,* 2:14–15; *Istoriia narodov Severnogo Kavkaza,* pp. 446; S. Sh. Gadzhieva, *Dagestanskie Terekementsy, 19–nach. 20 v.* (Moscow: Nauka, 1990), pp. 22–23.

9. *Dvizhenie gortsev severo-vostochnogo Kavkaza,* pp. 23–42 (nos. 4–21).

10. *Istoriia Dagestana,* 2:67. *Istoriia narodov Severnogo Kavkaza,* 36–37.

11. *Narody Dagestana* (Moscow: Nauka, 2002), pp. 334–48; Dibir Ataev, *Putevoditel' po Dagestanu* (Makhachkala: Dagestanskoe knizhnoe izd-vo, 1965), pp. 104–6, 119–19; Bronevskii, *Istoricheskie vypiski,* pp. 170–72.

12. *Narody Dagestana,* p. 295; *Istoriia Dagestana,* vol. 1 (Moscow: Vostochnaia literatura, 1967), pp. 328–29.

13. Fahrettin Kirzioglu, *Osmanlilar'in Kafkas-elleri'ni Fethi (1451–1590)* (Ankara: Sevinc Matbaasi, 1976), pp. 307–17; Bekir Kütükoglu, *Osmanli-Iran Siyasi* Münasabetleri (Istanbul: Edebiyat Fakültesi Matbaasi, 1962).

14. M. M. Ikhilov, ed., *Russko-dagestanskie otnosheniia 17–pervoi chetverti 18 vv.: Dokumenty i materially* (Makhachkala: Dagestanskoe knizhnoe izd-vo, 1958), pp. 31–59 (nos. 2–14); *Istoriia Dagestana,* vol. 1, pp. 248–49.

15. Kusheva, *Narody Severnogo Kavkaza,* p. 47; B. Aliev, Sh. Akhmedov, and M.-S. Usmanov, *Iz istorii srednevekovogo Dagestana* (Makhachkala: Institut istorii, iazyka i literatury, 1970), pp. 72–77.

16. V. V. Bartold, "Dagestan," in *Sochineniia,* vol. 3 (Moscow: Nauka, 1965), pp. 419–10.

17. The course of the war in the Caucasus is vividly related by the Russian officer R. A. Fadeev, who was a close assistant to Prince Bariatinskii and participated in the military actions at Gunib. Prince Bariatinskii rewarded Fadeev with Shamil's personal banner and entrusted him with writing the history of the war. R. A. Fadeev, *Kavkazskaia voina* (Moscow: Eksmo,

2003), pp. 7, 98–100. Other classic books on the subject are N. I. Pokrovskii, *Kavkazskie voiny i imamat Shamilia* (Moscow: ROSSPEN, 2000), and Gammer, *Muslim Resistance to the Tsar.*

18. Iu. D. Anchabadze and N. G. Volkova, *Staryi Tbilisi. Gorod i gorozhane v 19 veke* (Moscow: Nauka, 1990), p. 29.

19. Butkov, *Materialy,* 1:215. D. Ataev, K. Gadzhiev, *Putevoditel' po Dagestanu,* pp. 70–72, 93–94. *Istoriia narodov Severnogo Kavkaza,* p. 177.

20. *Dvizhenie gortsev severo-vostochnogo Kavkaza,* pp. 31–32 (no. 9), pp. 59–62 (nos. 33–35).

21. *Narody Dagestana,* pp. 180–85.

22. Belokurov, *Snosheniia Rossii s Kavkazom,* p. 33 (no. 4); U. Iaudaev, "Chechenskoe plemia," in *Sbornik svedenii o kavkazskikh gortsakh,* vol. 6 (Tiflis, 1868–81), p. 3. The word "Chechen" first appeared in 1708. *Polnoe sobranie zakonov Rossiiskoi imperii. Sobranie pervoe (PSZ),* vol. 4 (St. Petersburg, 1830), p. 421. It is found on a Russian map of 1719. *Kabardino-russkie otnosheniia,* 1:289; 2:364 (no. 256); N. G. Volkova, *Etnonimy i plemennye nazvaniia Severnogo Kavkaza* (Moscow: Nauka, 1973), pp. 133–50.

23. Berzhe, *Chechnya i chechentsy,* pp. 27, 42, 92; Pokrovskii, *Kavkazskie voiny,* p. 476.

24. Kabuzan, *Narody Rossii v 18 veke,* p. 227.

25. One of the better-known examples of resistance occurred at Shali in January 1864, an incident that would become deeply ingrained in Chechen memory. The events unfolded as follows. With the arrest by the Russian authorities of the popular leader of the Sufi branch, Sheikh Kunt Haji, no fewer than three thousand of his murids gathered at Shali demanding his release. Three times the sheikh's followers sent their delegates to the nearby Russian garrison where they believed Kunt Haji was held, and each time the Russian commander rejected their demands. Kunt Haji's followers had no idea that their sheikh was already far away inside Russia, sent there earlier in great secret. Soon after their delegates returned with another rejection, the crowd was brought into frenzy with the traditional chants (*zikr*). Relying on their prayers and the power of the Almighty, the murids left their firearms behind, unsheathed their sabers and daggers, and with chants and dances began to advance toward the Russian garrison. When the crowd approached, the Russian troops opened fire with rifles and cannons. The result was a massacre with 164 murids dead and many wounded. Hundreds were arrested, and the leaders were sentenced to hard labor and exiled to Siberia. Sheikh Kunt Haji found himself in exile in a small town in northern Russia, where he died three years later. Those massacred by the Russian troops in 1863 and others who fell resisting Russian authorities became martyrs; they were buried at a place on Shali's southern outskirts that became known as the ghazawat cemetery. *Ocherki istorii Checheno-ingushskoi ASSR* (Groznyi: Checheno-ingushskoe izd-vo, 1967), 1:129; *Toponimiia Chechni,* p. 489.

26. Pokrovskii, *Kavkazskie voiny,* p. 139; Gammer, *Muslim Resistance,* p. 30

27. Pokrovskii, *Kavkazskie voiny,* p. 139.

28. *Zapiski A. P. Ermolova,* pp. 304–11.

29. *Gorod Groznyi* (Groznyi: Checheno-ingushskoe izdatelstvo, 1984) pp. 8–15; *Stranitsy istorii goroda Groznogo* (Groznyi: Checheno-ingushskoe izdatelstvo, 1989), pp. 3–6.

30. L. N. Tolstoy, "Rubka lesa," in *Polnoe sobranie sochinenii,* vol. 3 (Moscow: Khudozhestvennaia literatura, 1932), pp. 40–74.

31. L. N. Tolstoy, *Kazaki* (Moscow-Leningrad: Khudozhestvennaia literatura, 1949), pp. 16–22.

32. Sholokhov, *Tikhii Don,* 2: 162–63.

4. Inside Ermolov's "Iron Fist"

1. M. M. Medvedeva, "Griboedov pod sledstviem i nadzorom," *Literaturnoe nasledstvo* 60 (1956): 485–86.

2. "Zapiska generala Ermolova o posolstve v Persiiu v 1817 godu," in *Zapiski Alekseia Petrovicha Ermolova* (Moscow: Universitetskaia tipografiia, 1868), 2:1–74.

3. *AKAK*, vol. 5, pp. 265–67; "Zapiska generala Ermolova o posolstve v Persiiu," p. 66.

4. Ermolov married his first wife, Siuida, during his stay at Tarki in November 1819. She bore him a son, Bakhtiyar (Viktor), who at the age of two was sent to be raised in Russia while Siuida stayed at Tarki. His second and favorite wife, Totay, was from the Koka-shura aul in central Daghestan. She was already betrothed when Ermolov ordered her kidnapped and brought to him in January 1820. In the following six years she would give birth to two sons, Allah-Yar (Sever) and Omar (Klavdii), and a daughter, Satiyat (Sofiia). Finally, in 1823, Ermolov married his third and final wife, Sultanum Bamat from Bolshye Kazanishchi. She bore him a son, Isfendiyar, who died at an early age. A. P. Berzhe, "Aleksei Petrovich Ermolov i ego kebinnye zheny na Kavkaze, 1816–27 gg.," *Russkaia starina* 15 (September 1884): 523–28; *Istoricheskii vestnik* 22 (1885): 732; *Russkaia starina* 5 (March 1872): 436–54. I am grateful to Alexander Mikaberidze for providing me with these references. For general information on this type of marriage, see entry under *nikah* in *The Encyclopedia of Islam*, new ed., vol. 8 (Leiden: E. J. Brill, 1995), p. 28, and Maksim Kovalevskii, *Zakon i obychai na Kavkaze*, vol. 2 (Moscow: Tip. A. N. Mamontova, 1890), pp. 177–79.

5. "Prilozheniia k zapiskam A. P. Ermolova," in *Zapiski Alekseia Petrovicha Ermolova*, 2:114.

6. A. S. Griboedov, *Polnoe sobranie sochinenii v trekh tomakh*, vol. 2 (St. Petersburg: Notabene, 1999), p. 293. For a wonderful discussion of Russian literature and the Caucasus, see Susan Layton, *Russian Literature and Empire*.

7. M. K. Azadovskii, "O literaturnoi deiatel'nosti A. I. Iakubovicha," *Literaturnoe nasledstvo* 60, pt. 1 (1956): 281.

8. *Zapiski A. P. Ermolova*, p. 317.

9. Ibid., pp. 316–20.

10. Ibid., pp. 338–39.

11. *Mnogonatsional'nyi Peterburg: Istoriia/ Religiia/ Narody* (St. Petersburg: Iskusstvo, 2002), p. 663; *Istoriia narodov Severnogo Kavkaza*, pp. 222, 503.

12. *Zapiski A. P. Ermolova*, p. 347.

13. Ibid., pp. 289, 314.

14. Ibid., p. 388; Pokrovskii, *Kavkazskie voiny i imamat Shamilia*, p. 135. The story became well known to the nineteenth-century Russian readers through a fictionalized account by Alexander Bestuzhev-Marlinskii, "Ammalat-Bek."

15. This scene is from a short story by Leo Tolstoy, "Nabeg," in *Polnoe sobranie sochinenii*, vol. 3 (Moscow: Khudozhestvennaia literatura, 1932), p. 32. Though Tolstoy was principally a writer of fiction, his descriptions heavily relied on his own military experience in the North Caucasus in the early 1850s and on his extensive familiarity with contemporary accounts of the war.

16. *Zapiski A. P. Ermolova*, p. 389; Pokrovskii, *Kavkazskie voiny i imamat Shamilia*, p. 136.

17. Pokrovskii, *Kavkazskie voiny i imamat Shamilia*, p. 142.

18. *Zapiski A. P. Ermolova*, pp. 410–15.

19. Ibid., pp. 423–24.

20. Ibid., pp. 424–27.

21. Ibid., p. 392; F. A. Shcherbina, *Istoriia Kubanskogo kazach'ego voiska*, vol. 2 (Ekaterinodar: Pechatnik, 1913), pp. 826–27.

22. "Prilozheniia," in *Zapiski Alekseia Petrovicha Ermolova*, 2:192–93, 209–10. In 1810 Alexander I likewise chastised the Caucasus commander General S. A. Bulgakov, who "in relying on extreme cruelty and inhumanity had crossed the boundaries of his duty." See Kosven, "Kabardinskii patriot Izmail Atazhukov," in *Etnografiia i istoriia Kavkaza*, pp. 143–44.

5. St. Petersburg and Poland

1. Tornau, "Vospominaniia o Kavkaze i Gruzii," p. 153.

2. *Ocherki istorii Leningrada*, vol. 1 (Moscow-Leningrad, Akademiia Nauk, 1955); A. B. Granville, M. D. *Guide to St. Petersburgh*, 2 vols. (London: Henry Colburn, 1835);

A. V. Kornilova, *Karl Briullov v Peterburge* (Leningrad: Lenizdat, 1976); F. M. Dostoevskii, "Peterburgskaia letopis," in *Polnoe sobranie sochinenii v 30 tomakh*, vol. 18 (Leningrad: Nauka, 1978), pp. 11–34; A. V. Darinskii, *Geografiia Leningrada* (Leningrad: Lenizdat, 1982).

3. Sh. B. Nogmov, *Istoriia Adygeiskogo naroda* (Nalchik: Kabardino-balkarskoe izd-vo, 1958), app., pp. 197–98.

4. Initially the Circassian Guard consisted of three senior officers, one clergyman (*efendi*), six cadets, forty arms bearers, and twenty-three servants. Its first commander was Sultan Azamat-Giray. A year later, by April 1830, the guard's staff had been expanded to include a treasurer, a translator, a scribe, three trumpeters, and a medical attendant. S. Petin, *Sobstvennyi Ego Imperatorskogo Velichestva konvoi, 1811–1911* (St. Petersburg, 1911), p. 28.

5. Nogmov, *Istoriia Adygeiskogo naroda* (Nalchik: Kabardino-balkarskoe knizhnoe izd-vo, 1958), pp. 5–11; Sh. B. Nogmov, *Istoriia Adygeiskogo naroda*, introduction by T. Kh. Kumykov, (Nalchik: Elbrus, 1994), pp. 16–20; Khan-Girei, *Cherkesskie predaniia: Izbrannye proizvedeniia* (Nalchik: Elbrus, 1989), pp. 8–11; Kosven, "Adygeiskii istorik i etnograf Khan-Giray," in *Etnografiia i istoriia Kavkaza*, pp. 184–86; Aleksandr Siver, *Shapsugi: Etnicheskaia istoriia i identifikatsiia* (Nalchik, 2002).

6. Richard S. Wortman, *Scenarios of Power* (Princeton: Princeton UP, 1995, 2000), 1:308–16, 327–28; 2:129–33; *St. Petersburg: A Traveller's Companion*, selected and introduced by Lawrence Kelly (New York: Atheneum, 1983).

7. In 1836 his story "The Valley of Adzhigutai" was published in the first volume of the journal *Sovremennik*, edited by Alexander Pushkin. Russia's foremost critic, Vissarion Belinskii, commented that the story "was remarkable as the work of a Circassian whose command of Russian is much better than that of many of our respectable writers. *Istoriia narodov Severnogo Kavkaza*, p. 242.

8. I. K. Zagidullin, *Islamskie instituty v Rossiiskoi imperii. Musul'manskaia obshchina v Sankt-Peterburge 18–nachalo 20 vv.* (Kazan: Kazanskii Universitet, 2003), pp. 23–25, 36.

9. For more on the Polish exiles in the Caucasus, see chapter 10 below.

10. For details of the Polish insurrection, see W. F. Reddaway et al., eds., *The Cambridge History of Poland: From Augustus II to Pilsudski* (Cambridge: Cambridge University Press, 1951), pp. 295–310.

11. RGVIA f. 395, op. 145, d. 205, ll. 4ob., 15; Petin, *Sobstvennyi Ego Imperatorskogo Velichestva konvoi*, p. 32; A. A. Kuznetsov, *Ordena i medali Rossii* (Moscow: Moscow University, 1985), pp. 62–64.

12. In order to collect them in Vilno, their leader, Khan-Giray, made an unauthorized detour that met with the disapproval of his superiors. Gosudarstvennyi Arkhiv Krasnodarskogo Kraia (GAKK) f. 332, op. 1, d. 6, ll. 125–26 (I am grateful to Sufian Zhemukhov for providing me with this reference).

6. Return to the North Caucasus

1. Pokrovskii, *Kavkazskie voiny*, pp. 148–64.

2. Ibid., pp. 165–94. For a discussion of the Sufi movement in the North Caucauss, see Anna Zelkina, *In Quest for God and Freedom: The Sufi Response to the Russian Advance in the North Caucasus* (London: Hurst, 2000), and Knysh, *Islamic Mysticism*, pp. 289–300.

3. Pokrovskii, *Kavkazskie voiny*, pp. 185–218.

4. About sixty Chechen settlements alone were destroyed during two weeks of August 1832. *Dvizhenie gortsev*, p. 724.

5. F. F. Tornau, *Vospominaniia kavkazskogo ofitsera* (Moscow: Tip. M. Katkova, 1864; repr. Moscow: AIRO-XX, 2000), p. 24.

6. Ibid., pp. 23–27.

7. Pokrovskii, *Kavkazskie voiny*, pp. 218–22.

8. *Istoriia narodov Severnogo kavkaza*, p. 35; Tornau, *Vospominaniia kavkazskogo ofitsera*, p.134–35.

9. The northwest Caucasus was originally understood to include the lands south and north of the Kuban River. By the early nineteenth century, however, the fertile lands to the north had been conquered and distributed among the Cossacks, as well as the ever-growing number of Russian, Ukrainian, and German settlers. The native populations of the Nogays and Circassians were pushed south and west across the river, and the new territories formed the Ekaterinodar and Stavropol districts of the Russian Empire. Between 1808 and 1811, 41,534 peasants moved from Ukraine to the Kuban, while in 1821 alone, 16,500 peasants from the Chernigiv and Poltava districts were resettled in the Kuban region. See V. A. Golobutskii, *Chernomorskoe kazachestvo* (Kiev: AN Ukrainskoi SSR, 1956), p. 218; *Istoriia narodov Severnogo Kavkaza,* p. 33).

10. *Ocherki istorii Karachaevo-Cherkessii,* vol. 1 (Stavropol: Stavropol'skoe knizhnoe izd-vo, 1967), p. 284; *Entsiklopedicheskii slovar' po istorii Kubani,* pp. 83–83.

11. *Entsiklopedicheskii slovar' po istorii Kubani,* pp. 250, 520–21, 525–26.

12. Ibid., p. 42.

13. Georgii Atarshchikov, "Zametki starogo kavkaztsa o boevoi i administrativnoi deiatel'nosti na Kavkaze general-leitenanta Barona G. Kh. Zassa," *Voennyi sbornik,* St. Petersburg 74, no. 8 (1870): 309–37.

14. Ibid, pp. 316–20.

7. Interpreter and Administrator

1. The description of Tiflis is taken from Tornau's memoirs of his stay in Tiflis in 1832. See *Russkie na Kavkaze* (St. Petersburg: Dmitrii Bulanin, 2004), pp. 310–50, and his "Vospominaniia o Kavkaze i Gruzii," p. 209. Also see Johann Anton Gildenstadt, *Puteshestvie po Kavkazu v 1770–73 gg.* (St. Petersburg: Peterburgskoe vostokovedenie, 2002), pp. 106–8; "Vospominaniia kniazia Dondukova-Korsakova," *Starina i novizna* 5 (1902): 211–16; Anchabadze and Volkova, *Staryi Tbilisi,* pp. 88–97; and Ronald Grigor Suny, *The Making of the Georgian Nation* (Bloomington: Indiana University Press, 1988), pp. 93–94.

2. Sh. B. Nogmov, *Istoriia Adygeiskogo naroda* (Nalchik: Kabardino-balkarskoe knizhnoe izdatelstvo, 1958), pp. 11–12; S. N. Zhemukhov, *Zhizn' Shora Nogmy* (Nalchik: Elbrus, 2002), pp. 103–8.

3. Iraklii Andronikov, *Lermontov. Issledovaniia i nakhodki* (Moscow: Khudozhestvennaia literatura, 1964), pp. 363–69; Tadeusz Swietochowski, *Russia and Azerbaijan. A Borderland in Transition,* (New York: Columbia University Press, 1995), pp. 26–30.

4. Tornau, *Vospominaniia,* 21–26.

5. Pokrovskii, *Kavkazskie voiny,* p. 277

6. *Ocherki istorii Karachaevo-Cherkessii,* 1:292.

7. RGVIA, f. 14719, op. 3, d. 168, pp. 1–3; *AKAK,* vol. 8, p. 743 (no. 644).

8. RGVIA, f. 14719, op. 3, d. 168, pp. 4–15.

9. Ibid., pp. 16–34.

10. For a historical geography of the Karachays and Balkars, see Volkova, *Etnicheskii sostav,* 94–110.

11. Ibid., p. 279.

12. Umar Aliev, *Karachai* (Rostov-na-Donu: Krainatsizdat-Sevkavkniga, 1927), pp. 89–97. Volkova, *Etnicheskii sostav,* pp. 101–2.

13. The group included German scientists in Russia, A. Ia. Kupfer, E. Kh. Lentz, K. A. Meyer, and Eduard Menetries, as well as the government official Vansovich and the architect of Mineralnye Vody, Giuseppe Bernardazzi.

14. Prince N. B. Golitsyn, *Zhizneopisanie generala ot kavalerii Emmanuelia* (St. Petersburg, 1851; repr. Moscow: Sobranie, 2004), pp. 257–61.

15. *Ocherki istorii Karachaevo-Cherkessii,* 1:296–97.

16. Ibid., 1:167.

17. Kosven, "Pervaia ekspeditsiia v volnuiu Svanetiiu 1838g i mnimye nekrasovtsy," in *Etnografiia i istoriia Kavkaza*, p. 252. A. I. Robakidze, *Svaneti* (Tbilisi: Metsniereba, 1984), pp. 68–69; David Marshall Lang, *A Modern History of Soviet Georgia* (London: Weidenfeld & Nicolson, 1962), pp. 9–10.

18. W. E. D. Allen, *A History of the Georgian People Down to the Russian Conquest in the Nineteenth Century* (London: K. Paul, Trench, Trubner, 1932), pp. 27–28; Robakidze, *Svaneti*, pp. 3–6.

19. Allen, *A History of the Georgian People*, pp. 300–303; Kosven, "Pervaia ekspeditsiia," p. 250.

20. RGVIA, f. 395, op. 145, d. 205, p. 25; Kosven, "Pervaia ekspeditsiia," p. 250–51; Ekaterina Pravilova, *Finansy imperii. Den'gi i vlast' v politike Rossii na natsional'nykh okrainakh, 1801–1917* (Moscow: Novoe izd-vo, 2006), p. 313. Paper money was of little value because of the runaway inflation that in the same year compelled the government to initiate major financial reform.

21. Lang, *A Modern History of Soviet Georgia*, pp. 96–97.

8. Russian Policies and Alternatives

1. For the Great Game and the *Vixen* incident, see Martin Ewans, ed., *The Great Game: Britain and Russia in Central Asia*, 8 vols. (London: RoutledgeCurzon, 2004) and Vladimir Degoev, *Bol'shaia igra na Kavkaze: Istoriia i sovremennost'* (Moscow: Russkaia panorama, 2003).

2. M. Polievktov, *Nikolai I: Biografiia i obzor tsarstvovaniia* (Moscow: M. i S. Sabashnikovy, 1918), pp. 191–93, 343–45; V. O. Bobrovnikov, *Musul'mane Severnogo Kavkaza. Obychai, pravo, nasilie* (Moscow: Vostochnaia literatura, 2002), p. 153.

3. Gammer, *Muslim Resistance to the Tsar*, pp. 91–95; John F. Baddeley, *The Russian Conquest of the Caucasus* (London: Longmans, 1908), pp. 307–10; For an Arab account of these events by Muhammad Tahir al-Qarakhi, see Thomas Sanders, Ernest Tucker, and Gary Humburg, eds., *Russian-Muslim Confrontation in the Caucasus*, (London: RoutledgeCurzon, 2004), p. 37.

4. A. P. Berzhe, "Imperator Nikolai na Kavkaze v 1837g," *Russkaia starina, no. 8* (1884): 377–98; "Memuary generala Musa-Pashi Kundukhova," pp. 100–101.

5. For a description of Stavropol, see E. Khamar-Dabanov, *Prodelki na Kavkaze* (St. Petersburg: Tip. E. Zhernakova, 1844), 2:25–28.

6. Tornau, *Vospominaniia kavkazskogo ofitsera*, pp. 297–98; Moritz Wagner, *Der Kaukasus und das Land der Kosaken in den Jahren 1843 bis 1846*. Dresden und Leipzig: Arnoldische Buchhandlung, 1848, p. 221.

7. *Arkhiv Raevskikh, vol. 3* (St. Petersburg: Izd-vo P. M. Raevskogo, 1910), pp. 342–50, 362–80.

8. A. Kh. Bizhev, *Adygi Severo-Zapadnogo Kavkaza i krizis vostochnogo voprosa v kontse 20-kh nachale 30-kh gg. 19 veka* (Maikop: Meoty, 1994), pp. 295–306.

9. A. Sokht, "Chernomorskaia beregovaia liniia: Sushchnost' i funktsii," in *Rossiia i Cherkessiia (vtoraia polovina 18–19 vv.)*, edited by Z. Iu. Khuako (Maikop: Meoty, 1995), pp. 147–57; James Stanislaus Bell, *Journal of a Residence in Circassia during the Years 1837, 1838, 1839*, vol. 1 (London: Edward Moxon, 1840), p. 117.

10. Edmund Spencer, *Travels in Circassia, Krim-Tartary, &c.* (London: Henry Colburn, 1839), 2:235–42, 374–75.

11. Sefer-bey's numerous peace proposals to the Russian government had a moderate agenda modeled on the Greek War of Independence from the Ottomans: Russia's withdrawal from Adyge lands back to the Kuban River in exchange for Circassian independence and a pledge of neutrality. A. Kerashev, "Politicheskaia deiatel'nost' kniazia Sefer-beia Zanoko v gody Kavkazskoi voiny," in *Rossiia i Cherkessiia*, pp. 102–14; A. Panesh, "Magomet-Amin na Severo-Zapadnom Kavkaze (1848–1859 gody)," in *Rossiia i Cherkessiia*, pp. 115–37.

12. The inadequacy of the Russian forts was made painfully obvious during the Crimean War when the appearance of the British and French fleets in the Black Sea forced Prince M. S. Vorontsov to evacuate all Russian garrisons along the coast to avoid capture.

13. Sufian Zhemukhov, *Mirovozzrenie Khan-Gireia* (Nalchik, 1997), pp. 25–26. In the atmosphere of strict censorship, others had a little more luck if only for a very short time. In 1844, 1,200 copies of a novel titled *Prodelki na Kavkaze* appeared in St. Petersburg. Deemed damaging to the image of the Russian military in the Caucasus, it was banned three days later, with most of the copies burned by the publisher and confiscated by the police. The censor who had allowed the publication of the book was fired and jailed for eight days. The author, E. P. Lachinova—who wrote under the pseudonym E. Khamar-Dabanov and turned out to be the wife of a retired Russian general—was put under police surveillance. Nicholas I personally ordered that particular attention be paid to any future manuscripts she might submit for publication. His police instincts proved to be right. Six years later Lachinova submitted a new manuscript titled *Two Imams, or the Destruction of the Avar Dynasty*. This time the imperial censors were on guard and quickly condemned the novel as sympathetic to the highlanders and critical of the Russian military campaigns. The manuscript never saw the light of day and vanished without a trace. E. Khamar-Dabanov, *Prodelki na Kavkaze*; L. I. Lavrov, *Istoriko-etnograhicheskie ocherki Kavkaza* (Leningrad: Nauka, 1978), pp. 175–81.

14. *Khan-Girei. Zapiski o Cherkessii*, ed. V. K. Gardanov and G. KH. Mambetov (Nalchik: Elbrus, 1992).

15. Zhemukhov, *Mirovozzrenie Khan-Gireia*, p. 79.

16. Ibid., p. 103.

17. RGVIA, f. 38, op. 7, d. 4, ll. 2–4.

18. Kosven, *Etnografiia i istoriia Kavkaza*, p. 187; Zhemukhov, *Mirovozzrenie Khan-Gireia*, pp. 48, 63.

19. Each court was to include one elder prince from each principality, two nobles, a notable, a qadi, a scribe, and a mufti. RGVIA, f. 38, op. 7, d. 4, l. 4.

20. Ibid., ll. 8–10.

21. Ia. A. Gordin et al., comps., *Kavkaz i Rossiiskaia imperiia: Proekty, idei, illiuzii i real'nost', nachalo 19—nachalo 20 vv.* (St. Petersburg: Zvezda, 2005), document no. 5, pp. 265–69; *Istoriia narodov Severnogo Kavkaza*, pp. 26, 28, 39.

22. V. S. Beslaneev, *Malaia Kabarda (13–nachalo 20 veka)*, 2nd ed. (Nalchik: Elbrus, 1995), pp. 116–18.

23. *Arkhiv Raevskikh*, 3:34–41, 338–50.

24. N. Sh. [*sic*], "General Veliaminov i ego znachenie dlia istorii Kavkazskoi voiny," *Kavkazskii sbornik* 7 (1883): 1–156; app., 67–77, 124–33, 144–54.

25. Edmund Spencer, *Travels in Circassia*, 2:245–46.

9. The First Desertion

1. Tornau, *Vospominaniia*, p. 139.

2. N. I. Lorer, *Zapiski dekabrista* (Irkutsk: Vostochno-sibirskoe izd-vo, 1984), pp. 258–59; A. I. Rozen, *Zapiski dekabrista* (Irkutsk: Vostochno-sibirskoe izd-vo, 1984), pp. 374–75. At the time, most of the European academic world was obsessed with phrenology. Skulls from the Caucasus were of particular interest and led the German scholar Johann Friedrich Blumenbach to conclude that the region was the birthplace of modern humans and to coin the term "Caucasian" for the white race. Adrian Desmond and James Moore, *Darwin's Sacred Cause: How a Hatred of Slavery Shaped Darwin's Views on Human Evolution* (Boston: Houghton Mifflin Harcourt, 2009), pp. 27–48.

3. Bell, *Residence in Circassia*, vol. 2, p. 14.

4. Golobutskii, *Chernomorskoe kazachestvo*, p. 218; Shcherbina, *Istoriia Kubanskogo kazach'ego voiska*, 2:55; *Zapiski A. P. Ermolova*, p. 370.

5. Another Atarshchikov, Georgii, played an important role in the resettlement of one group of these Armenians from the lower Laba River. GAKK, f. 261, op. 1, d. 491, p. 99; *Entsiklopedicheskii slovar'po istori Kubani*, pp. 24–25, 243.

6. Volkova, *Etnicheskii sostav,* pp. 62–63, 71; Butkov, *Materialy dlia novoi istorii Kavkaza s 1722 po 1803 gg.*, 3:369; Pokrovskii, *Kavkazskie voiny*, p. 298.

7. Shcherbina, *Istoriia Kubanskogo kazach'ego voiska*, 2:470, 814.

8. Gammer, *Muslim Resistance to the Tsar*, pp. 122–29; Pokrovskii, *Kavkazskie voiny*, pp. 281–98; Leo Tolstoy, "Khadji-Murat," in Sanders, Tucker, and Humburg, *Russian-Muslim Confrontation in the Caucasus*, pp. 69–152.

9. "Otryvok iz ispovedi Lachinova," *Kavkazskii sbornik* 2 (1877): 100.

10. T. E. Lawrence, cited in Ben Macintyre, *The Man Who Would Be King: The First American in Afghanistan* (New York: Farrar, Straus and Giroux, 2004), p. 251.

11. Degoev, *Bolshaia igra na Kavakaze*, pp. 234–50.

12. Shcherbina, *Istoriia Kubanskogo kazach'ego voiska*, 2:412.

13. GAKK, f. 356, op. 1, d. 217; f. 261, op. 1. d. 491; Georgii Atarshchikov, "Zametki starogo kavkaztsa o boevoi i administrativnoi deiatel'nosti na Kavkaze general-leitenanta barona G. Kh. Zassa," *Voennyi sbornik* 74, no. 8 (1870): 321. There is some confusion as to how many Atarshchikovs served in the region. Kosven believed that Semën had two brothers in the military. Kosven, *Etnografiia i istoriia Kavkaza*, p. 255. Fedor Tornau, writing from memory decades later, mentioned twin brothers, Ivan and Egor, in the service of commander Zass in 1832, and a translator from Chechen, "an old Mozdok Cossack Atarshchikov." Tornau, "Vospominaniia o Kavkaze i Gruzii," pp. 219, 255. Available records confirm the existence of only two Atarshchikovs, Semën and Georgii, who were unrelated.

14. The actual request was made for the Order of St. Stanislav fourth degree, but since it had been recently abolished, Atarshchikov was awarded the slightly more prestigious third degree. RGVIA, f. 395, op. 145, d. 205, ll. 4 ob., 15, 25, 26; Kuznetsov, *Ordena i medali Rossii*, pp. 88–89.

15. RGVIA, f. 395, op. 145, d. 205, ll. 5–7; *AKAK*, vol. 8, pp. 631, 633 (nos. 582, 583); Pokrovskii, *Kavkazskie voiny*, pp. 217–19. For more details on the battle at Germenchug, see chapter 6. The Russian poet Mikhail Lermontov, who served in the Russian army in the Caucasus at the same time, left a vivid description of Russian atrocities. M. Iu. Lermontov, "Izmail-bei," in *Polnoe sobranie stikhotvorenii*, (Leningrad: Sovetskii pisatel', 1989), 2:249–50).

16. For instance, in one scheme in 1839, under the pretext of disarming the Chechens, Pullo demanded one valuable musket from every ten Chechen households. He then substituted old and useless weapons for them, sold the good muskets, and pocketed the profit. "Memuary generala Musa-pashi Kundukhova," p. 102; Pokrovskii, *Kavkazskie voiny*, pp. 278–80).

17. RGVIA, f. 395, op. 145, d. 205, l. 7; *Dvizhenie gortsev severo-vostochnogo Kavkaza*, pp. 137–38 (no. 88); Pokrovskii, *Kavkazskie voiny*, pp. 256, 260, 278–79; Gammer, *Muslim Resistance to the Tsar*, pp. 77–79.

18. Kosven, *Etnografiia i istoriia Kavkaza*, p. 256; Volkova, *Etnicheskii sostav*, p. 74.

19. *Abaziny: Istoriko-etnograficheskii ocherk* (Cherkessk: Stavropol' skoe izd-vo, 1989), pp. 89–90, 105–7; *Istoriia narodov Severnogo*, pp.79–82.

20. Kosven, *Etnografiia i istoriia Kavkaza*, p. 257.

21. Just as the Caucasus served as a place of military exile for those imperial subjects who were deemed subversive, Finland seemed to be Nicholas I's favorite destination for dispatching troublemakers from the Caucasus. For example, a decade earlier, the same fate had befallen another Cossack officer and historian of the Caucasus, V. D. Sukhorukov, who was charged with sedition. "Dekabristy-kavkazovedy," in Kosven, *Etnografiia i istoriia Kavkaza*, pp. 178–81. Also see the anonymous story published in 1829. Layton, *Russian Literature and Empire*, p. 106.

10. From Semën Atarshchikov to Hajret Muhammed

1. Gammer, *Muslim Resistance*, pp. 119–29.

2. *Dvizhenie gortsev*, p. 303 (no. 159).

3. Leontovich, *Adaty kavkazskikh gortsev,* p. 138; Pokrovskii, *Kavkazskie voiny,* p. 306–7; Gammer, *Muslim Resistance,* pp. 163, 249.

4. Volkova, *Etnicheskii sostav,* pp. 58–61.

5. For a short time he settled among the Barakays, and there too he quickly found himself locked in a power struggle with Aitek Kanokov and was eventually forced to flee. D. Sokolov, "Haji-Muhammed," *Kubanskii sbornik* 11 (1904): 53–64, reprinted in *Muhammed-Amin i narodno-osvoboditel'noe dvizhenie narodov Severo-Zapadnogo Kavkaza v 40–60 gg. 19 veka* (Makhachkala, 1998), pp. 38–48.

6. Originally a Nogay dynasty, at the time the Enarukovs were well assimilated among the Kabardin notables and had their own *tamga* (a family seal). A. K. Baskakov, M. K. Baskakov, and N. D. Egorov, *Lineitsy. Ocherki po istorii stanitsy Labinskoi i Labinskogo otdela Kubanskoi oblasti* (Nicosia, 1996), pp. 88–89; Lavrov, Istoriko-etnograficheskie ocherki Kavkaza, p. 129.

7. Kovalevskii, *Zakon i obychai na Kavkaze,* 2:185–98; Kalmykov, *Cherkesy: istoriko-etnograficheskii ocherk,* pp. 214–18.

8. Valerii Sokurov, "Institut vyezda na sluzhbu u cherkesov," *Elbrus,* no.1 (1999): 113–14; *Adygeiskaia (Cherkesskaia) entsikolopediia* (Moscow: Fond im. B. Kh. Akbasheva, 2006), p. 906.

9. R. Kh. Khashkhosheva, *Adygskie prosvetiteli 19–nachala 20 veka* (Nalchik: Elbrus, 1993). Believing that linguistics was to serve the interests of the empire, Uslar played an early and crucial role in creating Cyrillic-based alphabets for the indigenous languages of the Caucasus. For instance, in 1862 with the help of a Chechen informant, Uslar created the Chechen alphabet and proceeded to create others for the languages of Daghestan. Austin Jersild, *Orientalism and Empire: North Caucasus Mountain Peoples and the Georgian Frontier, 1845–1917* (Montreal: McGill-Queen's University Press, 2002), pp. 80–84.

10. A. Iurov, "1843 god na Kavkaze," *Kavkazskii sbornik* 6 (1882): 1–220, Supplement pp. 21–30.

11. Shcherbina, *Istoriia Kubanskogo kazach'ego voiska,* 2:471–72.

12. RGVIA, f. 38, op. 7, d. 93, ll. 1–2. It is probably this letter that gave the Caucasus commander A. I. Neidgardt (1842–45) the idea to dispatch 250 letters to the highlanders with an appeal of his own. The idea was a fiasco given the widespread illiteracy among the native population. Lapin, *Armiia Rossii,* pp. 167–68.

13. At the time, ten silver rubles was a ransom for a soldier or a Cossack. Bell, *Journal of a Residence in Circasssia,* 2: 429–30, 435–38 (app.).

14. Teofil Lapinskii, also known under his Ottoman name as Teffik bey, left a valuable if tendentious account of his life among the peoples of the northwest Caucasus. It was published in Hamburg in 1863. Lapinskii, *Gortsy Kavkaza i ikh osvoboditel'naia voina protiv russkikh,* trans. V. K. Gardanov (Nalchik: EL-FA, 1995). For the important political and diplomatic role that Polish exiles in Europe played in the North Caucasus, see Ludwik Widerszal, *Sprawy kaukaskie w polityce europejskiej w latach 1831–1864* (Warsaw: Nakladem Towarzystwa Naukowego Warszawskiego, 1934).

15. Lapinskii, *Gortsy Kavkaza,* pp. 143–47; Lapin, *Armiia Rossii,* pp. 246–51.

16. *Dvizhenie gortsev,* pp. 329–30 (no. 176).

17. Ibid., pp. 364–68 (no. 203); Gadzhiev, *Rol' Rossii v istorii Dagestana,* pp. 243–46.

18. *Dvizhenie gortsev,* pp. 356–57 (no. 197), 486 (no. 261).

19. Shcherbina, *Istoriia Kubanskogo kazach'ego voiska,* 2: 473–75; *Entsikolopedicheskii slovar' po istorii Kubani,* p. 47.

20. Curiously, it was another Russian deserter, a former ensign named Jamal, who wrote a letter to the Russians advising them to withdraw peacefully. *Dvizhenie gortsev,* pp. 424—28 (no. 223-27).

21. *Dvizhenie gortsev,* pp. 393–94 (no. 217).

22. At times the raiding activity was almost reminiscent of a tournament of medieval knights or a gentlemanly duel. In the spring of 1838, for example, General Zass led an expeditionary force against two Abadzekh auls. As usual, the Russian troops put the auls to sword and fire and took away cattle and captives. During the battle Zass was wounded in the

leg. Because the wound was a mark of honor among the highlanders, the Abadzekhs sent a delegation to pay respect to the general and to inquire about his health. They admitted that Zass had outwitted them and warned that they would soon pay him back. Zass asked them to wait for a month while his leg healed so he could confront them properly. The Abadzekh agreed and did not launch their raids until the fall. *Entsiklopedicheskii slovar' po istorii Kubani*, p. 178.

23. *Dvizhenie gortsev*, pp. 360–63 (no. 202).

24. Shcherbina, *Istoriia Kubanskogo kazach'ego voiska*, 2:465–88.

25. Ibid., p. 476; *Adygskie pesni vremen Kavkazskoi voiny* (Nalchik, 2005), pp. 114–16, 158–62, 247–52.

26. GAKK, f. 256, op. 1, d. 63; Kosven, "Delo sotnika Atarshchikova," in *Etnografiia i istoriia Kavkaza*, p. 257; Shcherbina, *Istoriia Kubanskogo kazach'ego voiska*, vol. 2, p. 815.

27. During the late 1840s–'50s, Vorontsov oversaw a physical transformation of Tiflis: rebuilding the city, opening the first theater and public library, founding schools and the Caucasus section of the Russian Geographical Society, publishing the Russian newspaper *Kavkaz*, issuing invitations to scholars to travel and collect scientific data, and planning an expedition to the top of the Mount Ararat. See Anthony L. H. Rhinelander, *Prince Michael Vorontsov; Viceroy to the Tsar* (Montreal: McGill-Queen's University Press, 1990), chs. 11–14; O. Iu. Zakharova, *Svetskie tseremonialy v Rossii 18–nachala 20 v.* (Moscow: Tsentrpoligraf, 2001), pp. 41–47.

28. M. V. Pokrovskii, *Iz istorii adygov v kontse 18–pervoi poloviny 19 veka* (Krasnodar: Knizhnoe izdatel'stvo, 1989), pp. 212–36; *Entsikolopedicheskii slovar' po istorii Kubani*, pp. 410–12.

Glossary

Abrek. Ossetian term for a refugee or outcast who chooses the path of war.

Adat. Customary law.

Amanat. Hostage from among the non-Christians.

Atalyk. Adoptive father entrusted with bringing up a boy from a different family.

Atarshchik (otarshchik). Cattle hand watching a herd of horses.

Aul. Native village.

Barymta. Custom of seizing herds or humans as bargaining chips when adjudicating a dispute.

Beg (bey). Title of an indigenous notable.

Ghazawat. A holy war, specifically the raiding and combat in such a war.

Hajret. Term used by the Circassians for a refugee who embarked on the path of war.

Imamate. Islamic state.

Kanly. Kin-based vendetta against the perpetrator and his kin, possibly lasting several generations.

Konak (*kunak*). Guest under the full protection of his host.

Krym-shamkhal. Heir apparent to the shamkhal.

Mahkeme. Kabardin court that combined sharia and adat.

Maisum. One of the rulers of Tabasaran in Daghestan.

Maslahat. Truce and an alliance against a common enemy.

Muftiat. In the Russian Empire's official Islam, a body invested with the highest spiritual authority.

Mullah. A term of respect for an educated Muslim.

Murid. Disciple of the Sufi sheikh.

Naib. Shamil's deputy commander.

Pasha. Ottoman title for a general.

Pristav. Russian district superintendent in the Caucasus.

Pshi. Kabardin princely title.

Qadi. Islamic judge.

Shamkhal. Title of a Kumyk ruler in Daghestan.

Sharia. Islamic law.

Sheikh. Religious leader among the Sufis.

Shert. Peace treaty between Russia and an indigenous people.

Stanitsa. Cossack fortified village.

Sufism. Mystical tradition within Islam.

Taip. Chechen term for clan.

Tariqat. A school of Sufism.

Tukkhum. Alliance of Chechen clans.

Ulema. Muslim legal scholars.

Uork. Title of lesser nobility among the Kabardins.

Utsmii. Title of a ruler of Kaytag in Daghestan.

Uzden. Title of nobility among the Kumyks.

Vali. Title of an Ottoman governor.

Waqf. Pious religious endowment in Islam.

Bibliography

ARCHIVAL SOURCES

Rossiiskii Gosudarstvennyi Voenno-Istoricheskii Arkhiv *(RGVIA)*
f. 38, op. 7, d. 4, 93.
f. 395, op. 145, d. 205.
f. 14719, op. 3, d. 168.

Gosudarstvennyi Arkhiv Krasnodarskogo Kraia (GAKK)
f. 256, op. 1, d. 63.
f. 261, op. 1, d. 491.
f. 332, op. 1, d. 6.
f. 356, op. 1, d. 217.

PRIMARY SOURCES

Akty sobrannye Kavkazskoiu arkheograficheskoiu komissieiu. 12 vols. Tiflis: Tip. Glavnogo upravleniia namestnika Kavkazskogo, 1866–1904.
Arkhiv Raevskikh. 5 vols. St. Petersburg: Izd-vo P. M. Raevskogo, 1910.
Atarshchikov, Georgii. "Zametki starogo kavkaztsa o boevoi i administrativnoi deiatel'nosti na Kavkaze general-leitenanta Barona G. Kh. Zassa." *Voennyi sbornik*, St. Petersburg. 74, no. 8 (1870): 309–37.
Bell, J. S. *Journal of a Residence in Circassia during the years 1837, 1838, and 1839.* 2 vols. London: E. Moxon, 1840.
Belokurov, S. L., comp. *Snosheniia Rossii s Kavkazom. Materialy izvlechennye iz Moskovskogo Ministerstva inostrannykh del, 1578–1613.* Moscow: Universitetskaia tip., 1889.
Berzhe, A. P. *Chechnya i chechentsy.* Tiflis, 1859. Reprint, Groznyi: Kniga, 1991.
Bronevskii, S. M. *Istoricheskiia vypiski o snosheniiakh Rossii s Persieiu, Gruzieiu i voobshche s gorskimi narodami v Kavkaze obitaiushchimi, so vremen Ivana Vasilievicha donyne.* Edited by I. K. Pavlova. St. Petersburg: Peterburgskoe vostokovedenie, 1996.

Butkov, P. G. *Materialy dlia novoi istorii Kavkaza s 1722 po 1803 god.* 3 vols. St. Petersburg: Tip. Imp. Akademii Nauk, 1869.

Cook, John. *Voyages and Travels through the Russian Empire, Tartary, and Part of the Kingdom of Persia.* 2 vols. Edinburgh, 1770. Reprint, Boston: Oriental Research Partners, 1997.

Dvizhenie gortsev severo-vostochnogo Kavkaza v 20–50 gg. 19 veka: Sbornik dokumentov. Makhachkala: Dagestanskoe knizhnoe izd-vo, 1959.

Epigraficheskie pamiatniki Severnogo Kavkaza na arabskom, persidskom i turetskom iazykakh, compiled by L. I. Lavrov. 3 vols. Moscow: Nauka, 1966–80.

Gadzhiev, V. G., ed. *Russko-dagestanskie otnosheniia v 18–nachele 19 v.: Sbornik dokumentov.* Moscow: Nauka, 1988.

Gamrekeli, V. N., comp. *Dokumenty po vzaimosviaziam Gruzii s Severnym Kavkazom v 18 veke.* Tbilisi: AN Gruzinskoi SSR, 1968.

Gildenstadt, Johann Anton. *Puteshestvie po Kavkazu v 1770–73 gg.* St. Petersburg: Peterburgskoe vostokovedenie, 2002.

Golitsyn, Prince N. B. *Zhizneopisanie generala ot kavalerii Emmanuelia.* St. Petersburg, 1851. Reprint, Moscow: Sobranie, 2004.

Gordin, Ia. A. et al. *Kavkaz i Rossiiskaia imperiia: Proekty, idei, illiuzii i real'nost', nachalo 19—nachalo 20 vv.* St. Petersburg: Zvezda, 2005.

Griboedov, A. S. *Polnoe sobranie sochinenii v trekh tomakh.* St. Petersburg: Notabene, 1999.

Ikhilov, M. M., ed. *Russko-dagestanskie otnosheniia 17-pervoi chetverti 18 vv.: Dokumenty i materialy.* Makhachkala: Dagestanskoe knizhnoe izd-vo, 1958.

Kabardino-russkie otnosheniia v 16–18 vv.: Dokumenty i materialy. 2 vols. Moscow: AN SSSR, 1957.

Khamar-Dabanov, E. *Prodelki na Kavkaze.* 2 vols. St. Petersburg: Tip. E. Zhernakova, 1844.

Khan-Girei. *Cherkesskie predaniia: Izbrannye proizvedeniia.* Nalchik: Elbrus, 1989.

——. *Izbrannye proizvedeniia.* Nalchik: Elbrus, 1974.

——. *Zapiski o Cherkessii.* Edited by V. K. Gardanov and G. Kh. Mambetov. Nalchik: Elbrus, 1992.

Kusheva, E. N., comp. *Russko-chechenskie otnosheniia: Vtoraia polovina 16–17 vv. Sbornik dokumentov.* Moscow: Vostochnaia literatura, 1997.

Lachinov, E. E. "Otryvok iz ispovedi Lachinova," *Kavkazskii sbornik* 2 (1877): 100.

Lapinskii, Teofil [Teffik-bei]. *Gortsy Kavkaza i ikh osvoboditel'naia voina protiv russkikh.* Translated by V. K. Gardanov. 1862. Reprint, Nalchik: El-Fa, 1995.

Lorer, N. I. *Zapiski dekabrista.* Irkutsk: Vostochno-sibirskoe izd-vo, 1984.

"Memuary generala Musa-Pashi Kundukhova (1837–1865)." *Zvezda,* no. 8 (2001): 100–123.

Osmanli Devleti ile Azerbaycan Türk Hanliklari arasindaki Münasabetlere dair Arsiv Belgeleri. Vol. 1 (1578–1914). Ankara: T. C. Basbakanlik, 1992.

Polnoe sobranie zakonov Rossiiskoi imperii. Sobranie pervoe. 45 vols. St. Petersburg, 1830.

Rozen, A. I. *Zapiski dekabrista.* Irkutsk: Vostochno-sibirskoe izd-vo, 1984.

Sbornik svedenii o kavkazskikh gortsakh. 10 vols. Tiflis, 1868–81.

Spencer, Edmund. *Travels in Circassia, Krim-Tartary, &c.* 3rd ed. 2 vols. London: Henry Colburn, 1839.

Tornau, F. F. *Vospominaniia kavkazskogo ofitsera.* Moscow: Tip. M. Katkova, 1864. Reprint, Moscow: AIRO-XX, 2000.

——. "Vospominaniia o Kavkaze i Gruzii." In *Vospominaniia russkogo ofitsera.* Moscow: AIRO-XX, 2000.

"Vospominaniia kniazia Dondukova-Korsakova." *Starina i novizna* 5 (1902): 208–36.

Wagner, Moritz. *Der Kaukasus und das Land der Kosaken in den Jahren 1843 bis 1846.* Dresden und Leipzig: Arnoldische Buchhandlung, 1848.

"Zapiska generala Ermolova o posolstve v Persiiu v 1817 godu." In *Zapiski Alekseia Petrovicha Ermolova.* Moscow: Universitetskaia tipografiia, 1868, 2:1–74.

Zapiski A. P. Ermolova, 1798–1826. Edited by V. A. Fedorov. Moscow: Vysshaia shkola, 1991.

Secondary Sources

Abaziny: Istoriko-etnograficheskii ocherk. Cherkessk: Stavropol'skoe knizhnoe izd-vo, 1989.

Adygeiskaia (Cherkesskaia) entsikolopediia. Moscow: Fond im. B. Kh. Akbasheva, 2006.

Adygskie pesni vremen Kavkazskoi voiny. Nalchik, 2005.

Aliev, B., Sh. Akhmedov, and M.-S. Usmanov. *Iz istorii srednevekovogo Dagestana.* Makhachkala: Institut istorii, iazyka i literatury, 1970.

Aliev, B. G., and M.-S. K. Umakhanov. *Istoricheskaia geografiia Dagestana 18–nach. 19 v.* 2 vols. Makhachkala: Institut istorii, arkheologii i etnografii, 1999–2001.

Aliev, Umar. *Karachai.* Rostov-on-Don: Krainatsizdat-Sevkavkniga, 1927.

Allen, W. E. D. *A History of the Georgian People Down to the Russian Conquest in the Nineteenth Century.* London: K. Paul, Trench, Trubner, 1932.

Anchabadze, Iu. D., and N. G. Volkova. *Staryi Tbilisi. Gorod i gorozhane v 19 veke.* Moscow: Nauka, 1990.

Andronikov, Iraklii. *Lermontov. Issledovaniia i nakhodki.* Moscow: Khudozhestvennaia literatura, 1964.

Ataev, Dibir. *Putevoditel' po Dagestanu.* Makhachkala: Dagestanskoe knizhnoe izd-vo, 1965.

Atkin, Muriel. *Russia and Iran, 1780–1828.* Minneapolis: University of Minnesota Press, 1980.

Azadovskii, M. K. "O literaturnoi deiatel'nosti A. I. Iakubovicha." *Literaturnoe nasledstvo* 60 (1956): 271–82.

Baddeley, John F. *The Russian Conquest of the Caucasus,* London: Longmans, 1908.

Barrett, Thomas M. *At the Edge of Empire: The Terek Cossacks and the North Caucasus Frontier, 1700–1860.* Boulder, CO: Westview, 1999.

Bartold, V. V. *Raboty po istoricheskoi geografii.* Moscow: Vostochnaia literatura, 2002.

——. *Sochineniia.* 9 vols. Moscow: Izd-vo vostochnoi literatury, 1963–77.

Baskakov, A. K., M. K. Baskakov, N. D. Egorov, N. D. Lineitsy. *Ocherki po istorii stanitsy Labinskoi i Labinskogo otdela Kubanskoi oblasti.* Nikosiia, 1996.

Beituganov, S. N. *Kabardinskie familii: Istoki i sud'by.* Nalchik: Elbrus, 1990.

Berzhe, A. P. "Aleksei Petrovich Ermolov i ego kebinnye zheny na Kavkaze, 1816–27 gg." *Russkaia starina* 15 (September 1884): 523–28; *Istoricheskii vestnik* 22 (1885): 732; *Russkaia starina* 5, no. 3 (1872): 436–54.

——. "Imperator Nikolai na Kavkaze v 1837g." *Russkaia starina*, no. 8 (1884): 377–98.

Beslaneev, V. S. *Malaia Kabarda (13–nachalo 20 veka).* 2nd ed. Nalchik: Elbrus, 1995.

Bilge, M. Sadik, *Osmanli Devleti ve Kafkasya.* Istanbul: Eren, 2005.

Bizhev, A. Kh. *Adygi Severo-Zapadnogo Kavkaza i krizis vostochnogo voprosa v kontse 20-kh nachale 30-kh gg. 19 veka.* Maikop: Meoty, 1994.

Bobrovnikov, V. O. *Musul'mane Severnogo Kavkaza. Obychai, pravo, nasilie.* Moscow: Vostochnaia literatura, 2002.

Braudel, Fernand. *The Mediterranean World in the Age of Philip II.* Translated by Sian Reynolds. New York: Harper and Row, 1972.

Darinskii, A. V. *Geografiia Leningrada.* Leningrad: Lenizdat, 1982.

Davis, Natalie Zemon. *The Return of Martin Guerre.* Cambridge, MA: Harvard University Press, 1983.

——. *Trickster Travels: A Sixteenth Century Muslim between Worlds.* New York: Wang and Hill, 2006.

Degoev, Vladimir. *Bol'shaia igra na Kavakaze: Istoriia i sovremennost'.* Moscow: Russkaia panorama, 2003.

Desmond, Adrian, and James Moore. *Darwin's Sacred Cause: How a Hatred of Slavery Shaped Darwin's Views on Human Evolution.* Boston: Houghton Mifflin Harcourt, 2009.

Dostoevskii, F. M. *Polnoe sobranie sochinenii v 30 tomakh.* Vol. 18, *Peterburgskaia letopis'.* Leningrad: Nauka, 1978.

Dzamikhov, K. F. *Adygi v politike Rossii na Kavkaze (1550–nachalo 1770-kh godov).* Nalchik: El-Fa, 2001.

Egorov, V. L. *Istoricheskaia geografiia Zolotoi Ordy v 13–14 vv.* Moscow: Nauka, 1985.

Entsiklopedicheskii slovar' po istorii Kubani. Krasnodar: Edvi, 1997.

Fadeev, R. A. *Kavkazskaia voina.* Moscow: Eksmo, 2003.

Gadzhiev, V. G. *Rol' Rossii v istorii Dagestana.* Moscow: Nauka, 1965.

Gadzhieva, S. Sh. *Dagestanskie Terekementsy, 19–nach 20 v.* Moscow: Nauka, 1990.

——. *Kumyki: Istoriko-etnograficheskoe issledovanie.* Moscow: AN SSSR, 1961.

Gammer, Moshe. *Muslim Resistance to the Tsar: Shamil and the Conquest of Chechnia and Daghestan.* London: Frank Cass, 1994.

Gardanov, V. K. *Obshchestvennyi stroi adygskikh narodov: XVIII–pervaia polovina XIX v.* Moscow: Nauka, 1967.

Golobutskii, V. A. *Chernomorskoe kazachestvo.* Kiev: AN Ukrainskoi SSR, 1956.

Gordin, Ia. A. et al., comps. *Kavkaz i Rossiiskaia imperiia: Proekty, idei, illiuzii i real'nost', nachalo 19—nachalo 20 vv.* St. Petersburg: Zvezda, 2005.

Gorod Groznyi. Groznyi: Checheno-ingushskoe izd-tvo, 1984.

Granville, A. B. *Guide to St. Petersburgh,* 2 vols. London: Henry Colburn, 1835.

Grant, Bruce. *The Captive and the Gift: Cultural Histories of Sovereignty in Russia and the Caucasus.* Ithaca: Cornell University Press, 2009.

Gurlev, I. et al. *Derbent: Putevoditel' po gorodu i okrestnostiam.* Makhachkala: Dagknigoizdat, 1976.

Islammagomedov, A. I., and G. A. Sergeeva, eds. Traditsionnoe i novoe v sovremennom byte i kulture dagestantsev pereselentsev. Moscow: Nauka, 1988.

Istoriia Dagestana, 2 vols. Moscow: Vostochnaia literatura, 1967–68.

Istoriia narodov Severnogo Kavkaza, konets 18v.–1917. Moscow: Nauka, 1988.

Iurov, A. "1843 god na Kavkaze," *Kavkazskii sbornik* 6 (1882): 1–220.

Jersild, Austin. *Orientalism and Empire: North Caucasus Mountain Peoples and the Georgian Frontier, 1845–1917.* Montreal: McGill-Queen's University Press, 2002.

Kabuzan, V. M. *Narody Rossii v 18 veke. Chislennost' i etnicheskii sostav.* Moscow: Nauka, 1990.

Kaimarazov, G. Sh. *Ocherki istorii kultury narodov Dagestana.* Moscow: Nauka, 1971.

Kalmykov, I. Kh. *Cherkesy: Istoriko-etnograficheskii ocherk.* Cherkessk: Karachaevo-cherkesskoe otdelenie Stavropol'skogo izd-va, 1974.

Kazemzadeh, F. *The Cambridge History of Iran.* Vol. 7. Cambridge: Cambridge University Press, 1991.

Kazharov, V. Kh. *Traditsionnye obshchestvennye instituty kabardintsev i ikh krizis v kontse 18—pervoi polovine 19 veka.* Nalchik: El-Fa, 1994.

Kemper, Michael. *Herrschaft, Recht und Islam in Daghestan: Von den Khanaten und Gemeindebunden zum Jihad-Staat.* Wiesbaden: Reichert, 2005.

Kemper, Michael, and Marius Reinkowski, eds. *Rechtspluralismus in der Islamischen Welt. Gewohnheitsrecht zwischen Staat und Gesellschaft.* Berlin: Walter de Gruyter, 2005.

Kerashev, A. "Politicheskaia deiatel'nost' kniazia Sefer-beia Zanoko v gody Kavkazskoi voiny." In *Rossiia i Cherkessiia (vtoraia polovina 18–19 vv.).* Edited by Z. Iu. Khuako. Maikop: Meoty, 1995, pp. 102–14.

Khan-Magomedov, S. *Derbent. Gornaia Stena. Auly Tabasarana.* Moscow: Iskusstvo, 1979.

Khashkhosheva, R. Kh. *Adygskie prosvetiteli 19'nachala 20 veka.* Nalchik: Elbrus, 1993.

Khodarkovsky, Michael. "Of Christianity, Enlightenment and Colonialism: Russia in the North Caucasus, 1550–1800." *Journal of Modern History* 71, no. 2 (1999): 394–430.

——. *Russia's Steppe Frontier: The Making of a Colonial Empire, 1500–1800.* Bloomington: Indiana University Press, 2002.

King, Charles. *The Ghost of Freedom: A History of the Caucasus* Oxford: Oxford University Press, 2008.

Kirimli, Hakan. "Crimean Tatars, Nogays, and Scottish Missionaries." *Cahiers du Monde Russe* 45, nos. 1–2 (2004): 61–108.

Kirzioglu, Fahrettin. *Osmanlilar'in Kafkas-Elleri'ni Fethi (1451–1590).* Ankara: Sevinc Matbaasi, 1976.

Knysh, Alexander. *Islamic Mysticism: A Short History.* Leiden: Brill, 2000.

Kornilova, A. V. *Karl Briullov v Peterburge.* Leningrad: Lenizdat, 1976.

Kosven, M. O. *Etnografiia i istoriia Kavkaza: Issledovaniia i materialy.* Moscow: Izdatel'stvo vostochnoi literatury, 1964.

———, ed. *Narody Kavkaza.* 2 vols. Moscow: AN SSSR, 1960–62.

Kovalevskii, Maksim. *Zakon i obychai na Kavkaze.* 2 vols. Moscow: Tip. A. I. Mamontova, 1980.

Kudriavtsev, A. A. *Feodal'nyi Derbent.* Moscow: Nauka, 1993.

Kurtynova-D'Herlugnan, Liubov. *The Tsar's Abolitionists: The Slave Trade in the Caucasus and Its Suppression.* Leiden: Brill, 2010.

Kusheva, E. N. *Narody Severnogo Kavkaza i ikh sviazi s Rossiei: Vtoraia polovina 16–30-e gody 17 veka.* Moscow: Izd-vo AN SSSR, 1963.

Kütükoglu, Bekir. *Osmanli-Iran Siyasi Munasabetleri.* Istanbul: Edebiyat Fakültesi Matbaasi, 1962.

Kuznetsov, A. A. *Ordena i medali Rossii.* Moscow: Moskovskii Universitet, 1985.

Lang, David Marshall. *A Modern History of Soviet Georgia.* London: Weidenfeld and Nicolson, 1962.

Lapin, Vladimir. *Armiia Rossii v Kavkazskoi voine 18–19 vv.* St. Petersburg: Evropeiskii Dom, 2008.

Lavrov, L. I. *Istoriko-etnographicheskie ocherki Kavkaza.* Leningrad: Nauka, 1978.

Layton, Susan. *Russian Literature and Empire: Conquest of the Caucasus from Pushkin to Tolstoy.* Cambridge: Cambridge University Press, 1994.

Leontovich, F. I. *Adaty Kavkazskikh gortsev. Materialy po obychnomu pravu Severnogo i Vostochnogo Kavkaza.* Vol. 1. Odessa: Tip. P. A. Zelenago, 1882. Reprint, Nalchik: El-Fa 2002.

Lermontov, M. Iu. "Izmail-bei." In *Polnoe sobranie stikhotvorenii.* 2 vols. Leningrad: Sovetskii pisatel', 1989.

Macintyre, Ben. *The Man Who Would Be King: The First American in Afghanistan.* New York: Farrar, Straus and Giroux, 2004.

Malakhova, G. N. *Stanovlenie i razvitie Rossiiskogo gosudarstvennogo upravleniia na Severnom Kavkaze v kontse 18–19vv.* Rostov-on-Don: SKAGS, 2001.

Mamakaev, Mokhmad. *Chechenskii taip v period ego razlozheniia.* Groznyi: Checheno-Ingushskoe knizhnoe izd-vo, 1973.

Maremkulov, A. N. *Osnovy geopolitiki Rossiiskogo gosudarstva na Severnom Kavkaze v 18–nachale 19 veka.* Nalchik: Elbrus, 2003.

Medvedeva, M. M. "Griboedov pod sledstviem i nadzorom." *Literaturnoe nasledstvo* 60 (1956): 475–96.

Mnogonatsional'nyi Peterburg: Istoriia/Religiia/Narody. St. Petersurg: Iskusstvo, 2002.

N., Sh. [sic] "General Veliaminov i ego znachenie dlia istorii Kavkazskoi voiny" *Kavkazskii sbornik* 7 (1883): 1–156.

Narody Dagestana. Moscow: Nauka, 2002.

Nogmov, Sh. B. *Istoriia Adygeiskogo naroda.* Nalchik: Elbrus, 1994.

Novosel'skii, A. A. *Bor'ba Moskovskogo gosudarstva s tatarami v pervoi polovine 17 veka.* Moscow-Leningrad: AN SSSR, 1948.

Ocherki istorii Checheno-ingushskoi ASSR, 2 vols. Groznyi: Checheno-ingushskoe izd-vo, 1967.

Ocherki istorii Karachaevo-Cherkessii, 2 vols. Stavropol: Stavropol'skoe knizhnoe izd-vo, 1967.

Ocherki istorii Leningrada. Vol. 1. Moscow: Akademiia Nauk, 1955.

Orazaev, G. M.-P. "Tiurkoiazychnye dokumenty iz arkhiva Kizliarskogo komendanta—Istochnik po sotsial'no-ekonomicheskoi istorii narodov Severnogo Kavkaza." In *Istochnikovedenie i tekstologiia Blizhenego i Srednego Vostoka.* Moscow: Vostochnaia literatura, 1984.

Panesh, A. "Magomet-Amin na Severo-Zapadnom Kavkaze (1848–1859 gody)." In *Rossiia i Cherkessiia*, pp. 115–37.

Petin, S. *Sobstvennyi Ego Imperatorskogo Velichestva konvoi, 1811–1911.* St. Petersburg, 1911.

Pokrovskii, M. V. *Iz istorii adygov v kontse 18–pervoi poloviny 19 veka.* Krasnodar: Knizhnoe izd-vo, 1989.

Pokrovskii, N. I. *Kavkazskie voiny i imamat Shamilia.* Moscow: Rosspen, 2000.

Polievktov, M. *Nikolai I: Biografiia i obzor tsarstvovaniia.* Moscow: M. i S. Sabashnikovy, 1918.

Pravilova, Ekaterina. *Finansy imperii. Dengi i vlast' v politike Rossii na natsional'nykh okrainakh, 1801–1917.* Moscow: Novoe izd-vo, 2006.

Reddaway, W. F. et al., eds. *The Cambridge History of Poland: From Augustus II to Pilsudski.* Cambridge: Cambridge University Press, 1951.

Rhinelander, Anthony L. H. *Prince Michael Vorontsov; Viceroy to the Tsar.* Montreal: McGill-Queen's University Press, 1990.

Robakidze, A. I. *Svaneti.* Tbilisi: Metsniereba, 1984.

Russkie na Kavkaze. St. Petersburg: Dmitrii Bulanin, 2004.

Sanders, Thomas, Ernest Tucker, and Gary Humburg, eds. *Russian-Muslim Confrontation in the Caucasus.* London: RoutledgeCurzon, 2004.

Severnyi Kavkaz v sostave Rossiskoi imperii. Moscow: Novoe literaturnoe obozrenie, 2007.

Shcherbina, F. A. *Istoriia Kubanskogo kazach'ego voiska.* 2 vols. Ekaterinodar: Pechatnik, 1913.

Sholokhov, Mikhail. *Sobranie sochinenii.* Vols. 2–5, *Tikhii Don.* Moscow: Khudozhestvennaia literatura, 1966.

Siver, Aleksandr. *Shapsugi: Etnicheskaia istoriia i identifikatsiia.* Nalchik: Poligrafservis, 2002.

Smirnov, V. D. *Krymskoe khanstvo pod verkhovenstvom Otomanskoi Porty do nachala 18 veka.* St. Petersburg: Tip. A. S. Suvorina, 1887.

Sokht, A. "Chernomorskaia beregovaia liniia: Sushchnost' i funktsii." In *Rossiia i Cherkessiia, (vtoraia polovina 18–19 vv.).* Edited by Z. Iu. Khuako. Maikop: Meoty, 1995, 147–67.

Sokolov, D. "Haji-Muhammed." *Kubanskii sbornik* 11 (1904): 53–64. Reprinted in *Muhammed-Amin i narodno-osvoboditel'noe dvizhenie narodov Severo-Zapadnogo Kavkaza v 40–60 gg. 19 veka.* Makhachkala, 1998, pp. 38–48.

Sokurov, Valerii. "Institut vyezda na sluzhbu u cherkesov." *Elbrus*, no. 1 (1999): 116–25.

St. Petersburg: A Traveller's Companion. Selected and introduced by Lawrence Kelly. New York: Atheneum, 1983.

Stranitsy istorii goroda Groznogo. Groznyi: Checheno-ingushskoe izd-vo, 1989.

Suleimanov, Akhmad. *Toponimiia Chechni.* Nalchik: El-Fa, 1997.

Suny, Ronald Grigor. *The Making of the Georgian Nation.* Bloomington: Indiana University Press, 1988.

Swietochowski, Tadeusz. *Russia and Azerbaijan: A Borderland in Transition.* New York: Columbia University Press, 1995.

Toledano, Ehud R. *The Ottoman Slave Trade and Its Suppression, 1840–1890.* Princeton: Princeton University Press, 1982.

Tolstoy, L. N. *Kazaki.* Moscow: Khudozhestvennaia literatura, 1949.

——. "Khadji-Murat." In Sanders, Tucker, and Humburg, *Russian-Muslim Confrontation in the Caucasus,* pp. 69–152.

——. "Nabeg." In *Polnoe sobranie sochinenii.* Vol. 3. Moscow: Khudozhestvennaia literatura, 1932.

——. "Rubka lesa." In *Polnoe sobranie sochinenii.* Vol. 3. Moscow: Khudozhestvennaia literatura, 1932.

Volkova, N. G. *Etnicheskii sostav naseleniia Severnogo Kavkaza v 18–nachale 19 vekov.* Moscow: Nauka, 1974.

——. *Etnonimy i plemennye nazvaniia Severnogo Kavkaza.* Moscow: Nauka, 1973.

Widerszal, Ludwik. *Sprawy kaukaskie w polityce europejskiej w latach 1831–1864.* Warsaw: Nakladem Towarzystwa Naukowego Warszawskiego, 1934.

Wortman, Richard S. *Scenarios of Power.* 2 vols. Princeton: Princeton University Press, 1995, 2000.

Zagidullin, I. K. *Islamskie instituty v Rossiiskoi imperii. Musulmanskaia obshchina v Sankt-Peterburge 18–nachalo 20 vv.* Kazan: Kazanskii Universitet, 2003.

Zakharova, O. Iu. *Svetskie tseremonialy v Rossii 18–nachala 20 v.* Moscow: Tsentrpoligraf, 2001.

Zasedateleva, L. B. *Terskie kazaki. Istoriko-etnograficheskie ocherki.* Moscow: MGU, 1974.

Zelkina, Anna. *In Quest for God and Freedom. The Sufi Response to the Russian Advance in the North Caucasus.* London: Hurst and Co., 2000.

Zhemukhov, Sufian. *Mirovozzrenie Khan-Gireia.* Nalchik, 1997.

——. *Zhizn' Shora Nogmy.* Nalchik: Elbrus, 2002.

Index